# THE HOLOCAUST AND THE HISTORIANS

*Lucy S. Dawidowicz*

# THE HOLOCAUST
# AND THE
# HISTORIANS

Harvard University Press

Cambridge, Massachusetts
and
London, England

Permission was kindly granted to reprint excerpts from the following: From "Psalm," in *New and Selected Poems*, by Irving Feldman. Copyright © 1967 by Irving Feldman. Reprinted by permission of Viking Penguin Inc. From "Elegy for a Dead Soldier," in *Selected Poems*, by Karl Shapiro. Copyright © 1944 by Karl Shapiro. Reprinted by permission of Random House, Inc.

10   9   8   7   6   5   4   3

Library of Congress Cataloging in Publication data
Dawidowicz, Lucy S.
The Holocaust and the historians.
Includes index.
1. Holocaust, Jewish (1939–1945)—Historiography.
I. Title.
D810.J4D32        934.086        80-29175
ISBN 0-674-40566-8 (cloth)
ISBN 0-674-40567-6 (paper)

*In memory of the murdered Jewish historians*

Simon Dubnow (1860–1941)
Meir Bałaban (1877–1942)
Ignacy Schipper (1884–1943)
Emanuel Ringelblum (1900–1944)

# CONTENTS

# ACKNOWLEDGMENTS

This book began as a lecture on "The Holocaust in Contemporary History," which I delivered as part of the Aaron-Roland Lectures in Jewish Studies at Stanford University in 1975. I presented another aspect of the subject in the Harry Spindel Memorial Lecture at Bowdoin College in 1977.

With great pleasure I acknowledge my gratitude to the Memorial Foundation for Jewish Culture and especially to Jerry Hochbaum, its associate executive director, for a grant during the year I was writing this book.

Many people generously assisted me with information, encouragement, and stimulation. For unstinting help in locating a wide variety of materials, I am happy to thank Dina Abramowicz, librarian at the YIVO Institute for Jewish Research; Fred Bogin, librarian at the Leo Baeck Institute in New York; and Cyma M. Horowitz, director of the Blaustein Library of the American Jewish Committee.

Conversations with many friends and colleagues helped me to develop my ideas and clarify my thinking. Those who read parts or all of the manuscript spared me from errors of fact and lapses in judgment. I value their help more than the formal expression of these acknowledgments can indicate. My debt of gratitude to Neal Kozodoy is an obligation I am happy to bear, though I doubt that I can adequately repay it. To Alexander Erlich, Alfred Kazin, William Korey, George L. Mosse, Ismar Schorsch, and Isaiah Trunk I tender many many thanks for their time, their insight, and their friendship. Of course, none is responsible for my opinions.

My greatest debt is to my late husband, Szymon. He was my dearest friend, my wisest counselor, my severest critic, and my most rigorous editor. He died when the manuscript was half done. I tried faithfully to complete the work so that it would have satisfied his standards and fulfilled his expectations.

New York, New York                                          L.S.D.

THE HOLOCAUST AND THE HISTORIANS

# FOREWORD

History, as everyone knows, is the record of the past. It is also what historians write. The past, whether it is the moment just gone by, last year, or a thousand years ago, disappears as it is ceaselessly consumed by the present. The past survives only in memory and in the testimony of records and relics. Consequently, we depend on historians to tell us about the past. It is they who constitute it for us out of memory and records. Rather, they reconstitute it, for the past can never be restored as it existed in its original bewildering and intricate entirety. It can, however, be constructed as an account of the events of yesterday that speaks to our own sensibilities and addresses our contemporary concerns. The present is, after all, a relic of the past, a historical deposit left by the wash of time.

When historians knowingly or unknowingly omit from their historical writing an account of any given course of events, those events disappear from history. For if they are not recorded in history, the events of the past vanish into memory-lessness, irretrievably lost to the present and the future.

While I was working on *The War Against the Jews 1933–1945* and *A Holocaust Reader*, I was dismayed to find how inadequately the murder of the European Jews had been recorded in the history books. I became haunted by the fear that the history of the 6 million murdered Jews would vanish from the earth as they themselves and their civilization had vanished.

After I had completed both those books, I decided to look

into this historiographical mystery of why the Holocaust was belittled or overlooked in the history books. I wanted to learn whether the failure to give this subject its due recognition grew out of anti-Jewish bias or just indifference; whether it was a side effect of narrow academicism; whether it was the by-product of an obsession with one's own national history; or, finally, whether, as in the case of the Communist regimes, it was the result of the constraints some regimes impose on their historians.

As I studied the subject, I came to see that the neglect of the Holocaust in histories written by Americans could not be explained in the same way as the treatment accorded the Holocaust in Polish or German history books. Different national traditions or political situations accounted for the absence of the Holocaust from the history books in the different countries. That is why this book is organized as it is. Obviously, I could not read everything published in the different countries I have discussed, but I tried to deal with the more important works or works characteristic of each country's histories.

No doubt, historians and readers of history in any one country, of any one nationality, or of any one religion are saddened and often displeased and angered by the way historians of other countries, other nationalities, and other religions portray them. The Ukrainians, especially Ukrainian historians, for instance, have for generations resented the dominance of the Russian point of view in writing the history of the Ukrainians. The Poles and the Germans offer fundamentally different historical accounts of the same city that the first call Gdańsk and the second call Danzig. The history of Alsace has been told differently on either side of the Rhine. Given these defects, which universally afflict the vision of historians who write about peoples other than their own, it was to be expected that non-Jewish historians would not approach the history of the murder of the European Jews with the same empathy and moral concern that they would normally apply when writing the history of their own people.

But national partisanship alone cannot explain why so many historians in so many countries have failed to deal even adequately with the Holocaust. As this book demonstrates, other factors besides the narrow range of historical imagination account for this particular lapse from professional standards. Not the least of these factors has been a lack of interest in the fate of the Jews. In this book I have tried to analyze those factors of methodology and prejudice, politics and personality, tradition and ideology that explain why so many contemporary historians have neglected a subject that has, in other intellectual circles, raised fundamental questions about Western civilization and Christian morality.

A word needs to be added about an apparent paradox that we are now witnessing. Despite the historians' neglect, courses in the history of the Holocaust, its literature, and its theological implications have proliferated, especially in those colleges and universities with substantial Jewish enrollments. These courses often function as a Jewish equivalent to Black Studies, that is, as ethnic gratification rather than bona fide academic offerings. Actually, just a few history departments have incorporated the history of the Holocaust into their curricula of modern European history. Only when the Holocaust is accepted as a suitable subject for such study and is not regarded merely as an adjunct of ethnic studies will it have attained its proper academic recognition.

A people dies intestate, its benediction
lost. And the future succeeds, unfa-
thered . . .

IRVING FELDMAN, "Psalm"

# 1

# THINKING ABOUT THE SIX MILLION:

# FACTS, FIGURES, PERSPECTIVES

Rosa Luxemburg, a Jew who lived with a universal perspective, once upbraided a friend who lived with a Jewish perspective: "Why do you come with your special Jewish sorrows? I
feel just as sorry for the wretched Indian victims in Putamayo,
for the Negroes in Africa." In our time that kind of univer-
salism has prompted questions about the particularity of the 6
million European Jews murdered during the Second World
War by the Germans and their helpers. Why, it is sometimes
asked, should the Jews be singled out from the statistics of the
millions who were killed during the Second World War?
Surely, it is argued, there is no hierarchy of suffering, for all
peoples and nations suffered enormous losses of life. Surely, it
is contended, to dwell only on the murder of the 6 million Jews
is narrow and parochial, for that obscures the universal human
condition of suffering and death.

In truth, the awesome statistics of the uncounted and unac-
counted millions who lost their lives during the Second World
War stun us into reverential silence for all the dead without
distinction. The enormity of their numbers baffles the mind's
comprehension and numbs the heart's feeling. How does one
apprehend the vacancies left by millions who are missing and
dead? The poet turns from the impersonal anonymity of statistics to grieve just for one person:

4

> We ask for no statistics of the killed . . . .
> However others calculate the cost,
> To us the final aggregate is *one,*
> One with a name, one transferred to the blest . . .[1]

Still, intellectual honesty demands a reckoning of the terrible statistics. The bottom line alone does not truly render the account. Statistical calculations may even quicken the historical imagination. By counting all the dead and recounting the manner of their deaths, we can better fathom the course of the entire war and the import of that single statistic of 6 million murdered Jews.

## Statistics of Death: The War

It has been estimated that at least 35 million persons, perhaps even as many as 50 million, were killed during the Second World War in all theaters of operation in Europe, Africa, Asia, and the South Pacific, on land, on sea, and in the air. They were combatants and civilians, men, women, and children, killed on the battlefields and at home. Among some European peoples the statistics of the killed were so immense as to depress the statistics of those to be born in the next generation.

In Europe the scope of the war extended from the Atlantic to the Black Sea. The war began on September 1, 1939, when Germany invaded Poland and thereafter, in partnership with its then ally, the Soviet Union, occupied and despoiled Poland. Britain and France, committed to Poland's aid, declared war against Germany on September 3. The war engulfed Western Europe when Germany invaded and occupied Norway, Denmark, The Netherlands, Belgium, and France in April and May 1940, with Italy joining the hostilities as Germany's partner. By spring 1941, most countries of Southeast Europe fell under German rule or influence, by force or choice. In June 1941, when Germany launched the surprise invasion of its former ally, sweeping into Soviet territory, the war overwhelmed the whole European continent. Fighting the Russians on the Eastern front, the Germans conducted mainly a motorized, mechanized ground warfare. In the West, they engaged mainly in air warfare, at first offensive but increasingly defensive.

After the Allied landings in Italy in 1943 and in Normandy in 1944, Germany was compelled to fight land and air warfare on two fronts. Early in 1945, the Allied armies and Soviet forces began to converge on Germany and by May forced Germany's unconditional surrender.

Of all European countries, the USSR suffered the greatest loss of life in the war. According to the *Great Soviet Encyclopedia*, Soviet military and civilian losses amounted to some 20 million. Other sources estimate Soviet losses at about 11 million combatants and 7 million civilians. (Polish sources put Soviet losses at barely 7 million, the lowest of any estimate, suggesting that statistics can serve political ends, as a weapon of the weak against the strong.) The civilian losses included those killed in air raids and bombardments, those who died of starvation and disease, the millions deported to Germany for forced labor who are counted among the missing, and about 1.5 million murdered Soviet Jews.[2]

Most of the military losses were combat casualties, but about 3.5 million Soviet prisoners of war are believed to have been murdered by the Germans, gassed at Auschwitz, machine-gunned en masse, or shot in military-style executions. A month before the Germans invaded the Soviet Union, Hitler had issued a decree guaranteeing his armed forces immunity from subsequent prosecution for shooting enemy civilians, "even if the action is also a military crime or misdemeanor." On June 6, 1941, the German High Command, implementing Hitler's decree, issued the infamous *Kommissarbefehl* (Commissar Order), which authorized combat troops to single out from their captured prisoners "political commissars of all kinds" and to kill them. Thus, millions of Soviet prisoners of war were removed from the rights and protection of international law and murdered.[3]

Poland ranks second in the number of war losses. The Bureau of War Indemnities of the Polish People's Republic issued official figures of Poland's wartime losses, estimating a total of 6,028,000 deaths, about 22 percent of the prewar population.[4] (If the Jewish losses are computed separately, the number is about 3 million, or 12.5 percent of the Polish population.) The wartime deaths are categorized in four odd and unsystematic rubrics, without any subdivisions. The first, classified as "direct military action," gives the number of deaths as 644,000, presumably military personnel killed in combat and civilians killed in air raids and artillery fire. The second category, "victims of death camps, raids, executions, annihilation of ghettos, etc.," gives a total of 3,577,000 deaths, of whom 3 million were Jews, though the statistical table does not specify that. The third category, "deaths in prison and other places of confinement, due to epidemics, emaciation, ill treatment etc.," gives 1,286,000 deaths, without any further clarification as to how this estimate was derived. The fourth category, classified as "deaths outside prisons and camps, caused by wounds, mutilation, excessive work etc.," lists 521,000 deaths.

Even if these figures are high, as several Polish scholars acknowledge privately, the Poles did suffer great losses, for the German military and civilian occupation authorities dealt ruthlessly with the Polish population. In the first months of the German invasion, the SS's armed security forces rounded up and murdered thousands of Poland's leadership elite: political and military leaders, church authorities, and top educators. Their murder was intended to leave the Poles leaderless and thus less likely to resist their German despoilers. About 10,000 Poles were killed in the first year of German occupation. In the later years, about 25,000 Poles were killed in mass executions, many in reprisal for resistance activities.[5] No one can say with any exactness how many thousands, or perhaps tens of thousands, of Poles died in concentration and labor camps.

Yugoslavia sustained great wartime losses. Some 1.5 million Yugoslavs, about 9 percent of the population, were killed or disappeared. About 1.2 million of these were civilian casualties, mainly victims of German reprisals for the continuing guerrilla warfare that the Yugoslavs conducted during the German occupation. In Greece, where similar conditions prevailed, the loss of life has been estimated at about 250,000, some 3 to 4 percent of the population.

In Western Europe, in contrast, losses were fewer.* In France, for example, the number of persons killed or missing

* The Germans, who launched the war that brought these unprecedented statistics of death and destruction and who had to fight on both Eastern and Western fronts, suffered about 3.5 million combat casualties and 430,000 civilian casualties (mostly victims of air raids), about 8 percent of the German population in 1939.

has been put at 600,000, about 1.5 percent of the population. Of these, some 200,000 were combat casualties, and 400,000 were civilians (including about 90,000 Jews) who were killed in air raids, executed, or deported.[6] Belgium's losses are put at 50,000, out of a population just under 10 million. In Great Britain, deaths were estimated at about 360,000, comprising both military combat losses and civilians killed in air raids, amounting to less than 1 percent of the population. The English and French probably lost more men in the Battle of Verdun in the First World War than in all of the Second World War.

All over Europe, wherever the Germans had the power, they enforced their total rule by arresting masses of the civilian population whom they regarded as politically dangerous, socially harmful, or economically expendable. The categories were diverse: Communists, socialists, and other political opponents; outspoken members of the clergy and especially Jehovah's Witnesses, who refused to recognize the secular sovereignty of National Socialism; prostitutes, homosexuals, perverts, and professional criminals. To make room for all these prisoners, the National Socialist regime constructed a vast network of concentration camps. In time, to exploit the available human resources under their control, the Germans developed a system of forced labor in the camps, and in the later years of the war, when German manpower needs were desperate, the slave labor of these prisoners from all over Europe became a staple of the German war economy. It has been estimated that over the years about 1,650,000 persons were incarcerated in these camps. Over a million of them died or were killed. Some died of "natural" causes: hunger, exhaustion, disease. Those who lingered, the ailing, the sick, and the dying, no longer able to work and consequently, in the Nazi view, no longer worth keeping alive, were sent to the gas chambers that nearly every camp maintained to dispose of what Hitler called the "useless eaters."[7]

### Statistics of Death: Mass Murder

While planning and conducting the military war to gain *Lebensraum*—"living space" for the German people—and mastery over the whole European continent, Germany simultaneously planned and carried out a systematic program of mass murder. The National Socialists regarded this mass murder as nothing less than an ideological war and its prosecution was synergized with the conventional military war. The High Command of the German Armed Forces conducted the military war, while the SS, the dreaded armed police force of the National Socialist movement, conducted the ideological war. Both wars were concurrent undertakings, strategically and operationally meshed. The success of the mass-murder offensive was made possible by the SS's parasitic dependence upon Germany's military establishment and its national wartime resources, and the operations of the military war provided the cover for the mass murder.

The mass murder represented itself as a holy war to annihilate Germany's "mortal enemy." The mortal enemy—*Todfeind* was Hitler's word—consisted of the Jews, who were, according to the doctrines of National Socialism, the chief antagonists to the German "Aryans." In Nazi ideology the Jew was the primal adversary, the biological archenemy of the German people, whose physical presence, it was alleged, threatened the purity and even the very existence of the "Aryan" race.[8] No other people, nation, or "race" held that status.

Racial purity was a Nazi obsession and embraced every aspect of life in the German dictatorship. Racial eugenics became a matter of state policy. "Positive" racial eugenics encouraged "pure" Aryan Germans to have children. "Negative" eugenics discouraged—to the point of murder and mass murder—the procreation of life that the racists regarded as "valueless." Hitler himself had initiated a racially motivated program of murder, euphemistically called "euthanasia." Its purpose was to kill mentally ill "Aryan" adults, because their abnormalities were believed to infect the "Aryan" race and defile its national health. Within Germany itself, the euthanasia program claimed about 100,000 lives. During the war, convoys of patients from mental institutions from various countries arriving at Auschwitz were sent straight to the gas chambers. No records were kept of their arrival or their murder; their numbers were estimated to be in the thousands.[9]

In the hierarchy of Nazi racism, the "Aryans" were the superior race, destined to rule the world after the destruction of their racial archfoe, the Jews. The lesser races over whom the Germans would rule included the Slavs—Poles, Russians, Ukrainians.

It has been said that the Germans also planned to exterminate the Poles and the Russians on racial grounds since, according to Hitler's racial doctrine, Slavs were believed to be subhumans (*Untermenschen*). But no evidence exists that a plan to murder the Slavs was ever contemplated or developed. The German racists assigned the Slavs to the lowest rank of human life, from which the Jews were altogether excluded. The Germans thus looked upon Slavs as people not fit to be educated, not able to govern themselves, worthy only as slaves whose existence would be justified because they served their German masters. Hitler's racial policy with regard to the Slavs, to the extent that it was formulated, was "depopulation." The Slavs were to be prevented from procreating, except to provide the necessary continuing supply of slave laborers. Whether the Russians—or other "non-Aryan" peoples—lived or died was, as Himmler once put it to his top SS officers, "a matter of indifference." In contrast, he justified and even extolled the murder of the Jews as "an unwritten and never-to-be-written page of glory" in German history.[10]

The European Gypsies, too, suffered enormous losses at the hands of the Germans, yet the National Socialist state had no clear-cut racial policy with regard to them. Hitler appears to have overlooked them in his racial thinking. The Germans regarded the Gypsies primarily as an antisocial element, consisting of thieves and vagrants, rather than as an alien racial group. When the National Socialist regime began to incorporate its racial ideas in legislation, the Ministry of Interior ordered investigations to be made as to whether Gypsies were racially fit to be educated. (The answer was no.) But not until August 1941 did the German bureaucracy make any systematic attempt to classify the Gypsies racially. At that time Nazi officials established two basic categories, dividing the native Gypsy tribes from the foreign ones. The native tribes were defined as those who had settled in Germany since the fifteenth century, and hence were entitled to citizenship and the protection of German law. Distinctions also began to be made between "pure" Gypsies and "part" Gypsies (offspring of marriages between Gypsies and Germans), classifications that were patterned on the Nuremberg Laws promulgated in 1935 and frequently refined and implemented. When the Nazis began in 1941 to formulate a racial policy with regard to the Gypsies, no agreement on the matter had been reached by the top Nazi leaders. Late in 1943, the German occupying authorities in the Eastern areas ruled, with Himmler's approval, that sedentary Gypsies and their offspring were to be treated as citizens of the country, whereas nomadic Gypsies and their offspring were to be treated as Jews (that is, murdered). This distinction between two kinds of Gypsies blunted their classification as a racial group and strengthened the idea that nomadic Gypsies were antisocial. SS security forces, "cleansing" the occupied countryside of "dangerous elements," murdered many Gypsies on grounds that they were unreliable, unemployable, and criminal. Only in the last year of the war did the Nazi ideologues begin to regard the Gypsies not only as an undesirable social element, but also as an undesirable racial element.

During the war, tens of thousands of Gypsies living in Germany, Austria, and other German-occupied countries were deported to camps in Poland, including Auschwitz. The statistics of the murdered Gypsies are gross estimates: of about 1 million Gypsies in the countries that fell under German control, nearly a quarter of them were murdered—machine-gunned or gassed.[11]

### The Jews: A Special Case

The fate of the Jews under National Socialism was unique. They obsessed Hitler all his life and their presence in Germany, their very existence, preoccupied the policymakers of the German dictatorship. The *Judenfrage*—the question of the Jews—riveted all Germany. The age-old heritage of anti-Semitism, compounded of Christian prejudices, economic rivalries, and social envy, was fanned by Nazi racism. Every German city, town, and village applied itself to the Jews and the Jewish question with rampant violence and meticulous legalism.

Once the National Socialists came to power, they incorporated their racist beliefs into law, in a short time enacting a major corpus of anti-Jewish legislation. The laws established legal definitions of the Jews and then, step by step, deprived the Jews of their rights, their property, and their livelihoods. In time, the Jews became segregated and ostracized from German society and were deprived of the protection of the law—even such as it was in Nazi Germany.

But National Socialist Germany had a still more radical objective with regard to the Jews: total annihilation. The war which Hitler unleashed in September 1939 was intended to achieve that objective while the Germans also pursued their aggressive expansionism against the nations of Europe.

The German dictatorship devised two strategies to conduct its war of annihilation against the Jews: mass shooting and mass gassing. Special-duty troops of the SS's Security Service and Security Police, called *Einsatzgruppen*, were assigned to each of the German armies invading the Soviet Union. Following hard upon the armed forces and dependent upon them for basic services, the Einsatzgruppen were given the task of rounding up the Jews and killing them. The procedures used everywhere behind the Russian front were crude and primitive. (To talk of harnessing modern technology to mass murder is nonsense.) The Jews were loaded on trucks or forced to march to some desolate area with antitank trenches already dug or natural ravines. Otherwise, the Jews were ordered to dig what would become their own mass graves. Then they were machine-gunned at the rim of the trench or pit into which their bodies toppled. The International Military Tribunal at Nuremberg estimated that the Einsatzgruppen murdered about 2 million Jews.

To systematize the murder of the rest of the European Jews the National Socialist state built six installations with large-scale gassing facilities and with crematoria for the disposal of the bodies. These were all located on Polish territory: Oświęcim (better known by its German name, Auschwitz), Bełżec, Chełmno, Majdanek, Sobibór, and Treblinka. The technology applied here—discharging poison gas through shower-head vents in sealed chambers—was barely more sophisticated than the brute violence of the Einsatzgruppen. The logistics, however, were impressive, and in the three years during which these killing installations operated, about 3.5 million Jews from every country of Europe were murdered there.* (Approximately 1.5 million non-Jews were gassed in these camps, most at Auschwitz.)

Of the 9 million Jews who lived in the countries of Europe that fell under German rule during the war, about 6 million—that is, two-thirds of all European Jews—were murdered.[12] Their numbers and concentration in Eastern Europe and their uninterrupted cultural traditions there for a thousand years had rendered them the most vital Jewish community, whose creativity sustained Jews throughout the world. Though the Soviet Union suffered greater losses than the Jews in absolute figures, no other people anywhere lost the main body of its population and the fountainhead of its cultural resources. No other people was chosen for total extinction.

The deaths of the 6 million European Jews were not a by-product of the war. The Jews did not die as a consequence of the indiscriminate reach of bombs or gunfire or of the unselective fallout of deadly weapons. Nor were they the victims of the cruel and brutal expediency that actuated the Nazis to kill the Soviet prisoners of war and the Polish elite. Those murders were intended as means to practical ends: they were meant to protect and to consolidate the position of the Germans as undisputed masters over Europe. The murder of the Jews and the destruction of Jewish communal existence were, in contrast, ends in themselves, ultimate goals to which the National Socialist state had dedicated itself.

To refer to the murder of the 6 million Jews as distinctive, as unique, is not an attempt to magnify the catastrophe that befell them nor to beg tears and pity for them. It is not intended to minimize the deaths of the millions of non-Jews that the Germans brought about, or to underplay the immeasurable and

---

* In computing the statistics of the 6 million murdered Jews, it is estimated that in addition to the 2 million killed by the Einsatzgruppen and the 3.5 million in the gas chambers, about 500,000 died in the ghettos of Eastern Europe of hunger, disease, and exhaustion, and as victims of random terror and reprisals.

unendurable suffering of Russians, Poles, Gypsies, and other victims of the German murder machine. To speak of the singularity of the murder of the 6 million European Jews is not to deny the incontestable fact that the gas chambers extinguished without discrimination all human life.[13] The murder of the 6 million Jews stands apart from the deaths of the other millions, not because of any distinctive fate that the individual victims endured, but because of the differentiative intent of the murderers and the unique effect of the murders.

The intent on the part of the German dictatorship to annihilate the Jews was based on their judgment that the Jews had no right to live, a judgment that no one has the right to make. Karl Jaspers, German philosopher, explained the uniqueness of the murder of the 6 million Jews: "Anyone who on the basis of such a judgment plans the organized slaughter of a people and participates in it, does something that is fundamentally different from all crimes that have existed in the past."[14]

The effect of the murder of the 6 million Jews is still to be evaluated. From the Jewish point of view, we know one thing now for certain. The immensity of the Jewish losses destroyed the biological basis for the continued communal existence of Jews in Europe. Every country and people ravaged by the war and by the German occupation eventually returned to a normal existence. All the nations, the victims now become victors, the aggressors now defeated, once again assumed their positions in the political order. Having mourned their dead, commemorated their martyrs and heroes, all the peoples of Europe, including the Germans, recovered from their wounds, rebuilt their shattered cities. London, Warsaw, and Rotterdam, as well as Berlin and Dresden, were reconstructed. They restored their factories and their marketplaces. They resuscitated their institutions of learning and culture. They reestablished their armed forces. But the annihilation of the 6 million European Jews brought an end with irrevocable finality to the thousand-year-old culture and civilization of Ashkenazic Jewry, destroying the continuity of Jewish history.* This is the special

---

* The Jewish community in Israel, a state whose political existence was legitimated as a recompense for the murder of the European Jews, is producing a radically different Jewish culture from that of European Jewry. It is not yet evident whether Israel can develop the creative cultural energy that will succeed in binding Jews of the world together, while conserving the traditions of the past and evolving new ones.

Jewish sorrow. This is why the surviving Jews grieve, mourning the loss of their past and the imperilment of their future.

## The Holocaust Universalized: Metaphor and Analogy

The murder of the 6 million Jews, in its unparalleled scope, devastating effect, and incomprehensible intent, overtook the capacity of man's imagination to conceive of evil. The killing camps, an empire of death with their bulging gas chambers and smoke-belching crematoria operated by the SS Death's Head Division, eclipsed man's visions of hell. The names of these death factories—and especially the name of Auschwitz—replaced Dante's Nine Circles of Hell as the quintessential epitome of evil, for they were located not in the literary reaches of the medieval religious imagination, but in the political reality of twentieth-century Europe.

It was to be anticipated that Auschwitz would become a metaphor and a paradigm for evil. How could it be otherwise? But what was unexpected was the occasional attempt to turn Auschwitz into a metaphor for the "ecumenical nature" of the evil that was committed there or to render the murder of the Jews as mere atrocity, sheer blood lust. What was unexpected was the failure to understand—or to acknowledge—that the evil was not ecumenical, that the killing was not blood lust for its own sake, but that the evil and killing were specifically directed against particular victims. To make Auschwitz serve as the paradigm for universal evil is in effect to deny the historical reality that the German dictatorship had a specific intent in murdering the Jews.*

Auschwitz was a social and political reality. It was neither conceived nor constructed as a theater of atrocity to play out Everyman's capacity for evil, to satisfy a universal lust for killing. Auschwitz was the direct consequence of a specific and particular history of racist anti-Semitism. It was invented and assembled by National Socialist Germany to kill its mortal

---

* I am not here referring to those who altogether deny that the European Jews were annihilated, like Arthur R. Butz, author of an overtly anti-Semitic work called *The Hoax of the Twentieth Century*. Those people are outright Nazis or Nazi apologists. I find it difficult to believe that any person of good will, however ignorant of the recent past, can give credence to such notions. For more about the neo-Nazi attempt to deny the historicity of the murder of the European Jews see Lucy S. Dawidowicz, "Lies About the Holocaust," *Commentary*, 70, 6 (December 1980), 31–37.

enemy, the Jews. Once its killing facilities were devised and installed, once Auschwitz became an operational enterprise for mass-murdering the Jews, it became convenient for the Germans to use that equipment also to murder those non-Jews who had, for one reason or another, become expendable.

What underlies the attempt to deprive the Jews, as it were, of their terrible unique experience as a people marked for annihilation? Does it derive from a form of contempt for the Jews, from some personal resentment against Jews, or out of professional rivalry with Jews and envy of them, out of some barely conscious stirrings of anti-Jewish hostility? By subsuming the Jewish losses under a universal or ecumenical classification of human suffering, one can blur the distinctiveness of Jewish fate and consequently one can disclaim the presence of anti-Semitism, whether it smolders in the dark recesses of one's own mind or whether it operates in the pitiless light of history. Therefore, one can feel free to reject political or moral responsibility for the consequences of that anti-Semitism.

In denying the uniqueness of the fate the Jews experienced as the chosen victims of mass murder, the universalizers of Auschwitz do not necessarily deny the uniqueness of the mass murderers. At least they understand that the mass murder which the National Socialist state perpetrated stands alone in the annals of human murderousness, that something new in human history happened when Hitler's Germany arrogated to itself the right to decide who was entitled to live in the world and who was not. But all too often the necessary and essential distinction between the murder of the 6 million Jews and the accelerating violence and terror of our time is blurred, sometimes erased, whether mindlessly or with political intent.*

How commonplace nowadays the glib equation of the murder of the Jews with any disaster or atrocity, with any state of affairs one abhors or even merely dislikes. Extremist blacks, with careless disregard for linguistic precision or conceptual clarity, have abused words like "genocide," "Auschwitz," "ho-

* Those guilty of muddleheaded indiscriminateness include also Jews who are overwhelmed by anxiety for Israel's existence. For decades some have, with the intemperance of hysteria, equated Arab leaders with Hitler. Jewish poets and politicians alike often compare Auschwitz with Ma'alot, an Israeli settlement where in 1974 Arab terrorists killed 20 children and wounded 70 more.

locaust," exploiting them in excesses of rhetorical overkill to describe conditions in urban slums. Some American antiabortionists, with the fanaticism of zealots, have compared advocates of population control to Nazis who murdered the Jews. Vladimir Nabokov characterized this as *poshlost*, a Russian word whose many nuanced meanings he summarized as "corny trash, vulgar cliches, Philistinism in all its phases, imitations of imitations, bogus profundities." *Poshlost*, he said, "speaks in such concepts as 'America is no better than Russia' or 'We all share in Germany's guilt' . . . Listing in one breath Auschwitz, Hiroshima, and Vietnam is seditious *poshlost*."[15]

The extravagances that equate any offensiveness in contemporary life with the murder of the 6 million European Jews are not just the mouthings of imperceptive innocents or literary vulgarians. For one, they camouflage an underlying contempt for the Jews. By denying the particularity of the Jewish experience under the German dictatorship and, still more, the enormity of Jewish losses, by equating the destruction of the European Jews with other events, they succeed in obscuring the role of anti-Semitism in accomplishing that murder. All atrocities are reduced to the same rubble. For another, when they equate National Socialist Germany with the United States, they bespeak a vicious anti-Americanism. Their purpose is to depict America as Amerika, a Nazified United States, heir as it were of the unredeemed evil which the Nazis represented.

Thus, Hiroshima, the Japanese city upon which the Americans dropped the first atomic bomb in August 1945, becomes an accusatory byword against America. How valid is the equation? As for numbers, the A-bomb left 130,000 casualties in dead, injured, and missing. (At Nagasaki, where the second A-bomb was dropped, about 75,000 persons were killed or injured.) But numbers are not the only factor. America's decision to use the atomic bomb against Japan was not motivated by a wish to wipe out the Japanese people. The purpose of the bombing was to demonstrate America's superior military power and thus convince the Japanese that they had to capitulate, thereby ending the war and further killing. Merely to set down the bare outlines of what Hiroshima was intended to accomplish, and did in fact accomplish, is to expose the discongruity between the A-bombing of Hiroshima and the mass murder of the Jews, a discongruity not only with regard to extent, but more important, with regard to intent. (To say this is in no way to minimize Hiroshima's terrible cost of life and the fearful consequences of atomic radiation on the survivors.)

The ugly incident of My Lai, during the last years of United States involvement in the war in Vietnam, provided another spurious parallel with Auschwitz to fuel anti-American rhetoric. My Lai was a Vietnamese village where an American army unit in the course of combat operations against the Viet Cong in 1968 shot to death 347 unarmed civilians—men, women, and children. The army had covered up the incident, but when the story came to light a year later, public indignation prompted investigations and subsequently the responsible officer was brought to trial. Anti-Americanists, trying to justify their parallel between the Americans at My Lai and the Nazis, charged that the officer's decision ordering his men to kill the Vietnamese had been motivated by racism. (The more persuasive evidence indicated that the killings were prompted by fear that the civilians were in fact members of the Viet Cong.)

Furthermore, the argument that America committed crimes as monumental as those of the Nazis can justify a reverse claim: since the United States committed crimes as evil as those of Nazi Germany, then Nazi Germany committed no worse crimes than other states and was not unique among nations as a perpetrator of evil deeds. Thus, all states and all forms of government are reduced to a simplistic uniformity: differences between democracy and totalitarianism become unimportant. No distinction is made between a just war and an unjust war, between murdering 6 million Jews and, for instance, bombing Dresden. Thus Kurt Vonnegut in *Slaughterhouse-Five* baldly asserts that "the greatest massacre in European history" was the firebombing of Dresden.[16] Dresden, the historic German city, was bombed by British and American planes in February 1945, in retaliation for the launching of German V-2 rockets against London. The estimate of lives lost in the Dresden bombing is 35,000; the damage to the city was extensive. Though Vonnegut was himself held prisoner of war by the Germans in Dresden during the bombing, he leaned heavily for an account of that event and even for moral judgment on a

shamelessly fanciful anti-Allied version of the Dresden bombing by David Irving, an English journalist who has achieved a
measure of notoriety as a German apologist and even as a
Hitler apologist.[17]


## The Lesson of National Socialism

Jacob Burckhardt, the nineteenth-century Swiss historian, observed that "history is the record of what one age finds worthy
of note in another." The mountainous accumulation of histories about World War II and especially about the event-laden
twelve-year National Socialist era testifies to the consensus
among historians and consumers of history alike that the period was worthy of record. The rise and fall of the German
dictatorship, and especially the rise and fall of its dictator, con-
tinue to fascinate scholars and the public at large.

Why should this be so? The National Socialist regime effected no abiding transformations of society within Germany's
borders or beyond and left no lasting monuments to its once
overmastering presence on the European continent. To be
sure, when Hitler came to power, a revolution of political and
social magnitude erupted, but unlike other revolutions—political, industrial, scientific—the National Socialist revolution left
no enduring heritage. The Russian Revolution, in contrast, set
in motion political upheavals and economic convulsions whose
effects still reverberate around the world. The Communist revolution in China has already radically altered the social and political face of Asia itself. In the wake of the Second World War
the Third World nations emerged to transform the international arena and the struggle for world power. As for science
and technology, their development in the last three decades has
challenged the foundations of our past knowledge as well as of
our future existence. The terrifying capacity of the scientific
mind to destroy life may soon be outstripped by its still more
terrifying capacity to fabricate life.

National Socialist Germany achieved no comparable far-
reaching or fundamental impact on society. Yet even as the
events of its short reign and its still briefer dominion over Eu-

rope recede into the past, its ghostly ghastly presence continues to hover over us, to inhabit our political and moral universe. For Nazism, as we have seen, has come to represent the essence of evil, the daemon let loose in society, Cain in a corporate embodiment. The accomplishment of the National Socialist state was nothing less than the consummation of mass murder in the service of fanatic racism whose unconditional imperative was: destroy the Jews. Obsessed by its passion to kill the Jews, the Nazi state harnessed the energies of its people and of its institutions of government; of industry, technology, and science; of education, art, and religion. It succeeded in consolidating and systematizing them for that mission of monumental mass murder. Never before had the principles and methods of rational organization been employed on behalf of the irrational, the demonic. Never before had mass murder been so regulated and regularized, organized on scientific principles of industrial management, its standardized procedures for killing developed by a system of empirical testing and designed to achieve a maximum efficiency of operation. Never before in human history had a state and a political movement dedicated itself to the destruction of a whole people.

The destruction of the European Jews was and remains a special Jewish sorrow. But the National Socialist state and its capacity to organize mass murder on grounds of racist anti-Semitism was and remains a universal concern because it represents a terrifying juncture in human history. Things once unthinkable are now not only possible, but have actually happened. In 1897, when the Dreyfus Affair was tearing France apart, Bernard Lazare, a French Jew active in Dreyfus's defense, addressed a group of Jewish students in Paris on the subject of anti-Semitism. "For the Christian peoples," he remarked, "an Armenian solution" to their Jew-hatred was available. He was referring to the Turkish massacres of Armenians, which in their extent and horror most closely approximated the murder of the European Jews. But, Lazare went on, "their sensibilities cannot allow them to envisage that."[18] The once unthinkable "Armenian solution" became, in our time, the achievable "Final Solution," the Nazi code name for the annihilation of the European Jews.

What men do today, Karl Jaspers said, becomes the source of

their future actions. Nothing but the most lucid consciousness of the horror that happened can help avoid it for the future:

> That which has happened is a warning. To forget it is guilt. It must be continually remembered. It was possible for this to happen, and it remains possible for it to happen again at any minute. Only in knowledge can it be prevented.[19]

History never embraces more than a small
part of reality.

LA ROCHEFOUCAULD

# 2

# THE EYE OF THE BEHOLDER:
# THE HOLOCAUST ACCORDING TO
# ENGLISH AND AMERICAN HISTORIANS

An eminent English historian of Germany recently appraised
Hitler's place in contemporary history as follows:

> The curious thing—almost the paradoxical thing—is that the
> twentieth century has gone on its way almost as if [Hitler] had
> not existed. Not quite, of course. There is the division of Ger-
> many (though he was not really responsible for that . . .) and—
> the one thing, the only thing, for which he was entirely respon-
> sible, a dreadful and evil thing—the destruction of European
> Jewry. The monuments to his memory, the only lasting monu-
> ments . . . are the concentration camps, tidied up into neat show
> places and open to curious or mourning visitors. Otherwise, so
> far as the world today is concerned, he might not have lived.[1]

The appraisal underrates and overstates. Yet would we not
be justified to conclude from it that since the destruction of the
European Jews was Hitler's only lasting accomplishment, the
ideas and the progression of events which brought about that
destruction must now be considered, historically speaking, to
have been just as significant during Hitler's lifetime as they
would become after his death? Consequently, should we not
expect that the history of the Holocaust would be assured of its
place in the history of Germany, of the Second World War,
and even of the twentieth century?

But it is plain from even the most cursory review of textbooks and scholarly works by English and American historians that the awesome events of the Holocaust have not been given their historic due. For over two decades some secondary school and college texts never mentioned the subject at all, while others treated it so summarily or vaguely as to fail to convey sufficient information about the events themselves or their historic significance.[2]

## Lessons of the Textbooks

Consider a standard history of Germany by the eminent English historian whose appraisal of Hitler was quoted above. Geoffrey Barraclough's textbook, *The Origins of Modern Germany*, has served college students in England and the United States for well over a quarter of a century. Beginning with Charles the Great's coronation in 800 and closing in 1939, this volume takes the long perspective on the "German problem," defined somewhat apologetically as the need "to build a Germany of the German people, representing not the will of a predatory minority, but the sober interests and aspirations of the German-speaking millions in the historic German lands between France and the Slavonic east."[3]

Barraclough, who stresses the longer and wider perspective of German history, emphasizing continuity, never once in this book mentions the Jews, who were a continuous presence in the German lands at least since the tenth century. He never once mentions anti-Semitism, surely one of Germany's enduring historic traditions. In Barraclough's history, the Jews are not merely invisible, they are altogether nonexistent. Though their history in Germany was an integral part of every chapter in German history, Barraclough does not enter them anywhere in the record.

Still, the most astonishing omission is Barraclough's failure to mention that Hitler, the National Socialist party, and the National Socialist regime pursued anti-Jewish policies that started out by taking from the Jews their rights and ended by taking their lives. In his closing chapter Barraclough offers only one bare elliptical reference to National Socialism's "hateful racial doctrines," but nowhere are these specified or explicated.

Consider another instance, the *Columbia History of the World*, which begins with the formation of the universe and closes with a survey of the culture of the 1960s. Forty professors of Columbia University contributed to this 1,237-page volume, intended to serve as a world history text. Rene Albrecht-Carrié, a retired professor from Barnard College, wrote two chapters: "Europe Between the Wars" and "World War II." The first, covering Hitler's rise to power and his government up to 1939, contains only three sentences, and those overrun with errors, that deal with anti-Semitism, the Nazis' racial ideas and policies, and the situation of the Jews. We are told that Hitler was "a bitter and fervent nationalist" who "found his major scapegoat in the Jews," that decrees of 1935 and 1938 took up in earnest "the drive for 'racial purity,' " and that the SS and the Gestapo "were used to bring the entire country under subjection." Such fragments of information and misinformation can scarcely enhance a student's knowledge or understanding of the events referred to.

The chapter on the Second World War is no better. It contains one cryptic reference to Nazi racial policy with regard to the Slavs, and a general conclusion cited here in full:

> The impact of the Nazis' dreadful racial fantasies further exacerbated the situation. Some 6 million Jews and countless other innocents had been exterminated. The horrors of the concentration camps and gas chambers left memories that it would take a long time to erase.[4]

Finally a reference to the destruction of the Jews and the existence of the death camps, though no student could comprehend how or why such things had come about since no earlier account had been offered. The last sentence is a model of obtuseness.

From such accounts, it becomes evident that the neglect of the Holocaust in the history of Germany or twentieth-century Europe or the Second World War cannot be attributed to a mere lapsus, unfortunate but excusable. That neglect bespeaks professional deficiency. Textbooks generally reflect the accumulation of scholarship in special fields and textbook authors tend to rely on comprehensive works which have been accorded professional recognition. The Holocaust can claim few such authoritative scholarly works, yet they do exist: reliable works have been available for over twenty-five years to those who have chosen to look for them. Could one, for instance, write a competent history of the South or the Civil War without mentioning slavery or without referring to the black people? It is also clear that even the briefest and most perfunctory rendering of the Holocaust's history requires a coherent presentation, that it cannot be conveyed in dissociated fragments.

Ideally, the history of the Holocaust, however compactly composed, should consist of three fundamental components: (1) an exposition of how and by whom the European Jews were annihilated; (2) an explanation of why they were annihilated, with reference to the history of anti-Semitism; and (3) an appropriate account of their history before the rise of Hitler. To be sure, few textbooks do justice—or partial justice—to the subject, but there are some.

Consider, for instance, R. R. Palmer and Joel Colton, *A History of the Modern World*, a college text which succeeds in integrating Jewish history into the framework of European history and deals in an altogether admirable manner with the Nazi era.[5] As for textbooks of German history, the late Koppel S. Pinson combined his interests in modern German and Jewish history in an exemplary text in which the strands of Jewish social, cultural, and political history are woven into the fabric of German history.[6] More recently Gordon A. Craig's history of modern Germany, a work whose stylistic elegance enhances its intellectual distinction, has devoted space to the rise of political anti-Semitism in the German Empire and to the events leading to the destruction of the Jews in the Third Reich. Though this material is not integrated into the larger political perspectives of German history, standing, as it were, in isolation from other developments, Professor Craig has, by including this material, confirmed its place in the record of modern history.[7]

These books are, however, the exceptions. The frequency with which the Holocaust has been neglected or passed over, distorted or trivialized in history textbooks suggests that other factors besides professional competence are involved. How account for the blind spot which renders invisible the vast landscape of death and destruction of the Holocaust? The answer lies in a combination of professional and personal factors.

Good historians strive for fairness and objectivity. They do so by adhering to the methodological rules concerning the use of historical evidence, thus demonstrating that they have mastered the skills of their craft. But historians, being men and women like everyone else, are products of their time and place, shaped by their family, religion, culture, and class, and they write history out of those perspectives. Professor Arnaldo Momigliano noted: "Historians have evaluated the past either in accordance with their religious, social, political and philosophical beliefs or in order to test these beliefs against the results of their own historical explorations."[8]

American and English historians whose field is German history, who studied for years in Germany, formed lasting attachments to the country and its people, its language and literature. Older generations of historians saw Germany as the homeland of modern historiography, and were bedazzled by the illustrious names of Humboldt, Ranke, Sybel, Meinecke.[9] Those affective and intellectual influences that Germany exercised over historians eventually found some expression in their finished historical products, perhaps through the choice or avoidance of certain subject matter, perhaps in giving priority to one area over another, or, as with Professor Barraclough's text, in taking so long a perspective of German history and politics as to shrink the Nazi era into near nothingness.

## The Invisible Jews

An even more fundamental explanation for the absence of the Holocaust in so many history books and for the invisibility of the Jews can be sought in attitudes common among historians with regard to the place of Jews in history. For long centuries, Jews had been considered outsiders by those who wrote history. From the Middle Ages until the age of modernity, the writing of history, whether it was universal history or local chronicle, was largely in the hands of the Church and its advocates. Ever since the Church triumphed over the Synagogue, the Church determined the place of the Jews in history, if indeed they were to have a place at all. The story of the Jewish past and the exposition of Jewish ideas—especially the concepts and teachings of Judaism—were rewritten, distorted, and even falsified in order to assure the ascendancy of Christian doctrine and its superiority over Judaism. Besides, many scholars as well as Church militants believed that only by conversion to Christianity could Jews assure themselves of a place in history in this world and their salvation in the next.

The Reformation continued this tradition. In later times those liberal Protestants who wrote seemingly sympathetic histories of the Jews—like Pastor Jacob Christian Basnage, Hannah Adams, and Episcopal Dean Henry Hart Milman— were actually using the history of the persecuted Jews as a stick with which to beat the Catholic Church or to condemn the political despotism that they could not attack directly.[10] They themselves looked toward the conversion of the Jews, believing that someday Christian prophecies would come to pass and that "Jews and Gentiles unitedly" would "become the subject of Christ's universal empire."[11]

With the Enlightenment and the rise of the nation-states, history ceased to be the handmaiden of Christianity and its institutions and became instead the servant of the state. In the new political arrangements, the Jews continued to remain outsiders, persecuted and excluded because they were now considered alien to the developing national ethos. Also, in the newly developing discipline of critical historical scholarship of the nineteenth century, the Jews remained outsiders or were altogether nonpersons. Jews seldom appeared in the history books produced by the rapidly growing body of professional historians. Ranke, for example, wrote a six-volume history of Germany during the Reformation (1486–1555) with barely four references to the Jews.[12]

When the learned historians did not entirely excise the Jews from the history books, the Jews were cast in the same stereotypic images that the illiterate and superstitious masses held: the Jew as usurer or money-grubber, as dishonest businessman or avaricious banker; or the Jew was portrayed as deracinated intellectual, dangerous radical, cosmopolitan bohemian, cultural contaminator. One need only cite the now famous passage in Theodor Mommsen's history of Rome, in which he concluded, from the perspective of early German liberal nationalism, that "even in the ancient world Judaism was an effective leaven of cosmopolitanism and of national decomposition."[13] Though Mommsen, in later decades, vigorously opposed the rise of political anti-Semitism in Germany, that passage became a proof text for anti-Semites. (Hitler's frequent use of the phrase describing the Jews as the "ferment of decomposition" was derived from Mommsen.) In delineating the Jews in history, modern critical historians—Heinrich von Treitschke, for instance—scarcely differed from the methodically unsophisticated chroniclers and polemicist theologians of the Middle Ages—Isidore of Seville, for instance. In this regard critical history had made little progress since teleological history.

In a pioneering survey published in 1966, Professor Gavin I. Langmuir, a specialist in the history of anti-Semitism in medieval France and England, examined a series of textbooks and histories to see how the Jews were treated in post-Biblical history.[14] His findings led him to formulate the idea of "majority history," to explain the attitudes of historians toward Jews and their history: "Inheriting a historiographic tradition hostile towards or ignorant of Jews, or both, and writing for a society little interested in Jewish history or more or less hostile to Jews, historians of the majority have been little attracted to the history of the Jews, little inspired even to read the work of Jewish historians, let alone to study the matter themselves."

In the United States too, where anti-Semitism has not been widely prevalent in social life or political thought, the Jews have nonetheless been conspicuous by their absence from the history books. That absence can be accounted for in part by the fact that the historical profession for many generations consisted largely of white Anglo-Saxons, a predominance which has begun to be challenged only in recent decades. The Jews seldom occupied a place in the minds of those historians, an indifference that appears in sharp contrast to the preoccupations of many American historians with slavery. The extent to which the Jews and their history are nonpersons and nonsubjects is dramatically evident in a major work of American historiography, *History*, one of a series of studies commissioned by the Council of the Humanities of Princeton University.[15] Though two of its three authors have written on aspects of Jewish history, this work of theirs contains not one reference to Jews or Jewish history. The authors discuss every kind of history imaginable—ancient history and urban history, agricultural history and institutional history, Chinese history, Islamic history, Latin American history, but not Jewish history. Dozens of historians are mentioned, but not Professor Salo W. Baron, whose monumental *Social and Religious History of the Jews,* with sixteen volumes so far published by Columbia University Press, not only is a landmark in Jewish historiography, but also has set a standard for erudition and critical scholarship that few American historians can match. Nor does *History* mention Professor Jacob Rader Marcus, the dean of American Jewish historians, whose research in early American Jewish history has illuminated the social and economic life of early America.

## *Warps of Historical Method*

Many scholarly monographs and specialized histories are as flawed as the textbooks in their treatment, or nontreatment, of the Jews, and for the same reasons. But other factors contribute to the historiographical indifference, factors which have less to do with the Jews and more with professional methods prevalent among academic historians in America today.

Specialization, for example, the hallmark of academic research, eliminates from the field of view everything except that one small segment of historical matter chosen for dissection, thus encouraging tunnel vision. Neophyte historians soon adjust to the historical blinders that their teachers have prescribed. Not surprisingly, then, specialization will operate so as to eliminate from the historical perspective the Jews, whose presence does not fit anywhere into familiar categories.

Another factor to account for the absence of the Jews in works about Nazi Germany by many American and English historians is that they are not accustomed to dealing with ideology and with its political impact. It is a commonplace observation that Anglo-American political traditions, compounded of liberalism, libertarianism, utilitarianism, and pragmatism, are at complete variance with the political ideologies of communism, fascism, and Nazism. Ideological thinking, which entails a coherent and unitary view of human existence and of the universe (*Weltanschauung*), has been alien to American historians, not only because they have enshrined pragmatism as an integral part of the American ethos, but even more because America's religious, racial, and ethnic diversity and multiplicity have prevented the entrenchment of any one ideology in American political life. Academic historians, who have experienced only the happy provincialism of American politics, often fail to perceive the dynamism that those Central and East European ideologies generated in the newly emergent nation-states. American historians tend to approach the history of the Soviet Union as well as that of Nazi Germany with the conventional methods of nineteenth-century diplomatic, political, and military history or of twentieth-century socioeconomic history, neglecting inquiry into political ideas and ideology. They have thereby created a vacuum which has been penetrated mainly by the political scientists and philosophers.

Besides, American historians have been trained to scant the place of ideas in history. The progressive tradition in American historiography, which once cultivated empiricism and the social sciences, reinforced by the computer and the econometricians, is nowadays again in the ascendancy. Statistics often supplant ideas as the vital data for history. Few contemporary American historians would agree with Henry Adams that "the movement of thought" was "more interesting than the movement of population or of wealth."[16] American history not only has stinted on the history of ideas—Arthur O. Lovejoy notwithstanding—but has altogether begrudged acknowledging that ideas have a role in shaping and determining the great events in history. If noble and splendid ideas find little resonance in American historiography, how much more likely that mean and meretricious ones will be altogether overlooked, no matter that they were, and still remain, powerful historical propellants.

Indeed, the ugly complex of ideas, beliefs, opinions, attitudes, fancies, notions, and superstitions comprising anti-Semitism and racism has found little place in works by many American historians on Nazi Germany, even though those ideas nourished Germany's culture and politics. However competent such historical works may be according to prevailing professional standards, they are nevertheless flawed as history.[17] In slighting the relationship between Nazi ideas and the bloody events that proceeded from them, the historian reduces his own capacity to explain Nazi Germany's past.

To be sure, there are American historians—including some of the first rank—who have given the ideas and ideologies of anti-Semitism and racism their proper place in the history of modern Germany. George L. Mosse has established a reputation in modern historiography as the preeminent explicator and demythologizer of the ideas that shaped German nationalism and Nazism.[18] Fritz R. Stern, whose writings on modern Germany have established his international reputation, has shown a singular sensitivity to the presence of Jews in German history.[19] It is perhaps no coincidence that these scholars, and others in their company, came to the United States as refugees from Hitler's Germany. Their personal experience, sharpened by moral challenge, shaped their professional commitment. As Fritz Stern put it:

> For my generation and for those older than we, the Third Reich was the central, collective experience of our lives. The shadow of Hitler fell on our youth, and we remember still the mounting terror of his rule. We remember the frenzied enthusiasm he aroused and the tepid opposition he encountered; we remember his Reich as the meanest and most popular tyranny the world has ever seen. Hitler was a challenge to our lives that we survived; he was also a challenge to our moral and political traditions, to our assumptions about man's nature, and that challenge we are still in the midst of meeting.[20]

Some native American historians too, of Stern's generation and happily also of a younger generation, have pursued the matter of Nazi ideas and ideology, especially with regard to anti-Semitism, and they have shown as well an appreciation for the role of anti-Semitism and the spread of Nazi ideas in German society.[21]

## The British Perspective

The English historians of modern Germany, whose work has gained them international renown, astonish us with the minimal attention they give to German anti-Semitism and to the destruction of the Jews. Consider Alan Bullock's 800-page biography of Hitler, which for nearly two decades has been the standard work.[22] Its fifty-odd references to Jews and anti-Semitism (including Hitler's ideas about Jews and his program for their destruction) come to about fifteen pages, less than 2 percent of the whole book. Yet Lord Bullock himself asserts that "from first to last [Hitler's] anti-Semitism is one of the most consistent themes in his career, the master idea which embraces the whole span of his thought." Elsewhere Bullock writes that anti-Jewish legislation was a subject that always interested Hitler, yet Bullock's only reference to the massive anti-Jewish legislation Hitler introduced in 1933 is contained in one meager footnote.[23]

Method rather than bias explains the shallow treatment. Lord Bullock's biography is of the old school, with its conventional concentration on the external events of Hitler's life, especially the diplomatic aspects. Emphasizing Hitler's ambition for power, Bullock deals only lightly with Hitler's ideas, beliefs, opinions, and feelings—what the French call *mentalité*—as if these were without consequence in his drive for power.[24]

A. J. P. Taylor is the historian par excellence who consistently deemphasizes values and ideas as motivating factors in human behavior. In *The Course of German History*, he derided postwar Allied occupation efforts to "educate the Germans in democracy": "I never understood how this should be done. Democracy is learnt by practice, not by sitting on forms at a political finishing-school."[25] But practice grows out of a system of values and beliefs that, in turn, derive from one's religious and political culture and are inculcated at home and in fact taught in school.

Taylor's disdain for ideas as the substratum of history was most conspicuous in *The Origins of the Second World War*. There he argued that "in principle and doctrine, Hitler was no more wicked and unscrupulous than many other contemporary statesmen," though "in wicked acts he outdid them all."[26] In pushing the notion that Hitler behaved like any conventional political leader, Taylor tried to sidestep the question of Hitler's ideas by describing them as merely the commonplace thoughts of most Germans, different only because of Hitler's "terrifying literalism" (the "commonplace thoughts" include anti-Semitism). By taking "seriously what was to others mere talk"— so runs Taylor's argument—by translating "commonplace thoughts into action," Hitler brought about the Nazi dictatorship.[27] With this formulation, Taylor evades any historical analysis of the irrational ideas of race and anti-Semitism that exercised Hitler's mind. Taylor's contempt for ideas as a motivating force in history appeared in its most derisive form in a review in which he ridiculed with evenhanded impartiality both the serious and the silly approaches to Hitler's mind:

> Historians have often discussed the background of Hitler's so-called ideas. They have pointed to geopoliticians and racialist writers. I see now the true source of Hitler's inspiration. It was Karl May, a German who wrote thrillers about Red Indians. Hitler always saw himself in the dramatic role of a Red Indian brave.[28]

The work of H. R. Trevor-Roper is far more perplexing in regard to his treatment of Hitler's anti-Semitic ideas. In his now classic essay "The Mind of Adolf Hitler," Trevor-Roper argued that Hitler's mind was, to the historian, as important a problem as the mind of Bismarck or Lenin.[29] Yet this 24-page essay contained about a half dozen, mostly glancing, references to Hitler's racial anti-Semitism, without any analysis of the subject matter which Trevor-Roper acknowledges to have been Hitler's primary concern and which permeated Hitler's conversations. Even more curious is the bare citation, without comment, in Trevor-Roper's classic work *The Last Days of Hitler,* of the closing words of Hitler's political testament, composed just before his suicide in a Berlin bunker. There Hitler adjured the German people to uphold the racial laws and "mercilessly resist the universal poisoner of all nations, international Jewry."[30] (The rest of the book hardly ever refers to the Jews.)

Since Trevor-Roper has himself criticized Bullock's disregard of Hitler's mind and ideas, historical method cannot explain, as it does in Lord Bullock's case, his bypassing or substantially glossing over the cluster of ideas dealing with the Jews and with anti-Semitism. Perhaps the explanation may be

33

sought in English social manners, in the disdain with which members of the English upper class usually regard those they consider their inferiors, the Jews being such a category.

In Trevor-Roper's case the bias may be merely a form of social prejudice, but that kind of class snobbery in England has in other instances been associated with an anti-Semitism of contempt. A case in point was Sir Harold Nicolson, both historian and diplomat, a member of Parliament from 1935 to 1945. He exemplified this attitude in which snobbery and anti-Semitism were indivisibly coupled. His diary entry for December 17, 1942, describes that day in Parliament when Anthony Eden read a statement about the persecution of the Jews. (The Allied declaration was issued then; it stated the resolve of the United States, Great Britain, and the Soviet Union that the Germans responsible for the crimes against the Jews should "not escape retribution.") The members of the House then rose and stood in silence to mark their support of the declaration and to express the deep feelings which it stirred. Nicolson commented: "It is rather moving in a way." Three days later, at his home, he wrote a letter to his sons, describing the arrival of a tank brigade at the estate "heralded by a young officer of the name of Rubinstein. Recalling how but three days before I had stood in tribute to the martyred Jews of Poland, I was most polite to Captain Rubinstein."[31]

### "This Wicked Man Hitler"

Despite the recent outpouring of popular and scholarly books on Hitler, no work has yet been produced that satisfactorily explains Hitler's obsessive ideas about the Jews, the readiness of the German people to accept those ideas, and Hitler's ability to harness an enormous apparatus of men, institutions, and facilities just in order to murder the Jews. Hitler has proved to be an elusive and unrewarding subject for conventional biography because the explanations for the baffling mystique he exercised, for the power he came to wield, and for his unspeakable accomplishments are not to be found in the facts of a banal life, but in the ideas and feelings that created the symbiosis between him and the German people. Their mutuality and interdependence thrived, as Hitler first expressed and later gratified the Germans' most arrogant and abominable ambitions. He relieved their deepest fears and anxieties and, near the end, disburdened them of both guilt and responsibility for the wickedness they had given him warrant to commit. J. P. Stern, an English literary scholar and a refugee from Germany, perceived that the biographical approach was likely to trivialize rather than to illuminate this particular man: "If sociological interpretations lose sight of the man behind the trends, it is the common failing of biographies that they abstract a man from his world—a procedure that is particularly misleading in the case of one whose every public word and every public act expressed for almost the whole of his career the fears and aspirations of his contemporaries."[32]

That conclusion is borne out in the popular biographies by Robert Payne and John Toland, neither of which adds much to our knowledge or understanding of Hitler.[33] Payne, a prolific professional writer, produced a briskly told account of Hitler's life which is altogether devoid of ideas. He tells little about Hitler and the Jews: barely ten pages out of over 600 are devoted to the Final Solution, with a handful of other references to anti-Semitism, though not even a mention of the Nuremberg Laws.

Toland's book is more accomplished, yet despite massive research and countless interviews with countless persons, he has not succeeded in telling (in over a thousand pages) anything important that we had not known before. Asking few questions of historical significance of either his documents or his living subjects, Toland approached this book on Hitler, he admits, without a thesis. The "most meaningful" conclusion he reached was "that Hitler was far more complex and contradictory" than he had imagined.

But the nadir in Hitlerology is reached by David Irving's *Hitler's War*.[34] An amateur historian, whose reputation as a German apologist and as a writer without regard for accuracy or truth won him a measure of notoriety,[35] Irving produced a 926-page work intended to show that Hitler was kind to his animals and to his secretaries, that he was "probably the weakest *leader* Germany has known in this century," and that he did not murder the Jews or even wish to do so, but that the murder was committed behind his back, without his knowledge or consent. The killing of the Jews, Irving believes, "was partly of an *ad hoc* nature, what the Germans call a *Verlegenheitslösung*—the way out of an awkward dilemma, chosen by the middle-level authorities in the eastern territories overrun by the Nazis—and partly a cynical extrapolation by the central SS authorities of Hitler's anti-Semitic decrees."[36]

Irving claims to have new evidence and fresh interpretations of known documents, but in fact, all his evidence is familiar. He develops his arguments mostly by suppressing or ignoring the impressive body of existing evidence and partly by applying a guileful literalness to cases of Hitler's aesopian language.

Irving's thesis, which denies Hitler's responsibility for the murder of the Jews, is too preposterous to require refutation and argument, but one example will suffice to show his "scholarly" method. As seemingly irrefutable proof for his case, Mr. Irving offered an entry in Himmler's handwritten telephone log. On November 30, 1941, at 1:30 P.M., Himmler, then in Hitler's military headquarters bunker "Wolf's Lair," telephoned SS Obergruppenführer Heydrich, then in Prague. The gist of the telephone message was entered in four short lines in the log, though Mr. Irving cited only the last two lines:

Judentransport aus Berlin
keine Liquidierung.

That is: "Transport of Jews from Berlin. No liquidation."

From this Mr. Irving concluded that Hitler had somehow learned what Himmler was up to and had ordered him to stop. An obedient Nazi, Himmler had called Heydrich in Prague to transmit Hitler's order. But in view of everything we know about the destruction of the Jews, Irving's construction of events makes no sense. If Himmler continued to kill the Jews long after November 30, 1941, why did he order the liquidation of this one transport stopped? If he deceived Hitler before and after about the murder of the Jews, why should he be honest about it this once? Besides, what became of that transport of Jews from Berlin? Were they returned home? Irving's conclusion fails to provide a satisfactory explanation of those two lines in view of what actually happened, though it serves to

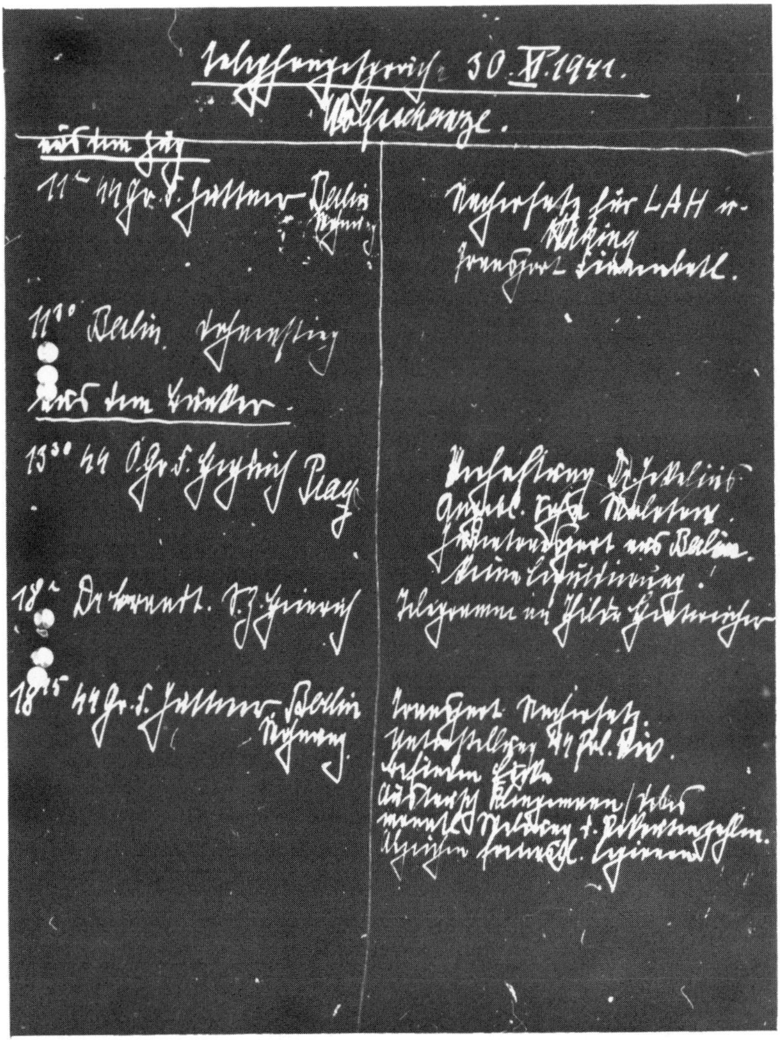

support his perversely fanciful interpretation of Hitler's character.

To understand those two lines it is necessary to read also the first two lines of the telephone conversation. Here is the full German text:

> Verhaftung Dr. Jekelius [name not fully decipherable]
> Angebl [ich] Sohn Molotovs.
> Judentransport aus Berlin.
> keine Liquidierung.[37]

That is: Arrest Dr. Jekelius. Presumably Molotov's son. Transport of Jews from Berlin. No liquidation.

The last two lines now make sense. Himmler called Heydrich to instruct him that a certain Dr. Jekelius, presumed to be the Soviet Foreign Minister's son, was to be taken in custody by the security police. Jekelius could be located in the transport of Jews from Berlin arriving in Prague and, unlike the rest of the transport, was not to be liquidated. (Perhaps the Germans intended to exchange Jekelius for one of their officers captured by the Russians.)

Irving, wittingly or unwittingly, has in fact disproved his own theory. For if Hitler was indeed responsible for Himmler's call (there is no evidence that he was), then Irving has shown that Hitler did in fact know all about the murder of the Jews. And indeed, how else could it have been? The murder of the Jews was Hitler's most consistent policy, in whose execution he persisted relentlessly, and obsessiveness with the Jews may even have cost him his war for the Thousand Year Reich.

### Hitler on the Couch

Given the unrewarding results of conventional biography and considering Hitler's patent pathology, it was to be expected that Hitler would attract the attention of the psychohistorians. The first such excursion, antedating by fifteen years Erik Erikson's pioneer work in psychohistory *Young Man Luther*, was a secret wartime report prepared for the United States Office of Strategic Services in 1943 by Walter C. Langer, a practicing psychoanalyst. The study of Hitler's personality was intended to help American policymakers understand the psychological nature of the German dictator and predict his possible courses of action. To carry out his assignment, Langer read all the then published material by and about Hitler and interviewed people who had known him. Nearly twenty years later, after the report had been declassified and made accessible to researchers at the National Archives, Langer had it published as *The Mind of Adolf Hitler*, a misleading title, for the study does not deal with Hitler's mind or ideas, but rather with his personality and behavior.[38]

Langer's report was path-breaking for its findings about Hitler's neuroses, perversions, and pathology, and many of Langer's surmises have since been confirmed. But few of his sources would be admissible as evidence in a court of historians, for they derived in large part from unverified accounts by people who knew, or claimed to have known, Hitler. The work suffered also from some misinterpretations of historical data as well as from the now universal failings of psychohistory—unsupported generalizations and reductive conclusions.[39]

Since Langer, two historians have completed works which combine the methods of psychoanalysis with the more conventional ones of history and biography. Rudolph Binion's work relies on Freudian analysis, interpreting "Hitler among the Germans" in terms of the traumatic mechanism.[40] Binion builds his argument on a progression of traumas. The first trauma, according to Binion, was experienced by Hitler's mother, whose first three children died in infancy. Traumatized by the guilt for their deaths, she breast-fed Hitler with incestuous passion, thereby transferring her trauma to him. Years later, his mother contracted breast cancer, which Binion diagnoses as a form of self-punishment. Hitler then encouraged Dr. Bloch, his mother's Jewish doctor, to treat her with iodoform, a chemical substance used as an antiseptic, whose persistent odor was reminiscent of poison gas. His mother died and Hitler was once again traumatized, the trauma now fixed on the Jewish doctor. Hitler was gassed eleven years later during the First World War, thereby—Binion explains—reviving the trauma of his mother's iodoform poisoning. The shock of Germany's defeat retraumatized him and he resolved to undo his mother's death and reverse Germany's defeat, the concept of "mother Germany" combining both the personal and national factors of his trauma. He would do so by murdering the Jews. Meanwhile, the German people, having suffered a national trauma in their defeat, needed to relive it. Hitler gave them that opportunity.[41]

The second psychohistory, by Robert G. L. Waite, offers a more sophisticated assortment of psychological and analytic explanations for Hitler's pathology, putting together all the bits of evidence, gossip, and hearsay about Hitler's coprophilia, monorchidism, his fears and obsessions. Though making more use than Binion of the data of political and social history, Waite nevertheless fails to integrate them into a coherent whole. Explaining the origins of Hitler's anti-Semitism, Waite too is betrayed by simplistic reductionism. Hitler, Waite tells us, was ambivalent toward his father. Through the process of displacement, Dr. Bloch, his mother's Jewish doctor, became his father substitute. But his mother's sufferings at the hands of the Jewish doctor kindled Hitler's anti-Semitic feelings. Hitler, according to Waite, identified his mother with Germany. Consequently he favored the word "motherland," rather than the more common "fatherland," for he associated his father with multiracial Austria. Loving Germany and hating Austria, Hitler therefore seized Austria in 1938 and attached it to Germany.[42]

Freud himself would probably have mocked these attempts to use his methods and try to explain complex historical developments by recourse to individual pathology rooted in childhood neuroses. He himself regarded social and political events as sufficiently real and significant to have formative influences on the individual. *Group Psychology and the Analysis of the Ego*, as well as the flawed *Moses and Monotheism*, reveal his preoccupation with the unresolved problem of applying the insights of individual psychology to the behavior of groups, crowds, and masses. Especially apposite is Freud's comment to Arnold Zweig, who was writing a novel about Nietzsche and probing the philosopher's psychic problems. Freud warned Zweig about the pitfalls in reconstructing motivations from pathology: "It is the case history of a sick man, and this is much more difficult to guess or reconstruct. I mean, there are psychical processes in a certain sequence, but not always psychical motivations generating them, and in the unravelling of these one could go very much astray."[43]

Psychohistory has not proved any more successful than conventional biography in unlocking the mysteries of Hitler's political career, for the answers are not to be found in his personal pathology but, as I argued earlier, in the symbiotic relationship between him and the German people. The historian will come closer to understanding the German past by investigating the mass pathology that made it possible for the Germans to accept Hitler as their leader.

## Mass Pathology in History

Only a bare handful of historians have undertaken to study historical phenomena of mass hysteria and social pathology—the witch crazes, religious apocalypticism, the contagions of anti-Semitism and racism, the role of superstition and occult beliefs in social behavior, fanaticism in war and peace, the varieties of political paranoia. For those who have ventured into these subterranean passages of the past, the imaginative use of conventional methods of history, reinforced by other disciplines where appropriate, has proved far more rewarding than any mechanical application of psychoanalysis. The work of Norman Cohn amply illustrates the possibilities of original and significant historical research. His exploration of revolutionary messianism in medieval Europe represented a breakthrough both in subject matter and method.[44] His book on the history of the Protocols of the Elders of Zion was a model work in the history of anti-Semitism.[45]

Most historians avoid such subject matter. Is it because they are uncomfortable with the irrationality which they would have to confront? Historians are, by the very nature of the enterprise in which they are engaged, systematic and rational. In writing history, they seek explanations, causes and effects, motives and goals. Mass delusions and popular crazes repel as much as baffle them. A historiographical case in point can be found in an altogether remote area of history—the study of Jewish enthusiast and antinomian mysticism, of the Sabbatian and Frankist movements, and even of East European Hasidism. Until the advent of Gershom Scholem, Jewish historians from the rise of *Wissenschaft des Judentums* until today, from Graetz to Dubnow and Baron, were committed to a rationalist perspective of Jewish history, whether that outlook derived from dedication to eighteenth-century Enlightenment, nineteenth-century Progress, twentieth-century Marxism, or universal humanism. So repelled were the Jewish historians by the irrational character of Jewish mystical messianism that they failed in their professional obligations to interpret such movements fairly. Scholem has characterized that outlook as the "rationalist perversion of sound judgment."[46]

Even taking into account the historians' aversion to historical phenomena that are intrinsically irrational, it still comes as a shock to see the extent to which anti-Semitism in all its forms and guises has been neglected as a subject of historical study. When one considers the deplorably abiding presence of anti-Semitism in human history, its geographic penetration into all the far and unlikely places of the world, and its adaptive character to all sorts of political, social, and economic environments, one sees the disproportion between the place of anti-Semitism in actual history and its place in the history books. Then one discovers, perhaps with more melancholy than shock, that most scholarly studies of anti-Semitism were produced by Jews and subsidized by Jewish institutions.[47] Anti-Semitism, like the Holocaust itself, it would seem, is a subject of merely parochial interest. The Nazi era notwithstanding, Jew hatred still appears to be of interest only to its victims.

There is no witness so dreadful, no accuser
so terrible as the conscience that dwells in
the heart of every man.

POLYBIUS

# 3

# THE SHADOW OF THE PAST:
# GERMAN HISTORIANS
# CONFRONT NATIONAL SOCIALISM

In 1946, amid the rubble of the Third Reich, Friedrich Meinecke, Germany's most eminent historian of the twentieth century, pondered the course of his nation's history. The scholar
who had devoted his long life to the study of German nationhood and the idea of the German state was now in dismay:
"Must we not always be shocked at the precipitous fall from
the heights of the Goethe era to the swamps of the Hitler period? Passionately we Germans ask ourselves how this was
possible within the selfsame nation."

Meinecke's question was twofold. It asked for the clarification that history could give and also for the chastening of moral
judgment. For in their acknowledgment that National Socialism had indeed been the catastrophe of the German people and
of their history, the Germans hoped for emotional release and
recovery of their national self-esteem. "The Third Reich,"
Meinecke wrote, "was not only the greatest misfortune that the
German people have suffered in their existence, it was also
their greatest shame."[1]

The fall of the Third Reich introduced into the writing of
German history a moral yardstick, long disdained by the German historical guild, which had dedicated itself for generations
to the principle of value-free scholarship. Thus, in 1954 Ger-

43

hard Ritter, second only to Meinecke among Germany's distinguished historians, could declare in his introduction to *The German Resistance* that it was "simply not true that the power-political interests of the nation can gloss over the fundamental difference between right and wrong." With that statement he called into question not only the sacred tenet of ethical neutrality in writing history. More drastically, he now appeared to renounce the substance of German historiography's still more venerable tradition: the justification of the German state in all its striving for power—over its subjects as well as over competing nations—as an ultimate value transcending all morality. Ritter could not have been more explicit in repudiating the ethical system of past generations of German historians: "There can be no national honor where no distinction is made between good and evil; there can be national honor only where a people and a state prove their worth by moral accomplishments too."[2]

Yet when we read German historical accounts of the Third Reich that appeared shortly after 1945, we are struck by the unbridged gulf between moral pronouncement and historical explanation. From many of these works, it would seem, the more things have changed in German historiography, the more they have remained the same. Despite the trauma that the collapse of the Third Reich called forth, despite their awareness of the past as history gone desperately wrong, the older German historians could not divest themselves of those still authoritative intellectual traditions in which they had been reared and professionally trained and in accordance with which they had conceived and written their works. Even the anguished recognition in 1945 by the historians who grew up in the age of German nation- and empire-building that the Third Reich, the regime of their nation and people, had committed the most heinous crimes in human history could not make them disown their loyalties to the past or discard the values of a lifetime.

### The German Historiographic Heritage

In 1916, in the midst of the Great War, some of Germany's most eminent historians published a collection of essays whose thrust was to justify Germany's political and military strategy as a necessary struggle against England's alleged claim to world supremacy. One historian, citing a nationalist poet of an earlier time, summed up the attitude then prevalent not only among German historians but also among most middle-class Germans: "One day the world will be restored to health by the German spirit."[3] That statement epitomized the unique character of the German nationalism which German philosophers and poets, historians and intellectuals had shaped and nurtured for a century.

From the start, German nationalism differed from the early nationalism of the French or the Italians or of the so-called nonhistorical peoples submerged in the Hapsburg Empire. For those peoples, nationalism had grown out of the universal values of liberty, equality, and fraternity. Each nation expressed its own particularity through pride in its origins and in the sense of community that derived from common language, customs, traditions, and memories. But German nationalism, from its earliest days, was marked by two distinctive characteristics. To begin with, a fundamental idea of German nationalism was the belief which German thinkers from Fichte and Arndt on had fostered—that the German nation was not merely different from other nations but superior to them. Endowed with supposedly unique and unsurpassed physical, mental, and moral qualities, the German nation—so the argument went—was destined for world leadership. Secondly, German nationalism had its roots in an idea whose origins have been traced back to Wilhelm von Humboldt—that the individual could best fulfill himself through subordination to his historic community, an entity whose ideal manifestation was seen to be the national state.[4]

The idea of the centrality of the state in human affairs became an explicit concept in German historiography in the early writings of Leopold von Ranke. In his view of history, the state, even—and perhaps especially—in its pursuit of political and military power, embodied the highest spirituality, to whose transcending ethical purposes all individual interests had to be subordinated. This concept became a fundamental tenet in German historiography. By the end of the nineteenth century the German state as *Machtstaat*—the state by virtue of its power—was regarded as history's driving force. Since the state represented the highest good, according to this view, German historians came to justify Germany's claim to world power and its imperialist drive in Europe and overseas as politically necessary and morally unimpeachable.

Little wonder, then, that most German historians, like most Germans, were carried away by patriotic euphoria when Germany declared war against Russia on August 1, 1914."The exaltation of spirit experienced during the August days of 1914," Meinecke would recall in the less exalted days of 1945, was "one of the most precious, unforgettable memories of the highest sort."[5] Little wonder that most German historians put their professional skills at the service of the state to sanction Germany's aggressiveness. But their political commitment so overwhelmed their professional capacity, their nationalist passion so befogged their intellectual faculties that they were unable to understand the reasons for Germany's defeat. "Delusions kept us from any sober recognition of the true causes of our failure," wrote Ludwig Dehio, one of Germany's more liberal historians. The German historians, he argued, "were not able . . . to produce a convincing interpretation of the first World War, firmly grounded in a comprehensive historical panorama and therefore immune to both national sensibilities and political interests."[6]

Given the entrenched tradition of nationalism among German historians, with its components of political conservatism, distrust of democracy, aversion to equality, and fear of the revolutionary masses, it is no surprise that many German historians—and most of those who held university professorships—had little enthusiasm for the Weimar Republic and its constitution. It was an outlook which they shared with the German middle class as a whole.[7] Meinecke himself, who came to be a lukewarm supporter of Weimar, defined his position this way: "I remain, in rapport with the past, a monarchist from the depths of my heart and will become, in rapport with the future, a republican by dint of reason."[8]

History written during the short-lived Weimar Republic was, for the most part, conceived in the spirit of the past, imbued with longing for the *Machtstaat*, indifferent to the presence of a constitutional government. In response to Germany's defeat and to the Versailles treaty, which formally held Germany responsible for the war and imposed upon her the obligation of reparations, many German historians devoted themselves to historical studies to disprove the charges of war guilt. Others dedicated themselves to investigating the Bismarck era, to seek moral comfort in the days when the German *Machtstaat* flourished.[9] The few German historians who cared about the Weimar Republic and democracy, who were attuned to what we call Weimar culture, like Eckart Kehr and Veit Valentin, remained outside the academic historical establishment.

Not a single historian undertook to examine the *Dolchstoss* legend, the myth about the stab-in-the-back, the betrayal from within, which German nationalists, in a blind refusal to account for Germany's military defeat in real historical terms, attributed to the Jews. The omission is significant, for it not only highlights the nationalist bias in German historiography, but also discloses the anti-Jewish bias that afflicted most German historians when forced to consider the place of Jews in Germany and in German history.

The Jews were, as a matter of fact, rare subjects in German history. When they occasionally surfaced in the history of modern Germany, they appeared not as subjects of intrinsic historical interest and worth, but only as a problem in German history which was designated as the "Jewish question." The "Jewish question," as German nationalists conceived it, was the threatened and threatening invasion into the German national community by a group whom the Germans almost universally regarded as racially alien, culturally unassimilable, harmful to the Christian ethos, and politically destructive. It was a view of the Jews which the German historians shared with the German nationalists and in which they felt themselves reinforced when confronted by the historical record of this people that had managed to preserve its individual character throughout its millennial history, while living "as an alien body" among the nations of the world.[10]

With respect to anti-Semitism as with respect to German nationalism, worship of the *Machtstaat*, and the indifference to constitutional government, the German historians were as firmly and ideologically situated in the German middle class as was the business bourgeoisie.[11] Given the pervasiveness of this nationalist conservatism in the historical profession, the acceptance of anti-Semitism, and the widespread disaffinity for the Weimar Republic, it is obvious that most German historians had little, if any, difficulty in negotiating a smooth political passage from Weimar to the Third Reich.

## The Historians and the Third Reich

Though no full professor of history in the German universities was said to have been a member of the Nazi party before Hitler came to power, the historical profession—not unlike all the other professions then in Germany—capitulated to the new regime quickly, readily, and even enthusiastically.[12] Thereafter historians began to demonstrate their loyalty by joining the National Socialist party. The most prominent among these joiners was Karl Alexander von Müller, from his earliest days an ultranationalist, professor of history at the University of Munich, once a Rhodes scholar at Oxford, and, in 1933, president of the Bavarian Academy of Sciences.[13]

Most German historians accepted the National Socialist regime without qualms of conscience. Some indeed were soon to strike a note of greater optimism in their work than they had ever felt during the lifetime of the Weimar Republic. Thus, Johannes Haller, then professor of history at the University of Tübingen, described his feelings of exuberance when Hitler came to power: "What had been faith and hope became reality ... Sooner than the keenest hopes had dared to think possible, the sun arose over Germany."[14]

The Nazification of the historical profession showed itself first in the wave of dismissals from various academic posts and honorary positions. Historians who were Jews or "non-Aryans"—that is, born of Jewish parents or grandparents—were driven from the universities along with those few in the profession (but not commonly in the universities) with leftist loyalties. Most of these historians left Germany in 1933, the rest a year or two later.[15] A few, like Dehio, joined the "inner emigration," withdrawing from participation in professional associations and publications. The places in the university now made available were filled with Nazi party members, some of whom might otherwise never have been appointed had academic merit and scholarly achievement remained the chief criteria for such appointments.

Several young historians who had hitched their career aspirations to the National Socialist regime actively sought to take over the historical profession and Nazify it. They did so through the customary means available to ambitious Nazis: denunciation, intrigue, and wire-pulling. The Nazi historians accused Germany's leading historians of being Jews, half-Jews, or under Jewish influence, of being Communists, Marxists, or opportunists. Creating an atmosphere of distrust and conspiracy, they used the protection of top Nazis in the state and party apparatus to gain power over the historical profession, to fire their enemies and hire their friends. By 1935 these enterprising young men, most notably one Walter Frank, had succeeded in liquidating the *Historische Reichskommission*, an influential national institution which had sponsored research on modern Germany, and in taking over control of the *Historische Zeitschrift*, Germany's most prestigious historical journal which Meinecke had edited for over 40 years. Frank successfully schemed to have Müller appointed editor in Meinecke's place.[16]

In place of the *Historische Reichskommission* a new historical institution called *Reichsinstitut für Geschichte des neuen Deutschland* (Reich Institute for the History of the New Germany) was established under the aegis of the Reich Ministry of Education. Walter Frank was appointed its president and as such was given civil service status and the rank of professor. Thus this man whose life and work were governed by obsessive anti-Semitism became a key figure in the historical profession in Nazi Germany.

Frank, born in 1905 and a suicide in 1945, received his doctorate in 1927 from the University of Munich with a dissertation on Adolf Stoecker, founder of the anti-Semitic Christian Social Workers' party in Berlin in 1878. Frank's academic sponsor was Müller, who shared his pupil's nationalist and anti-Semitic views. In 1928 Frank's dissertation was published and none other than Meinecke himself favorably reviewed it in *Historische Zeitschrift*, even though Frank had openly identified himself with Stoecker not only as populist but also as anti-Semite. (Meinecke even appointed Frank to be responsible for the modern history book review section of the *Historische Zeitschrift*.) Subsidized by a fellowship from the *Deutsche Forschungsgemeinshaft*, an influential foundation, Frank then went to Paris. There he worked for several years on a second book, *Nationalismus und Demokratie im Frankreich der dritten Republik*, which compared the France of Dreyfus's time with Weimar, both—according to Frank—corrupted by Jews and Jewish influences. Unable to get a university appointment, Frank took on a commission to write the biography of Nazi general Franz Ritter von Epp. Thereafter, Frank's career in history was achieved through service to the Nazi movement.

Frank intended to make the new Reichsinstitut the center of the historical profession in the Third Reich and to demonstrate that it represented the continuity of Germany's historical traditions. To this end he exploited whatever political and professional resources he could muster. He set up a six-man honorary council of the best people he could find in the academic community who were deeply committed to National Socialism. Three were historians: Karl Alexander von Müller, Erich Marcks, and Heinrich Ritter von Srbik.

Marcks (1861-1938) had been retired from his professorship at the University of Berlin since 1928. A German nationalist all his life, author of many books, and recipient of many honorary positions in the historical profession, Marcks, despite his age, was still a prominent name in German historiography and a prestigious addition to Frank's institute. (Marcks had once written a blurb for Frank's biography of Epp: "The book is a historical work of art, unified and full of the passion and color we have come to expect of him.")

Srbik (1878–1951), then professor of history at the University of Vienna, was a Pan-German, an ardent German nationalist. President of the Academy of Sciences in Vienna, he was elected a member of the Reichstag in 1938, after the Anschluss. His best-known work was a biography of Metternich, published in a series called "Masters of Politics," which, coincidentally, Marcks and Müller jointly edited.

The three nonhistorians Frank was able to coopt were Ernst

Krieck, professor of philosophy, who joined the National Socialist party early in 1932 and the following year became the first Nazi appointed rector of a university; Alfred Baeumler, professor of philosophy at the University of Berlin, who later headed a scholarly institute for Alfred Rosenberg, Hitler's ideological mentor; and Hans F. K. Günther, professor of anthropology at the University of Jena and since 1922 famous as the author of *Racial Science of the German Nation* and of *Racial Science of the Jewish Nation*.

Frank organized his Reichsinstitut in three research divisions: one on the "Jewish Question," one on "Political Leadership in World War," and one on "Postwar History," especially the history of the National Socialist movement. Frank named Munich as the site for the Research Division on the Jewish Question and appointed Müller to head this division. He then hired, as Müller's executive director, Wilhelm Grau, who had earned his doctorate under Müller with a study on "Anti-Semitism in the Late Middle Ages."* The Research Division on Political Leadership, to be located in Berlin, was headed by Colonel Walter Nicolai, formerly of the Army's General Staff, and once chief of intelligence under Erich Ludendorff. Frank himself was to head the Research Division on Postwar History, which had no specific location.

The formal opening of the Reichsinstitut took place on October 19, 1935, at Berlin University, the festive character of the occasion enhanced by the presence of SA and SS honor guards, flag bearers, and bands. The highest dignitaries were Frank's two top patrons—Rudolf Hess, Hitler's deputy, and Alfred Rosenberg. Heinrich Himmler, Baldur von Schirach, Generals Ludwig Beck and Wilhelm Keitel all sent personal representatives. The Interior and Education Ministries were represented by second-line officials and several university rectors were present. Not all the members of the Honorary Council showed up (Müller did not). Srbik, indisposed with bronchitis, sent a letter from Vienna, expressing his hopes for the harmonious cooperation between the older and younger scholars and for the union of scholarly integrity with the demands of national thought and will.

*After Müller took over the editorship of the *Historische Zeitschrift*, Grau became a regular contributor on the subject of the "Jewish question."

*Anti-Semitism in the Guise of Scholarship*

The Reichsinstitut functioned until the very end of the war, though Frank himself, because of his endless disputatiousness and his gift for intrigue, was ordered on compulsory paid leave in 1941 by the top Nazi hierarchy. The Reichsinstitut's accomplishments, that is, research and publication, were attained primarily by the Research Division on the Jewish Question. Its annual meetings provided a platform for the specialists in anti-Jewish studies, whose papers were later published in a serial, *Forschungen zur Judenfrage*, of which nine volumes were published between 1937 and 1944.

At the first annual conference, held in Munich on November 19, 1936, in the presence of Rudolf Hess and other top political, military, and academic dignitaries, Müller delivered the opening address. He characterized the Research Division on the Jewish Question as not just an ordinary scholarly undertaking, but, in the area of scholarship, "a revolutionary deed," part of the "great National Socialist revolution of Adolf Hitler." For the first time, he said, the "Jewish question," which he called "one of the most important and fateful subjects of history," would be studied from the German nationalist perspective.[17]

At the annual conferences held in 1937 and 1938, the professors and scholars of the "Jewish question" were honored by the active participation of Julius Streicher, Nazi party leader of the district of Franconia and editor of the anti-Semitic sheet *Der Stürmer*. Regarded as the patron saint of the Research Division on the Jewish Question, Streicher was invited to address the conference. He came to the 1937 meeting in the company of several prostitutes. On that occasion he harangued the audience with a three-hour address on his "struggle with world Jewry" and the professors responded with an ovation, according to the press.[18]

Nearly all the scholarly participants of the conferences and the contributors to *Forschungen zur Judenfrage* were professors at leading German universities. Not only historians, but also philosophers, anthropologists, economists, literary scholars, and jurists ventured into anti-Jewish studies. The following list, chosen at random from the nine volumes of *Forschun-*

*gen zur Judenfrage,* indicates the scholarly and moral caliber of this research:

"Jewry as an Element of Decomposition among the Nations: Reflections on World History"
"The Intellectual Foundations of Anti-Semitism in Modern France"
"The Invasion of the Jewish Spirit by Friedrich Julius Stahl in German State and Church Law"
"Jewry and Bolshevik Cultural Politics"
"The Literary Predominance of Jews in Germany, 1918–1933"
"The Penetration of Jewish Blood in the English Upper Class"
"Jewry in the Capitalist Economy"
"Laws Concerning the Receipt of Stolen Goods Among Jews and Pawnbrokers"
"Albert Einstein's Attempt to Subvert Physics"
"The Racial Origins and the Earliest Racial History of the Hebrews"

Gerhard Ritter, in a postwar survey of German historiography in the twentieth century, described Walter Frank and his "host of fanatic as well as ambitious young National Socialists" as men who wanted "to constitute the elite and the shock troops of a new National Socialist historiography." But, he concluded, they did not accomplish much except to publish some pamphlets and speeches, "besides several studies on the history of the Jewish question (a few also factually usable)," a judgment reflecting more on Ritter's attitude toward Jews and the "Jewish question" than on the manifestly spurious scholarly character of those studies.[19]

Frank's downfall had its origins in a quarrel with Wilhelm Grau, his underling in charge of the Munich Research Division on the Jewish Question. In March 1938, without first informing Frank or clearing with him, Grau had submitted a memorandum on the "Jewish question" to Hitler himself. In this document, "Tasks of Germany's Anti-Jewish Policy Abroad: Ideas and Proposals," Grau argued for a consistent application of Germany's anti-Jewish policies abroad on the ground that "the Jew was an international problem." He hoped that this memorandum would get him a job from Hitler himself. In April, Frank found out about Grau's memorandum from one of the many officials who had received a copy. The conflict that subsequently developed between Frank and Grau reached titanic proportions, eventually involving Himmler and Martin Bormann. Frank fired Grau, had Müller drop him as contributor to *Historische Zeitschrift*, and closed off Grau's access to fellowships and academic posts.

But Grau outwitted him. Grau turned to Fritz Krebs, mayor of Frankfort, who had the ambition to give his city a reputation as anti-Semitic terrain. At the center of Krebs's scheming was the confiscated Judaica collection of Frankfort's municipal library, some 25,000 volumes, including rare books and unica. In 1935 the collection had been offered for sale to Frank for his Munich Research Division on the Jewish Question, but while Frank was trying to raise funds, Krebs had decided that the collection should stay in Frankfort as part of an anti-Jewish research organization located there.

Grau's appearance in 1938 gave Krebs the opportunity he was waiting for. He approached top party officials with a proposal that the Judaica library be used as the basis for a national research institution on the "Jewish question." The idea met an enthusiastic reception from Alfred Rosenberg himself, chief Nazi philosopher and ideologue, who by now had a grudge against Frank. Within a year it was agreed that the Frankfort municipality would put the Judaica collection at the disposal of the National Socialist party and that Rosenberg would establish in Frankfort, under his direction and authority, an institute of the party to study the "Jewish question," of which Grau, of course, would be appointed director. The institute was named *Institut zur Erforschung der Judenfrage* (Institute to Study the Jewish Question) and it was established as an adjunct to a nonexistent Nazi party university.

The German invasion of Poland on September 1, 1939, and the war delayed the formal opening of the Institute until March 1941. Grau, meanwhile, went into the army. After the Germans seized France, he obtained leave to head up the Paris team of *Einsatzstab* Rosenberg, Rosenberg's special staff assigned to plundering, among others, Jewish libraries across Europe in order to enrich the Judaica collections of the Frankfort Institute. By that time, Rosenberg had already confiscated the collections of the Berlin Jewish Community, the Breslau Rabbinical Seminary, the Vienna Jewish Community, and the Vienna Rabbinical Seminary. Grau helped to appropriate the libraries of the Alliance Israélite Universelle and the École Rabbinique in Paris and the Rosenthaliana in Amsterdam. Later, after the invasion of the Soviet Union, other teams of *Einsatzstab* Rosenberg plundered the Jewish libraries of Eastern Europe, including the Strashun Library and the renowned library and archives of the Yiddish Scientific Institute—Yivo in Vilna.[20]

The exigencies of war restricted the Frankfort Institute's operations, though Rosenberg and Grau had ambitious plans for an international conference even as late as 1944. By then the larger ambition of the anti-Semites had been fulfilled, not in the "fighting scholarship of Nazism," but in the murder of 6 million Jews.

### The Unmastered Past: Nazism as Discontinuity

In 1965, in a sociological study of modern Germany that sought to explain how National Socialism had been possible, the most pointed question the author put was: "How was Auschwitz possible?" To this he replied: "I believe that for the time being this question transcends the horizons of scientific explanation: it is too close and too overwhelming to be studied *sine ira et studio*."[21] It was then twenty years after the event, a generation later. At about the same time, a German historian, in a survey of German history in modern times, touched only briefly on the murder of the European Jews. He explained his avoidance of the subject this way: "Darkness hides this vilest crime ever perpetrated by man against man."[22]

Both scholars, men of integrity and political honor, were unable to probe the depths of Nazi infamy even at the remove of twenty years. Their revulsion was compounded of pain and shame, guilt and torment, as they forced themselves to confront the accomplishments of the Third Reich. Thomas Mann most eloquently expressed that revulsion in *Doctor Faustus*, through the words of his most sympathetic character:

> Germany had become a thick-walled underground torture-chamber, converted into one by a profligate dictatorship vowed

to nihilism from its beginnings on. Now the torture-chamber had been broken open, open lies our shame before the eyes of the world. Foreign commissions inspect those incredible photographs everywhere displayed, and tell their countrymen that what they have seen surpasses in horribleness anything the human imagination can conceive.[23]

After 1945 the Third Reich became a trauma for most of those Germans who had never before regarded National Socialism as a trauma. Many Germans managed to suppress and repress the memories of the Third Reich and their participation in it, some going so far as to deny the evidence of the shameful events they had once not considered shameful. But German historians could not suppress the memories or deny the past. Most of them felt that it was their moral as well as their professional obligation to confront the National Socialist past, to ask not only how all that had come to pass, but also, even more urgently, how it *could* have come to pass. The heavy moral and emotional burden that freighted the historical problem had to be dealt with in historical terms.

Given the nature of his craft, the historian seeks to unravel the twisted chain of causality. As Carl Becker wrote long before the world knew of Adolf Hitler, the modern historian has "a concept, a preconcept, of continuity and evolution."[24] For more than a century, since natural science came to dominate the world of knowledge and since historians began to think of their discipline as a science, the principle of continuity has been accorded a central place in the scientific explanation of historical progress and change. According to this principle, everything in nature occurs by degree and there are no discontinuous changes. Indeed, even crisis and discontinuity are explained in history by the disclosures of hidden forces whose historic influence for continuity was not apparent at first.

Under the burden of conscience and of political morality, the matter of continuity became a central problem in postwar German historiography. For the historians tried to explain how the country of Kant, Goethe, and Beethoven had become the country of Hitler, Himmler, and Albert Speer. What then was the place of National Socialism in the span of modern German history? Did National Socialism and the Third Reich bespeak a continuity of German political traditions, a persistence of nationalism, authoritarianism, militarism, anti-Semitism? Or was it only some aberration, some freakish concatenation of unforeseen, accidental events that brought Hitler to the leadership of Germany?

It comes as no surprise that many German historians, especially those whose own long productivity embodied the continuity of German historiography from Empire to Republic to Third Reich, should have rejected the idea that National Socialism was a link in the chain of Germany's continuous history. For it assuaged the conscience and comforted the soul to believe that National Socialism was only a breach in the continuity of German political traditions, that it was no more than a fateful but capricious deviation from the calculated trajectory of German history.

In 1946 Meinecke published his reflections on the Third Reich in a little book called *The German Catastrophe*, cited at the beginning of this chapter. Then eighty-four years old (he died eight years later), Meinecke wrote this work in the weariness of his old age and in despair of Germany's recent history. His perspective, however, derived from his lifelong passionate identity with his people and with Germandom. Predictably the book was hardly more than an apologia for Germany and the Germans.

Meinecke's reading of history yielded an interpretation for the rise and ready acceptance of National Socialism in Germany that denied the continuity of specifically German political traditions. To begin with, he argued, National Socialism was not unique to Germany, but was the product of universal processes which operated with equal vigor also outside Germany. These processes he described as impersonal forces working in human history, depriving—it would appear—human beings of their freedom to determine their own fate and future. Meinecke once even referred to these vast impersonal forces as "higher historical necessity." These ineluctable forces included the synthesis of nationalism with socialism, the rise of technology and the concomitant growth of militarism, the spread of utilitarian ideas, and the decline of culture in the Western world. The most destructive of these processes he called "mass Machiavellism," embracing political democratization and the striving for power at any price, an idea suggestive of J. L. Talmon's later "totalitarian democracy" and also of the more popular theories of universal fascism and totalitarianism. All were variants of an approach which provided cosmic interpretations to account for what had happened in Germany.[25]

History, according to Meinecke, was made also by chance events. For instance, he attributed Hindenburg's appointment of Hitler to the Chancellorship to a "chance trait in Hindenburg's personality"—that is, a limited capacity for making political judgments.[26] Thus Meinecke afforded chance a role in making history not unlike that envisaged by the ancient Greek historians who saw the course of history affected by the gods' capricious turning of the wheel of fortune. For chance occurs outside of causality; it ruptures the continuity of history. When the historian designates chance as an event-producing factor, in effect he puts the event beyond historical causality and thus he no longer needs to provide a historical explanation for it.

Even the rise of Hitler Meinecke ascribed to a "chance chain of causes," thus combining causality with the concept of misfortune. But when Meinecke spoke of the "Hitler group," that "band of criminals" who succeeded "in forcing the German people under its leadership," he appeared to give credence to the devil theory of history. The German people, he said, though "not fundamentally diseased with criminal sentiments," were seduced by this evil man and his cohorts. Thus Meinecke saw Hitler and National Socialism as an intrusion, destructive of continuity in German history. The only serviceable explanation he could offer for Hitler's success was an otherworldly one: Hitler derived his power from his personality—"in this case . . . a downright demonic personality."

If Meinecke in *The German Catastrophe* dismays us by his inability to root National Socialism in German history, he actually shocks us by his failure to confront the essence of the German catastrophe. Writing in 1945–46, when the evidence of Germany's unspeakable crimes was exposed before the eyes of the world, when the International Military Tribunal at Nuremberg was trying those responsible for war crimes and crimes against humanity, Meinecke mentioned none of those crimes. No one reading *The German Catastrophe* would ever know about slave labor, concentration camps, mass shootings, death factories, the murder of 6 million Jews.

About the Jews and the consequences of anti-Semitism Meinecke appeared to have been frozen in the past, to have learned nothing from his meditations on the Third Reich. From his youth Meinecke was afflicted with the conventional anti-Semitism widespread in Germany, convinced that Jews were an alien element in German society. (There was, to be sure, the exception to the rule—Franz Rosenzweig, the Jewish philosopher whom Meinecke offered a university position in 1920.) There is no record that Meinecke ever expressed any objection to anti-Semitism or ever defended the Jews from defamation before, during, or after the Third Reich.[27] Given his conservative nationalism and the anti-Semitism which was as much a part of his nature as his Germanism, he failed to grasp the centrality of anti-Semitism in Hitler's appeal to the Germans. Meinecke's few comments about the Jews reveal him to have retained all his old-fashioned anti-Jewish prejudices.

Twice he blamed the Jews for having brought anti-Semitism upon themselves. Discussing the 1880s, in a passage that is a model of conventional anti-Semitism, Meinecke asserted that Jewish economic success had aroused "resentment of various sorts," and that Jews "contributed much to that gradual depreciation and discrediting of the liberal world of ideas," presumably because Jews as advocates of liberalism could, in the eyes of non-Jews, only discredit it. Though Jews achieved much "that was positive in the cultural and economic life of Germany," Meinecke nevertheless complained of "their negative and disintegrating influence," which he never described but his words resonated with that anti-Semitic rhetoric about Jews as a "ferment of decomposition." Discussing Weimar, Meinecke charged that "among those who drank too hastily and greedily of the cup of power which had come to them were many Jews." Such were the views of the man who supported "by dint of reason" the Weimar Republic and its constitution.

Meinecke's reflections should not be read as history, even though they were written by a man once universally regarded as Germany's greatest living historian. *The German Catastrophe* is rather to be taken as the poignant autobiographical record of a man who had misread the signs of the past and no longer had anything to say about the future. His prescription for a postwar renewal of the German spirit through the cultivation of Goethe communities lays bare a pitiful poverty of political understanding. Little wonder that he never fathomed the depths of the German catastrophe.

Meinecke's apologia for Germany was soon followed by Ritter's.[28] Ritter had been associated with the conservative anti-Hitler resistance since 1938 and, after the failure of the attempt on Hitler's life on July 20, 1944, was arrested and imprisoned until finally the Allied forces released him in April 1945. But he was still a nationalist at heart and his work betrays his conservative authoritarian bias. Ritter, like Meinecke, rejected the idea that National Socialism originated out of a specifically German historic context, arguing that "the firm ground of European political traditions was shaken, not by some event in German history, but by the French Revolution." Thus Ritter too attributed to the idea of mass democracy, which presumably the French Revolution unloosed, the pernicious influence that brought about National Socialism. Indeed, Ritter continued, Hitler and Mussolini were not "the first of their kind," for "Europe experienced grand-style dictatorship under Napoleon."[29]

As for the provenance of racist and anti-Semitic ideas, Ritter claimed that these were "not indigenous to Germany proper but rather to the southeastern parts of Europe with their chaotic mixture of nationalities and unceasing national rivalries." In all of two pages devoted to anti-Semitism, with the murder of the European Jews relegated to a footnote, Ritter altogether minimized the existence of German anti-Semitism. Where and when it existed, he blamed it on the Jews themselves. Anti-Semitism was either "based on the economic resentments of the peasantry and the petty bourgeois" or "related to the heavy influx of Jews" or "to certain symptoms of corruption" among Jews, a phrase which in itself is nothing more than an anti-Semitic charge.

But Ritter was unable to come to grips with the fundamental question of "the wild racist fanaticism of the National Socialists." In his text he explained that Hitler carried this racism "from the ferment of national hatreds prevalent in Austria into

Germany and, by his quite personal hysteria, intensified it until it became a major national peril." Hitler, it would then appear, had single-handedly imposed upon the whole German people this racist anti-Semitism which, according to Ritter, had never been a "widespread popular attitude." Yet Ritter contradicted himself in the footnote that mentioned the murder of the European Jews, by arguing, as if with himself, that it was nevertheless "impossible to speak of Hitler's ideas as an 'alien imposition' on German traditions," that Hitler was not the first to import "racist pride, 'völkische' arrogance and anti-Semitism into Germany." Ritter, then, like Meinecke, illustrates the bias in German historiography. Despite his long career as one of Germany's great historians, he could not resolve the historical question of the place of anti-Semitism in modern German history and in modern German society, even when writing from a postwar perspective on the Third Reich.

These views of Meinecke and Ritter were not just individualistic, peculiarly their own, but bespoke the nationalist tradition in German historiography which permeated their own generation and that of their students. Consider Hans Rothfels, who studied under Meinecke. A converted Jew, Rothfels was forced out of his professorship in 1934 for "racial" reasons. He went abroad, eventually teaching at Brown University and the University of Chicago. He returned to teach at a German university in 1951 and a few years later resettled there for good. In 1947 he had delivered an address at the University of Chicago in memory of the failed coup of July 20, 1944, subsequently elaborating it into a book on the German opposition to Hitler.[30] In this touching tribute to those who resisted Hitler actively or passively, in deed or in silent heart, Rothfels magnified the extent and the depth of the opposition to Hitler and to National Socialism and generally idealized it, but—precisely like Meinecke and Ritter—insisted that Nazism was not a specifically German phenomenon rooted in Germany's history. It was, he held, the product of a European malaise: "In many respects National Socialism can be considered as the final summit of an extreme consequence of the secularization movement of the nineteenth century."

In September 1950 the Federal Republic of Germany chartered the *Institut für Zeitgeschichte* (Institute for Contemporary History), with a mandate to study the history of the National Socialist party and the Third Reich. Organized and administered in cooperation with the regional states, the Institute was based in Munich. (No comparable research center was ever established in East Germany.)[31] Meinecke was made an honorary member along with Theodor Heuss, President of the Federal Republic of Germany. The Advisory Board included among its members Ritter and Rothfels, as well as a few somewhat more liberal historians. A library and archives were soon established. Staff members undertook research mostly for the government, to present material in trials of Nazi war criminals and also for cases involving restitution or pensions. At the beginning of 1953 the Institute's quarterly *Vierteljahrshefte für Zeitgeschichte* began to appear.[32]

In the lead article of the first issue, Hans Rothfels prescribed the approach and the tone which German historians were to take in dealing with what he euphemistically called "German matters." In a sentence with the characteristically German syntax of the impersonal verb in the passive voice Rothfels laid down ground rules for evenhandedness: "what is most urgently required is to keep distance from all tendencies toward self-abasement as also from apologetics"—that is, it would appear, neither overly to attack nor overly to defend the historical record of the German people with regard to Nazism. To be sure, Rothfels continued, while the greatest possible objectivity in research was wanted, this did not mean "neutrality with regard to the traditions and principles of European morality."[33] This preferred stance of noninvolvement has become the hallmark of the Institute's substantial accumulation of books, monographs, *Gutachten*, and the many volumes of the *Vierteljahrshefte*. Without doubt the Institute has made a signal contribution to knowledge about National Socialism and the Third Reich. Its studies are thorough, competently researched, and well documented. The Institute has also produced a number of excellent studies about anti-Jewish policies in the Third Reich and about various aspects of the murder of the European Jews.

Still, many of the Institute's publications have an antiseptic quality, sometimes merely cool and detached, but more often lifeless. In part, the overload of factual detail induces tedium.

In part, the style of calculated objectivity and the deliberate avoidance of what Institute researchers like to call "emotionalism" create distance from the subject matter and suggest an attitude of moral disengagement and a state of emotional anemia. But for the most part, the inert quality that pervades much of the Institute's work derives from its substantive approach, which isolates National Socialism and the Third Reich from the whole German past. Following the lead of Meinecke, Ritter, and Rothfels, Institute scholars do not look backward. They study National Socialism as if it were hermetically enclosed within the time span 1918–1945 or else they look for comparable universal European phenomena by which to explain the German experience.[34] In their view, the continuity of German history was shattered by the Third Reich.

## Continuity Restored to German History

In 1961, when Fritz Fischer's book *Griff nach der Weltmacht* appeared in Germany, it affected German historiography like a violent shock wave, setting off upheavals everywhere.[35] Working from documentary sources in the federal and state archives of Germany and Austria, Fischer probed German war aims during the First World War and analyzed the policies which German leaders pursued to realize those aims. From his research and critical analysis Fischer concluded that the German government, fully supported by the military, the industrialists, the bourgeoisie, and even the leftists, strove to create a German empire by annexation and colonization that would bestride Europe. Germany's aggressive, all-devouring aims were motivated not only by raw imperialism but also by a deep-seated nationalist ethos about German superiority over the rest of Europe. To attain its aim of European hegemony, Fischer argued, Germany engineered the outbreak of the war, for which it had long prepared itself.

Fischer's book displeased the historical guild and jolted German public opinion. Since Weimar, the historians had written what the politicians had propounded and what the public had come to believe, that is, that Germany had been the victim of the sinister machinations of the European powers, the object of a policy of hostile "encirclement." Consequently, so the conventional history went, Germany's need for security forced it into the war as justifiable self-defense. Indeed, the popular interpretations given for Germany's defeat in the First World War, especially that of the *Dolchstoss*, and the terms which the Versailles Treaty imposed were seen as the ultimate evidence of Germany's victimization. It was this self-pitying and self-righteous view of Germany's role in the war that Fischer overturned.

His book did even more damage to the edifice which the conservative German historians had erected, for Fischer showed that from the perspective of the First World War, in a long view which encompassed German history from Bismarck to Hitler, the Hitler era was no aberration from the true course of German history, but part of its continuous flow. In his foreword, Fischer expressed the hope that his book might "serve as a contribution towards the problem of the continuity of policy from the First World War to the Second."[36] Indeed, his work restored to the foreground those elements in German history that had endured since the eighteenth century—the nationalist ethos celebrating German superiority, the militaristic traditions that stamped Prussian character, the conservatism that afflicted every social class in Germany from the petty bourgeoisie to the aristocracy, and the pervasive mistrust of democracy.

Not only did Fischer confront the central question of continuity which German historians had evaded, he also exposed the integral links between foreign and domestic policy. Thus he contributed toward undermining another venerable tradition in German history—the concept of the primacy of foreign policy in the state's existence. Another departure for German historiography was Fischer's introduction of material about Jews and anti-Semitism, as these topics impinged on his writing.[37] The integration of this subject matter, however brief, in German history represented a methodological innovation.

Fischer's most eminent antagonist in the historical guild was Gerhard Ritter, who charged him with tendentiousness. Yet Ritter appeared to be more concerned with the matter of German national self-esteem than with historical truth. In his attack on Fischer, he expressed apprehension lest Fischer's view that Germany provoked the First World War prevail. For then, Ritter lamented, the German people's "national historical consciousness" would be "darkened" even more "than it was by the experiences of the Hitler period."[38]

Fischer yielded no ground to his critics with regard to either methodology or substance. He did however make one important idea explicit. His book, he explained, dealt with the similarities of German war aims in both wars, but there were also differences: "Genocide and the enslavement of entire nations were the exclusive domain of Nazi Germany and cannot be ascribed to Germany in World War I, despite a policy of expansion to the east."[39]

Fischer's books and the influence which his ideas and methods exerted on his students effectively opened a window on German historiography to let in fresh air. Younger German historians now tend to be less rigidly nationalistic in their political view and more flexible in their methodology. Their contacts with English, French, and American historians and their consequent increased familiarity with different techniques and approaches in the study of history may help to unfetter German historiography from its confining political and philosophic traditions.[40]

In 1969 the first comprehensive history of the Third Reich and its origins was published in Germany. Called *Die deutsche Diktatur* by Karl Dietrich Bracher, a professor of history at the University of Bonn,[41] it was also the first work on this subject to restore fully the continuity of German history to the era of the Third Reich. A model work of historical scholarship, this book combined scrupulous objectivity, moral judgment, and a passionate commitment to the democratic ethos. In his preface Bracher writes: "This book is dedicated to the hope that a sober picture of the German dictatorship may help Germany avoid both old and new dangers, primarily the traditional authoritarian concept of the state, but also a radical utopianism—both expressions of intolerance and conceit, and, moreover, profoundly unpolitical modes of behavior."

Nearly half the book deals with the history of modern Germany prior to 1933, in a wide-ranging effort to uncover the German roots of Nazism. Bracher emphatically rejects the theory of a universal, undifferentiated fascism to explain the rise of the Nazi dictatorship. Though he takes into account the rampant presence of nationalist, pseudosocialist, elitist, and racist ideas throughout Europe in the nineteenth and early twentieth centuries, he points out that these did not produce a uniform effect, the fascist phenomenon varying from locale to locale.

The German variety, Bracher demonstrated, is best understood by tracing it from its origins in Bismarck's Germany and in the Hapsburg Empire to the critical events in Germany after its defeat in the First World War. Bracher also rejects the once-fashionable theory of totalitarianism that viewed right- and left-wing dictatorships as similar phenomena but failed to make critical distinctions between authoritarian-traditional modes of rule and totalitarian-revolutionary ones in their premises, goals, and content. For Bracher, National Socialism was a purely German manifestation, without precise precedent or analogue. It was, he says, a "specifically German phenomenon" which operated "in a concrete political and social situation." National Socialism, according to Bracher, was given its unique shape and force by a series of specific developments in modern German history, all of which had one element in common: "the fragility of the democratic tradition and the powerful remnants of authoritarian governmental and social institutions."

Bracher further stresses the importance of ideology as a factor in the rise of Nazism, even though the movement's thinking was eclectic, its conduct opportunistic, and its "ideas of power politics vulgarly Machiavellian." Nevertheless, he argues, it would be a mistake to ascribe National Socialism's rapid success merely to chance or improvisation. Indeed, "the basic and fatal error" which was made prior to 1933 inside Germany and then later everywhere else was to underestimate the Nazi movement and the terrible directness with which Hitler moved to realize Nazi ideology on both domestic and foreign fronts. That ideology, as Bracher summarizes in plain words, consisted of three cardinal principles originally propounded in *Mein Kampf*: hatred of the Jews; *Lebensraum*—Germany's unique version of racial imperialism; and the supremacy of the Führer as dictator.

Bracher is the first German historian, indeed the first non-

Jewish historian anywhere, who has recognized that from the start the Nazis assigned primacy of place, in doctrine and in action, to make hatred of the Jews, with all its tragic consequences, a cardinal feature of the state's policy. He has placed anti-Semitism and the destruction of the Jews in the very center of his book, fully integrating that subject matter with the political and military developments of the time.[42]

Finally, what contributes to making *The German Dictatorship* a work of unparalleled distinction in all the historical literature on the Third Reich produced in any language is that it is not a value-free work, neither dispassionate nor evenhanded. Looking at a contemporary Germany, Bracher concludes:

> The German dictatorship has failed, but German democracy has not yet been secured. Securing it remains a task that demands full awareness that the road to a real and realistic democratization is a narrow one, still strewn with many obstacles. It runs between the continuing burden of the past and the increased demands of the future, between the threats of the authoritarian tradition and the exaggerated promises of ideological radicalism which prevented the maturing of democracy in Germany and paved the way for the most terrible dictatorship mankind has known. The heritage of National Socialism lives on— negatively in the dangers of a relapse, positively in the opportunities of an educational process drawing on the experience of the past.

Truth is the only merit that gives dignity
and worth to history.

LORD ACTON

# PALIMPSEST HISTORY:
# ERASING THE HOLOCAUST
# IN THE USSR

In 1800, when Friedrich Schlegel described the historian as a
prophet in reverse, he surely never dreamed that 150 years
later his words could apply ironically to the USSR. For there
historians have had to learn how to read the past in the light of
the present if their work is to have any chance of surviving into
the future.[1] M. N. Pokrovsky, the leading Soviet historian of an
earlier time, put the situation more bluntly when he said that
"history is politics projected into the past."

Whereas in non-Communist countries historians approach
their subject matter with the perspectives of their own culture
and beliefs, historians in the Soviet Union have no choice but
to write history that conforms to Communist ideology and also
to the current political line. Whereas historians in non-Communist countries turn for inspiration and guidance to Clio as
expressed in the words of their master-models—Herodotus,
Gibbon, Ranke, or Graetz—the Soviet historians must perforce
invoke the local deities: Marx and Lenin at all times; Stalin,
Khrushchev, or Brezhnev, depending on whose star is in the
ascendancy.

The Soviet Union demands of its historians (as of all its
scholars and artists) impossible feats of intellectual acrobatics.
While under the restraints of the straitjacket of the approved

ideology, the historian is required to perform the fitful flip-flops of the party line. Given a task that cannot be fulfilled without sacrifice of historical truth and moral integrity, historians in the Soviet Union often become little more than accessories of the gigantic propaganda mill operated by the Communist Party of the Soviet Union (CPSU), its Central Committee, and its top dictators.

## Style and Substance: Marxism-Leninism and the Party Line

Marxism-Leninism is the official ideology of the Communist Party of the Soviet Union. An economic and political philosophy, it is derived from the ideas of Marx and Engels, which first Lenin and later Stalin modified, tampered with, and manipulated for their own political uses. The CPSU nevertheless has at all times claimed to be the faithful guardian of orthodox Marxism and the only true Marxists.

The philosophic underpinning for Marxism-Leninism is provided by the theory of historical materialism, which explains the rise and fall of most social systems. Crudely summarized, the theory holds that the "material conditions of life" determine the structure of a society. Consequently, important changes in those conditions will bring about important changes in the legal, political, and ideological structures of that society. All human history has followed a course of development based on social dynamics, which Marx described in a theory of historical epochs succeeding one another in accordance with historical law.

Primitive communism, man's original social organization, gave way to slave-owning society, that in turn to feudalism, and then to capitalism. Capitalist society, as a consequence of its internal contradictions, must break down, to be followed by a period of the dictatorship of the proletariat. Ultimately a Communist society will take its place. The passage from one historical epoch to the next is made possible through the class struggle and the inevitable emergence of the most oppressed class—the proletariat—to its rightfully dominant position in society.

According to this philosophic view about the progression of

human society, history is a vast destructive process governed by universal laws operating with the force of inevitability whose course is therefore predetermined. Only those who understand the workings of these laws can follow the direction of history and see its goal. Thus, "scientific" Marxism-Leninism is in fact a Communist teleology, a doctrine of immutable laws of the universe driving human society toward a predetermined end. Beneath its philosophic language, Marxism-Leninism offers its believers a secularized eschatology.

Practically every historical work published in the Soviet Union gives lip service to this theory. Thus, an editorial article in *Voprosy istorii* ("Problems of History"), the leading Soviet historical journal for the profession, declared that "the experience of history has irrefutably demonstrated that the teaching of Marxism-Leninism gives the only explanation of the laws of the historical process that is true and conforms to objective reality."[2]

This dogmatic view of the course of history serves as the mold into which the substance of history is poured and shaped to the required conformity. The substance itself is determined by the party line which represents the interests of the Soviet regime. For in the Soviet Union the historian is not permitted freedom of historical inquiry, or the luxury of pluralist approaches, or the indulgence of reflection on the meaning of the events he is studying. The Soviet historian is at bottom in the position of a homager of the state, expected to show his allegiance by faithfully adhering in his writing to the party line. History, as far as the regime is concerned, is useful because it furnishes a heavy-duty undergirding for the more conventional forms of political propaganda.

The shifts in party line, which change the course of current policy and strategy, necessarily also operate retroactively. Each shift in policy demands the imputation of blame for the past policy, since it is impossible for the CPSU or Marxism-Leninism ever to be wrong. Because no allowance is ever made for human fallibility or misjudgment, the past has to be corrected, that is, rewritten in the light of the present. Thus the rewriting of history first occurs at the level of politics. The previous policy is now seen not as wrong, misguided, or uninformed, but as misprision, treason, a conspiracy perpetrated by counterrevo-

lutionaries, spies, wreckers, fascists, falsifiers, traitors, bourgeois intellectuals, and dangerous enemies who must be extirpated. In undoing past policy, the current dictator also must
undo those associated with that policy. And so they are
purged, consigned to labor camps, imprisoned, murdered.
Sometimes they just disappear down the dark hole of Soviet
history, becoming, as George Orwell called them in *1984*, "un-
persons."

Historians have not been exempt from this process. Like
millions of other Soviet citizens, many of them have undergone
the terrors of changes in the party line. "Many disputes that
began in the pages of scientific journals," wrote Roy A. Medvedev, "ended in the torture chambers of the NKVD."
Pokrovsky himself, once the veritable dictator over Soviet historians, was posthumously branded the great enemy of Soviet
history. A natural death was his good fortune, sparing him the
ignominy and torture which his successors underwent. For the
criticism launched against him and his school turned into "a
political pogrom."[3]

Given these dynamics, writing history in the Soviet Union
became a "process of continuous alteration," which Orwell described with uncanny insight: "Day by day and almost minute
by minute the past was brought up to date . . . All history was a
palimpsest, scraped clean and reinscribed exactly as often as
was necessary."[4] With each change in party line, the previous
histories disappeared and new works were ordered to take their
place. Many major historical personages and events disappeared altogether from the record or their historicity was otherwise falsified, while minor figures were elevated to historic
stardom. Half-truths and lies were inextricably interwoven.
Such histories succeeded one another according to the rhythm
of the purges and the changes in party line, piling up layer
upon layer. Western scholars, to find out what really happened
in the history of the CPSU, for instance, have had to resort to
what has been characterized as an "archeological method," as if
in search of a long-buried civilization. "They must dig through
the mutually contradictory, successive layers of relative truth
and calculated falsehood in an effort to determine which of the
many layers represents the true Homeric Troy."[5]

In the first decade after the Bolsheviks came to power, the

CPSU exercised its vigilant censorship primarily over the history of the party, but after 1929, when Stalin became undisputed dictator, the party extended its jurisdiction over all history, most notably that of the Soviet Union, going back deep into the Russian past and ranging far beyond Russia's borders. Still, the most critical areas in terms of political surveillance remain the history of the CPSU and the history of the Soviet Union. Certain subjects—the October Revolution and the Second World War, especially the period of Russia's participation in what is called the Great Patriotic War—remain high priorities on the historical/political agenda. Here the palimpsest character of Soviet history is most evident.

After Stalin's death early in 1953 and the subsequent struggle for power among his successors, the rewriting of history accelerated. In 1954, the publishers of the *Great Soviet Encyclopedia* advised their subscribers "carefully" to cut out the pages about Lavrenti Beria, former head of the security police, purged at the end of 1953, and to substitute in their stead a newly supplied article on the Bering Strait. Two years later, in a comparable case, the *Encyclopedia* editors recommended "using scissors or razor blade" to remove an article about a historical figure now consigned to the memory hole.[6] When Khrushchev took over Stalin's position as total dictator, he too became the custodian of Soviet history: "Historians," he once said, "are dangerous people" and because "they are capable of upsetting everything," he explained, "they must be directed."[7]

### The History of the Second World War Revised and Standardized

No subject has been as sensitive to the Soviet historian's touch or as dangerous to his political health as the Second World War. For every chapter of Soviet history bearing on the Second World War looms as a mine field through whose explosive terrain the historian needs a politically discriminating mine detector for safe guidance. Every subject he may wish to examine is laid with political traps: ideology (Communism versus Nazism) as well as practical politics (the Hitler-Stalin pact or the Grand Alliance); diplomatic affairs (relations with the

Western capitalist countries or with Nazi Germany) as well as military strategy and tactics (Soviet military unpreparedness for the Nazi invasion); the behavior of the Soviet population (collaboration of many Russians, Ukrainians, and other nationalities with the German occupiers) as well as the behavior of the great dictator himself (his failure to heed Western warnings about the planned Nazi invasion of the USSR); economic matters (the weaknesses of Russia's industrial and agricultural capacity and productivity) as well as social policy (the active collaboration of the Soviet population in the murder of the Jews, despite Soviet claims to have outlawed anti-Semitism).

The embarrassments of Soviet historiography begin with the Nazi-Soviet nonaggression pact of August 23, 1939, when the USSR signed not just a treaty of friendship with its ideological archenemy, but also a secret protocol that set forth the spheres of interest of both parties in Central and Eastern Europe and provided for their partitioning of Poland. The Soviet Union did not take part in the war which began on September 1, 1939, with Germany's invasion of Poland, but independently pursued its own ambitions of territorial aggrandizement by attacking Finland and annexing the Baltic countries and parts of Rumania. None of these subjects was a licit area for historical investigation. In fact, nowadays, forty years later, when Soviet historians have found reasons to justify the nonaggression pact, the secret protocol still remains unmentionable.

After the Germans invaded the Soviet Union, the realities of war transformed the politics and the propaganda. The Nazis, who had before 1939 been painted black and then became neutrally colored, once again became black, while the capitalist imperialists of the West became part of the Grand Alliance, joining the democratic freedom-loving peoples in their struggle against fascism. At this juncture, greater freedom of expression was accorded the Soviet journalists and writers. This was not just the consequence of the general disorder of war, but came about by a deliberate policy decision. Stalin believed that outpourings in newspapers, magazines, books, and the radio about the sufferings and the heroism of the Soviet people would effectively raise morale within the Soviet Union and serve as a powerful propaganda weapon outside.[8]

Accordingly, wartime journalistic reportage and fiction reflected—within the normal limits of omnipresent Soviet censorship, now somewhat relaxed—a fair measure of the social realities of war-torn Russia. Naturally, they presented the positive elements which the official propaganda demanded: national patriotism, sense of duty and self-sacrifice, courage, and all the standard virtues. But from time to time they also showed the darker aspects of individual behavior—cowardice, dishonesty, venality—and, even more daringly, flaws in Soviet society: the panic caused by lack of information, military blunders, political stupidity, and even collaboration with the enemy. To be sure, the negative features never predominated, being salted into the largely positive portraits.

After the tide of war changed and the Red Army—massively supplied by the United States, another embarrassing subject of the war's history—began to push back the Germans, Soviet historians undertook to gather materials for the history of the war and to discuss among themselves questions of methodology, that is, what the party line should be. But soon after the war's end, Stalin called a halt to all historical inquiry about the war. Thenceforth, until his death in 1953, the major sources of information about the war were his own wartime writings and speeches. Stalin's blackout on war historiography can be attributed only in part to the grave disparities between reality and propaganda apparent to everyone who experienced the war. But the more urgent reason for the obscuration was the drastic change in Soviet foreign policy, which entailed commensurate changes in the party line and in domestic policy as well.

Stalin's ruthless postwar subjugation of the East European countries into a host of Soviet satellites and his less successful attempts to gain footholds in the Mediterranean, Iran, and Manchuria, aroused fear and mistrust in the West, sparking the cold war. By mid-1946 the wartime Grand Alliance had come to an end. It now belonged to a past that had to be erased. The Sovietization of Eastern Europe demanded total conformity and justification in every area of Soviet society. It entailed the total mobilization of anti-Western sentiment throughout the USSR, and the condemnation of everything Western from American chewing gum to the United States Marshall Plan for European economic recovery. The entire propaganda machinery of the Communist party and the Soviet state had to be retooled to accomplish this end. The habitually brutal dictatorship became even more Draconian. To ensure total compliance and agreement, the regime stepped up the terror. Millions of Soviet citizens were arrested without reason and sent away to the rapidly expanding system of labor camps. Those postwar years were the most cruel period in Russia's history, with a near total eclipse of intellectual endeavor, even such as it was under the habitual restraints of Soviet censorship.

In the humanities, especially literature and history, the "anticosmopolitanism" campaign, first launched in late summer 1946 by A. Zhdanov, with its ugly anti-Semitic undertones, set the appropriate course of anti-Westernism and Great Russian chauvinism. The motif of patriotism became a fundamental feature of the history that was to be written. "Our duty," declared one of Russia's leading historians at a meeting in 1949, "is to struggle with all attempts to belittle the significance of our national history. We know that we have a glorious Motherland, which has its own glorious history, and we must not allow anyone to depreciate or debase it."[9] This Soviet jingoism, coupled with the conventional exaltation of the virtues of Communism over capitalism, has since remained a cardinal element of Soviet historiography.[10]

After Stalin's death on March 5, 1953, a struggle erupted among his successors to take over the power he had held. The next years brought changes in the leadership, in political policy, and also in the party line. In February 1956, at the Twentieth Party Congress, Nikita Khrushchev, by now the CPSU's first secretary, *primus inter pares*, delivered his famous secret speech accusing Stalin of having fostered a "cult of personality" and of having committed those very crimes of which the West had long accused him. By June 1957, during a week-long meeting of the CPSU's Central Committee, Khrushchev finally prevailed in the power struggle. His defeated opponents, including Vyacheslav Molotov, Georgy Malenkov, and Lazar Kaganovich, were then condemned as the so-called "Anti-Party Group."

These events profoundly affected the course of Second World War historiography. To begin with, Khrushchev lifted the blackout that Stalin had imposed. The strategy of the cold

75

war gave way to peaceful coexistence. In September 1957 the party's Central Committee authorized the preparation of a multivolume history of the war and created a Department of History of the Great Patriotic War at the Institute of Marxism-Leninism to do so. Historians and party ideologues, whose function was to clarify the party line, conferred about the character of the war and discussed the political framework within which the correct ideological interpretation could be presented. It was to be expected that the process of de-Stalinization which had already penetrated most other aspects of Soviet life would now turn up in the new histories.

In 1959, the Soviet journal of military history, *Voyennoistoricbesky zhurnal,* which had not been issued since the war, began to reappear, publishing articles and memoirs by top military officers. They uniformly presented a revisionist, anti-Stalinist view of the military conduct of the war.[11] Most unusual was the access provided to state archives. A Foreign Ministry Commission, headed by Andrei Gromyko, was empowered to edit diplomatic documents for publication. The Archives of the Ministry of Defense and of the Army and Navy were made available to scholars.

These developments appeared to indicate an unprecedented openness, offering Soviet historians hitherto undreamed of opportunities for their research. Actually the conditions for intellectual freedom had hardly changed. While the revised and newly standardized version of the history of the Second World War was much closer to the way things really were than the Stalinist version had been, the Khrushchev dictatorship allowed the Soviet historian no real freedom to explore the past or its documents.[12] The ideology of Marxism-Leninism continued to demand conformity to its fundamental view of the course of history and the party continued to demand adherence to the new line. If the external pressures of censorship were somewhat more relaxed, the self-censorship that prudent writers in the Soviet Union learned to exercise ensured that their work would remain within the prescribed bounds.

In 1960 the first volume of the history of the war prepared under the auspices of the Institute of Marxism-Leninism appeared; the sixth and final volume came out in 1965.[13] Like all official Soviet publications, this work justified and glorified the

Soviet Union and the Communist party which leads it. According to *Voprosy istorii*, its objective was "to disclose comprehensively and thoroughly the sublime epopee of the struggle of the Soviet people, led by the Communist Party, for their freedom and independence and for the liberation of the peoples of other countries from fascism."[14] In this period of de-Stalinization, at a time when even the cities and towns bearing Stalin's name were being renamed, it was to be predicted that the history of the war would be so rewritten as to attribute to Stalin and—to a lesser extent—to Beria and the Anti-Party Group the blame for everything that had gone wrong, and to restore prestige to the Red Army and its generals, in disgrace with Stalin in the last years of his life. The Soviet Union's state of military unpreparedness, the failure of its intelligence agencies to know about Germany's plans to invade the Soviet Union, and the shortcomings of Soviet industry and agriculture during the war were mentioned as the misdeeds of Stalin and Beria. The heroism of the Soviet people was extolled and it was made plain that the Soviet Union alone was responsible for the defeat of Nazi Germany. Grudging acknowledgment was made of Allied aid to the Soviet Union, but more space was assigned to condemning the Western countries for having delayed opening the second front, with the suggestion even of sabotage on their part in this matter.

By the time the last volume of this Khrushchev-sponsored history appeared, Khrushchev had already been removed from office and his place taken by Leonid Brezhnev. The change of guard meant a change of party line. The new party boss feared that the de-Stalinizers had introduced too much permissiveness in politics as in historiography. Now revisionism was to be revised.[15] A dramatic case in point was a historical study by Aleksandr M. Nekrich, then a senior research scholar at the Institute of General History of the prestigious and powerful Soviet Academy of Sciences. His book, *June 22, 1941*, was published in Moscow in 1965, having been sponsored by the Academy of Sciences. Its subject matter was Russia's lack of preparation for the invasion and the war. Nekrich had blamed not only Stalin, but also the CPSU and the Soviet regime. But the political climate had changed by the time this book appeared. It was condemned at a conference specially convened by the Institute of Marxism-Leninism, banned from circulation, and its copies ordered to be destroyed. Nekrich himself was expelled from the party and allowed to publish no more than "one article per year in an academic publication of limited circulation." Unable for years to break out of this enforced silence, Nekrich finally managed to leave the Soviet Union in 1976.[16]

Still, enough historians and memoirists have been ready to follow the new line which, though downplaying Stalin, no longer blames him for failures and occasionally even praises him, albeit mutedly and indirectly. The flow of publications that Khrushchev had released has increased to a torrent in the last decade. In 1966 the Ministry of Defense created an Institute of Military History which has been producing a twelve-volume *History of the Second World War, 1939–1945*, to have been completed by 1979.[17] But the continuing stream of histories, memoirs, essays, and documents have produced little of substantive interest to Western historians.[18]

## The Holocaust as Historiographic Problem

Any rendering of the fate of the Jews in the USSR during the Second World War is problematic, for the subject matter falls among perilous reefs of historical inquiry: the interpretation of Nazism, the persistence of anti-Semitism in the Soviet Union, and the voluntary collaboration of many Soviet citizens in the murder of the Jews. Besides, the history of the Jews in the Soviet Union, while not actually interdicted, is best ignored if one is a prudent Soviet historian.

Since the rise of National Socialism in Germany, Soviet scholars, dutifully following the prescriptions of Marxism-Leninism, have diagnosed Nazism as tool or bodyguard of "monopoly capitalism." Sometimes Nazism (or a generic fascism) is presented as the Tweedledum to the Tweedledee of "bourgeois parliamentarianism" and sometimes as the instrument used by monopoly capitalists to overthrow "bourgeois democracy." Recently a Soviet historian explained the outbreak of the Second World War with this abstract formula:

The pre-war political crisis . . . demonstrated the sharp aggravation of the contradictions in the imperialist camp. It had already become impossible to solve these contradictions by peaceful means. The Second World War proved to be the inevitable result of the development of world economic and political forces based on contemporary monopoly capitalism.[19]

The racist anti-Semitic character of Nazism has been generally disregarded in the USSR, while economic interests and class differences are stressed. Thus, Soviet analysts used to claim that the Nazis hated only working-class Jews, while welcoming the support of wealthy Jews, or that the Nazis expropriated the Jews only to win support among the German petty bourgeoisie who became enriched at the Jews' expense.[20] Lately Soviet historians make occasional references to Nazi racism, apparently to demonstrate their familiarity with the Western literature on the subject. But in the Soviet history books the fundamental anti-Jewish element of Nazi racism is seldom mentioned. The most recent edition of the *Great Soviet Encyclopedia* capsulizes Nazi ideology this way:

In preparing for the war for world domination and especially against the USSR, the Hitlerites instituted large-scale ideological preparation, preaching racism and extreme chauvinism—the "superiority" of the Aryan race and the historical "justice" of the conquest of "living space" (*Lebensraum*) among the German population and the army; instilling hatred against communism, the Soviet people, and the "lower races" (*Untermensch*); and moulding a special type of fascist soldier—a murderer and a predator.[21]

A recent history of the Second World War published in the Ukraine refers to Nazi racism as an "anti-humanistic racial theory," but never once mentions the Jews: "The fascist ideologists openly advocated extermination of whole nations . . . In their plans of physical annihilation of people the Nazis allotted the first place to the Slavs."[22]

Despite frequent declarations that anti-Semitism is incompatible with Communism and despite the repeated assurances that the Soviet regime had outlawed it, anti-Semitism, which has been deeply rooted in the superstitions of the Russian people for generations and which had always been exploited by tsarist officials, has continued its persistently long life under the Soviets. It has remained visible and audible throughout the history of the Soviet Union and especially so during the Second World War. At that time an impressive record of the anti-Semitism rampant in the USSR was amassed from a wide range of witnesses, including refugee Polish Jews in the Soviet Union and British Foreign Office staff.[23]

When the German armed forces and the murdering *Einsatzgruppen* swept into the Soviet Union, they found substantial numbers of Lithuanians, Latvians, Estonians, White Russians, Ukrainians, Great Russians, Tartars, Kalmyks, and others willing to collaborate with them. Reasons for hostility to the Soviet regime were many and varied. Some peoples, especially the Ukrainians, wanted national autonomy and political independence; others simply sought revenge for past Soviet brutality and persecution.

A common spirit binding the disaffected peoples with the Germans was their pervasive anti-Semitism. The *Einsatzgruppen* found many hands ready to assist in murdering the Jews. In all, the Germans and their helpers slaughtered about 1.5 million Soviet Jews: 245,000 in White Russia, 900,000 in the Ukraine, 107,000 in Russia proper, and 228,000 in the Baltic countries.[24] In Kiev, for instance, in September 1941, shortly after the Germans took the city, they rounded up over 33,000 Jews and shot them during two days at a ravine in outlying Babi Yar. The Ukrainians became Germany's most diligent collaborators. They even turned up as helpers in the murder of the Jews as far from home as Warsaw, where they served as auxiliaries to General Jürgen Stroop's SS troops in putting down the uprising in the Warsaw ghetto in April–May 1943.[25]

Helping the Germans kill the Jews must have become a commonplace experience in the Soviet Union, for the trace of bad conscience became a sardonic joke in Russian folk humor. Andrei Sinyavsky, in his testimony from the slave-labor camp of Dubrovlag, noted that when someone groaned and screamed in his sleep, the usual comment of the listeners was "dreaming of Yids":

> The "Yids" come at night to strangle and torment the sleeping man who, presumably, had taken part in atrocities against them at some time or other. Of course, he saw nothing wrong in help-

ing to "liquidate" them at the time, but now they come back—in dreams.[26]

Given the party line on Nazism and the anti-Semitism which was as intense at the highest levels of the Soviet bureaucracy as among the Ukrainian peasants, it was to be expected that in the period before the Hitler-Stalin pact whatever material critical of the Third Reich and Nazism the Soviet media published, it seldom referred to Nazi anti-Semitism and the persecution of the Jews. After the pact, during the period of "friendship" between Germany and the Soviet Union, criticism of Germany disappeared altogether from Soviet publications. The silence about the treatment of the Jews was deafening.[27]

But once Germany attacked the USSR, the policy changed, as noted earlier. Stalin launched a massive propaganda campaign to raise morale within the Soviet Union and to elicit political and financial support abroad. The sufferings of the Jews were exploited for this end. From 1942 until the end of the war the Jewish experience became a licit subject for the media. Reportages, eyewitness accounts, documentary material, fiction, and poetry describing the terrible fate of the Jews and also their heroic resistance began to be published in the general press.

The Soviet authorities established a Jewish Anti-Fascist Committee, which made its public appearance in April 1942 and began to issue a Yiddish newspaper called *Eynikayt* ("Unity") in June 1942. Western observers have long presumed that this Jewish Anti-Fascist Committee operated under the direction of the NKVD, having been created only to rally worldwide Jewish support for the Soviet Union.[28] The most distinguished writer mobilized in this effort was the novelist Ilya Ehrenburg, whose own sense of Jewish identity was deeply stirred by the murder of the European Jews. Working with the Soviet journalist Vasilii Grossman, Ehrenburg gathered documentary materials about the wartime experiences of the Soviet Jews—testimonies and narratives of the killings and of Jewish resistance, as well as accounts of Jewish participation in the Red Army and the partisan movement. These documents were to be issued as an accusatory *Black Book*, to be

81

published in Russian and Yiddish in the USSR, in English in the United States, and in Hebrew in Palestine.[29]

By mid-1944 Ehrenburg had assembled the materials. That year a small Yiddish book of documentary accounts of the German atrocities against the Jews appeared in Moscow with an introduction by Ehrenburg.[30] At that time, Ehrenburg sent copies of his documentation to New York for the English publication. Meanwhile, the Russian version began to be set in type. The English edition of the *Black Book* was published in 1946, but the Russian version never came out.[31] The history of the Holocaust and, with it, the Jewish Anti-Fascist Committee and many Jewish writers and intellectuals became the victims of the shift in the party line from cooperation with the West to the cold war.

### Erasing the Jews from Soviet History

In mid-December 1946, three months after the Central Committee of the CPSU had taken action against several Soviet journals in the wake of Zhdanov's attack against "cosmopolitanism," *Eynikayt* published an editorial article which criticized Jewish wartime literature for its parochialism. Jewish war literature, the editorial declared, suffered from a serious defect: "the German-fascist murders of the Jewish population are depicted as isolated and are not integrated with the Hitlerite killings of the Soviet people in general."[32] At this signal, the Holocaust began to be erased from the records of Soviet history, the facts of the Final Solution homogenized with the statistics of Soviet war losses.

In the next three years, the campaign against cosmopolitanism took on an explicitly anti-Semitic character, especially in the media, literature, and the humanities. It originated, as noted earlier, in the new anti-Western stance which demanded superpatriotism and elevated Great Russian nationalism over any other ethnic loyalty, but a specifically Jewish element intruded. The Soviet Jews had responded, it appeared to Soviet authorities, with excessive enthusiasm for the then newly established state of Israel. Consequently, as a corollary to anti-cosmopolitanism, the Soviet dictatorship launched an anti-

Zionist campaign in September 1948, choosing none other than Ehrenburg as its advocate. The thrust of the anti-Zionist argument was to deny that any bonds of solidarity existed among Jews of different countries. The Jews were now charged with "bourgeois nationalism," which was bad, even though it was the opposite of cosmopolitanism, also bad, with which the Jews were charged as well.

In the field of history the campaign against cosmopolitanism hit at the Jews, who were designated by the code term of "cosmopolitans without kith or kin." Historians in Oriental studies—where Jewish history had been pigeonholed—were assigned "the urgent task" of "unmasking and destroying the cosmopolitan ideology of 'a single Jewish nation.' "[33] The Jews began to disappear from the history books.

New secondary school textbooks issued in the 1950s and 1960s substantially abbreviated or altogether deleted the references to Jews, not just in modern and medieval history, but even in accounts of ancient history. The few remaining references to Jews cast them in an unfavorable light—as moneylenders or capitalists. The general textbooks on the Second World War gave no information about Nazi anti-Semitism and hardly anything about the murder of the Jews.[34] Rare references to the uprising in the Warsaw ghetto gave the credit to the Communist organizations and magnified, to the point of falsehood, the role of non-Jewish Communists in aiding the Jews, even in fighting alongside them.[35] The scholarly literature somehow managed totally to overlook the presence of the Jews in Soviet history, past and present. A multivolume history of the Ukraine, for example, never once mentioned the Jews, though major Jewish settlements were located there, once centers of revolutionary activity during the Revolution and the sites of the destructive pogroms during the Civil War and of the mass murders in the Second World War.[36]

Babi Yar was the most notorious instance of the Soviet erasure of the Holocaust. For years Soviet authorities denied petitions to set up a monument at the site to commemorate the murdered Jews. Soviet novelist Anatoli Kuznetsov reported that he had heard Communists in Kiev more than once ask: "What Babi Yar are you talking about? Where they shot the Yids? And who said we had to put a memorial up to some lousy Yids?"[37] Soviet authorities actually intended a literal cover-up: to fill in the ravine and build a sports stadium there. Then, in 1961, in the de-Stalinization era, Yevgeni Yevtushenko's poem about Babi Yar and his ringing denunciation of anti-Semitism made the memorialization of the murdered Jews an international issue.

But the Soviet authorities did not respond for years. Finally, in 1976, they erected a monument at Babi Yar. But it does not memorialize the Jews. Its bronze tablet bears this inscription: "Here in 1941–43 German fascist invaders executed over 100,000 citizens of the city of Kiev and prisoners of war." A news story in *Pravda*, describing the unveiling, elaborated:

> A terrible tragedy broke out at Baby Yar at the end of September 1941. Tens of thousands of totally blameless, peaceful residents of Kiev, including many children, women and old people, were shot to death there within a period of a few days. The invaders murdered Russians, Ukrainians, Jews, Byelorussians, Poles.[38]

During the 1960s, when a spate of war memoirs poured from the Soviet presses, only one Jewish survivor account was published. Issued simultaneously in Russian in Moscow and in Yiddish in Warsaw, the book purports to be a diary of life in the Vilna ghetto kept by a young Communist, Masha Rolnik, characterized as "the Lithuanian Anne Frank."[39] Even if the diary is an authentic document, it has unmistakably been doctored. For instance, accounts about the resistance movement that the diarist could never have known at the time are set down. She credits the Jewish resistance entirely to the Communists, though in fact the Zionist youth groups and the Jewish Socialist Bund were equal participants.

The diary's most flagrant falsification is in the account of the death of the Communist underground activist Itzik Wittenberg, who was head of the United Partisan Organization. Wittenberg, then in hiding, was wanted by the Gestapo, who threatened to destroy the entire ghetto unless he was handed over. Wittenberg's own party comrades, the Communists, decided to do just that. Of course the Gestapo murdered him, probably the same day. The Rolnik diary offers altogether a fanciful version of those events, with whose dramatic course the whole ghetto had become familiar and whose true history

Rolnik had been bound to know. In her purported diary entries, Rolnik records that Wittenberg voluntarily turned himself in to save the ghetto from Nazi wrath and that he had a capsule of cyanide to take his own life—a detail never before mentioned in the numerous accounts of Wittenberg's last days.[40] As if Wittenberg's death at the hands of the Germans were not sufficient warrant to make him a martyr, Rolnik turns him into a saint, at the same time absolving the Communists of handing over their own leader to the Nazis.

## The Tables Turned: Victims into Victimizers

Soviet anti-Semitism intensified in 1967 after the Six Day War in which Israel stunningly defeated the Arab states armed by the USSR. Soviet propaganda became more virulent against Israel and its supporters, all indiscriminately labeled as Zionists. That was just one more way for the Soviet regime to enhance its position among its Arab client-states. Meanwhile, the regime's continuing anti-Semitic and anti-Israel propaganda strengthened the sense of Jewish identity that the Soviet Jews had come to experience after the Holocaust and the establishment of Israel. They gained more courage in avowing their solidarity with Israel and in choosing to emigrate. Their actions reinforced Soviet anti-Semitism. Soon the dialectics of repression and dissidence contributed to the emergence of what is probably the most bizarre anti-Semitic argument ever propounded. Zionism, already characterized in both Communist and Arab propaganda as a tool of the white man's imperialism, was now branded first as a form of racism and then equated with fascism and anti-Semitism. (The only appropriate response to this upside-down version of history is in *Through the Looking Glass,* when Alice tells the White Queen that "one *can't* believe impossible things." To which the Queen remarks that Alice hasn't had much practice. "When I was your age, I always did it for half-an-hour a day. Why, sometimes I've believed as many as six impossible things before breakfast.")

In 1971 Vladimir Bolshakov, a writer assigned to produce anti-Zionist propaganda, wrote two articles in *Pravda,* in which he asserted that Zionism, characterized as "a ramified system of organization and political practice of the big Jewish bourgeoisie," had throughout its history collaborated with reactionaries, pogromists, and anti-Semites. The Zionists had even entered into "a dirty alliance with the Hitlerites." Making his case on the basis of an anonymous and no doubt fabricated letter, Bolshakov accused the Zionists of the ultimate crime— responsibility for Babi Yar:

> "The tragedy of Babi Yar," Soviet citizens of Jewish origin living in the Ukraine wrote in a letter to Pravda, "will forever remain the embodiment not only of the cannibalism of the Hitlerites but also the indelible shame of their accomplices and followers—the Zionists."[41]

That same year, the Soviet dictatorship ordered that the new anti-Zionist line be introduced also into scholarly literature, presumably to provide academic legitimation for the crude propaganda. The Soviet Academy of Sciences was told to establish an Israeli Studies Section and managed to do so by appointing academicians who knew no Hebrew. In 1972 the CPSU instructed the Academy to create a Permanent Commission attached to the Social Sciences Section of the Academy's Presidium. Its task, as the long-winded title put it, was "Coordination of Studies Concerned with the Exposure and Criticism of the History, Ideology, and Practice of Zionism." The chairman assigned to this new Permanent Commission was the director of the Academy's Institute of Oriental Studies and formerly first secretary of the Communist party in Tadzhikistan.[42]

A conference on Zionism was convened by the Permanent Commission in February 1976 at which scholars in related fields—Oriental studies, modern history, philosophy, legal studies—presented papers and discussed ground rules for dealing with Zionism "as one of the most fascist . . . forms of anti-Communism."[43] In July 1977 the Academy of Sciences published a collection of papers entitled *International Zionism: History and Politics.* One contributor, writing on the subject of the World Zionist Organization, charged that Zionism had a close working relationship with Hitlerism and was consequently to be held responsible for the Holocaust.

In the late 1970s this literally unbelievable charge that the Jews themselves were responsible for the Holocaust was given ever wider circulation in the Soviet press and in Soviet scholarly literature. Here are a few extracts from several writers, all published in 1976 and 1977:

Memoirs, chronicles and testimonies of eye-witnesses *unmasking the true role of the Zionists in organizing the mass destruction of Jews and the cooperation of leaders of the Zionist movement with the Nazis* are generally not published in Israel and those capitalist countries where publishing houses are in the hands of the Zionists.

Not without the help of the leaders of Zionism did hundreds of thousands of ordinary Jews meet their death in the gas chambers.

It is no longer a secret that Zionist capital helped to strengthen the Hitlerite regime in Germany and the fascists' preparations for their attack on the Soviet Union.

Israeli intelligence undertook to capture Eichmann and remove him to Israel primarily in order *to ensure secrecy over a number of Zionists' deals and the collaboration of their secret services with the Hitlerites during the Second World War.*[44]

This "impossible thing" to believe is now being repeated so often that the Soviet people will have sufficient practice to come to believe it before breakfast. Orwell's prophetic 1984 has already arrived in the USSR. The Soviet Union's propaganda apparatus, the equivalent of Orwell's Ministry of Truth, proclaims that war is peace, freedom is slavery, and the Holocaust was perpetrated by the Jews.

> Truth exists, only falsehood has to be in-
> vented.
>
> GEORGES BRAQUE

# 5

# APPROPRIATING THE HOLOCAUST: POLISH HISTORICAL REVISIONISM

Today barely 5,000 Jews live in Poland. A few decades ago there were 3.3 million. Jews had settled in Poland as far back as the eleventh century and by the sixteenth century had become the most populous of all European Jewish communities and the most creative. Invited by the Polish kings to a land of indolent nobility, landed gentry (*szlachta*), and a peasantry reduced to serfdom, the Jews became the middle class. They were rewarded for their mercantile and administrative skills, their financial experience, their craftsmanship, and their industriousness. Yet as the pendulum of history swung from tolerance to hostility, the Jews were persecuted and ravaged for those very qualities. Their enterprise was envied, their industriousness resented, their financial talent distrusted. The Jews became despised, even feared, when once they had been welcomed, cultivated, and esteemed.

For centuries Poland had been unable to govern itself, to maintain political or economic stability. The nobility and the clergy feuded endlessly with the royal and ducal powers, usurping from them ever more privileges and areas of governance. In the fifteenth century the Kingdom of Poland, having united with the Grand Duchy of Lithuania, routed the Teutonic Knights, at last extinguishing the Prussian influences in the country. In the next century the Jesuit Order became a major power in Poland and thus ensured the place of Roman

Catholicism as the supreme religion of the land. Soon the Catholic Church in Poland became Rome's firmest bulwark, halting the spread of the Protestant Reformation eastward and of Greek Orthodoxy westward. Within Poland, the Church fanned the hostility against the Jews, reinforcing the Poles' economic resentments with medieval superstitions and anti-Judaic arguments. Indoctrinated by a clergy insensible to Renaissance humanism and alienated from other Slavic peoples because of their adherence to Rome, the Poles came to regard themselves "as under the special protection of Providence, as chosen people."[1]

Trusting in Providence, the Poles did little to help themselves. A series of disastrous wars and uprisings in the seventeenth century sapped Poland's weak resources. Without a sense of national unity, its governance determined by the whims and greed of the *szlachta*, enfeebled Poland became a pawn of the great European powers. In the eighteenth century, foundering on their own helplessness, the nobles invited the assistance of the foreign powers, the lamb itself whetting the tiger's appetite. By that century's end, Poland's three powerful neighbors—Prussia, Austria, and Russia—had three times partitioned the country (1772, 1793, and 1795). Poland as a nation disappeared from the map.

## The Shaping of Polish National Consciousness

Smarting under foreign rule, the Poles underwent a "crisis of national consciousness." Polish nationalism emerged among the thousands of Polish exiles in Paris during the so-called Great Emigration of the 1830s, following the unsuccessful Polish uprising in 1830–31. Nurturing the memory of their homeland, the philosophers and romantic poets among the exiles evolved a concept of Polish national identity and unity that had never before been articulated, even in Poland itself.

Poland's political misfortunes shaped the idea of Polish messianism among the emigrés. Since Divine Providence had failed to intervene in human history to save Poland, the philosophers and poets—devout Catholics whose mysticism the comfortless course of Polish history had heightened—concluded that God had not turned His back on beloved Poland, the torchbearer of Catholicism in Eastern Europe, but that Poland's suffering had transcendent meaning. They fantasized Poland as the Christ of the nations, whose historical mission would be to redeem the world from its political sins. Poland's emigré romantic poets, including Adam Mickiewicz, the greatest among them, incorporated these mystical ideas in their writings, which soon assumed the character of a national gospel. According to these works, martyred Poland would be resurrected after three partitions, just as Christ rose three days after he was crucified. Arising from death, Poland would become the savior of the nations and bring to the world a new order of political morality.[2] This concept of Poland martyred and resurrected became an enduring national myth, continually reinforced by Poland's hapless political history. After the First World War Poland's reemergence as a national state was regarded as a resurrection, and Poland's partition and occupation by Germany and the Soviet Union in the Second World War further intensified the feelings of Poland's martyrdom. Today, as Poland remains in bondage to Soviet power, its people remain faithful to the Church and still cling to the national myth of a martyred Poland to be resurrected as part of God's design.

This myth, identifying the nation wholly with the faith, was the core out of which modern Polish nationalism evolved. Then, when Prussia, in its part of partitioned Poland, began to compel Germanization and Lutheranization as remorselessly as the tsarist regime enforced its Russifying policy in Congress Poland, the Polish language was added as a constituent element of the developing Polish national ethos. Attempted suppression of language and faith only intensified and politicized Polish nationalist passions and the appetite for independence. Indeed, their exaltation of martyrdom inclined the Poles to desperate, even suicidal, ventures to win their freedom. In 1863, the Poles once again mounted an unsuccessful uprising against the Russians. Once again tsarist suppression was harsh. Polish leaders, this time in a revulsion from romantic martyrdom, turned to a more realistic and altogether different political mode. They hoped now that by developing Poland's economy and industry rather than by engaging in quixotic gestures, they could provide a sound foundation upon which some day they would build an independent nation.

This new course in nationalist aspirations in the last third of the nineteenth century introduced anti-Semitism as another factor in Polish nationalism. As Poland belatedly entered the industrial age with an emerging Polish middle class and an embryonic urban Polish proletariat, the anti-Jewish prejudices long inculcated by the Church found new expression in economic competition, as the Poles aimed to displace the Jews in business and light industry. Still more pernicious was the importation, in the last two decades of the nineteenth century, of the anti-Semitic ideologies then rampant in Germany, Austria, and Russia. In that period the Polish nationalist movement split. The liberals opted for a federalist nationalism that accepted the presence and welcomed the cooperation of all national minorities—Ukrainians, Jews, Belorussians, and Germans—in a future independent Poland. The conservatives, however, regarded the Jews as an alien intrusion in the Polish body politic. In 1897, when the National Democratic party, known by its acronym Endecja, was founded under the leadership of Roman Dmowski, the Polish nationalist movement embarked on its inexorable anti-Semitic course. The Endecja, which placed anti-Semitism at the center of its nationalist goals, eventually became the dominant party in the politics of independent Poland.

The creation of an independent Polish republic in 1919 brought political power to the nationalists. The man who headed the Polish state for most of its brief life, Józef Piłsudski, originally a socialist, a federalist, and not an anti-Semite, as he confronted the raw and reckless anti-Semitism of the Endecja, concluded opportunistically that the tide of anti-Semitism was irresistible, that if he combated the Endecja's anti-Jewish nationalism he would lose power. For the Endecja commanded political muscle, manipulating a prejudiced population that had had little experience in representative government. Furthermore, the Endecja enjoyed the backing of the Roman Catholic Church, most of whose clergy were its active supporters.

Responding to the agitation fomented by the Endecja, in the 1920s the Polish government embarked on a campaign to deprive the Jews of their rights and their livelihoods. Like other newly created states under the Treaty of Versailles, Poland had obligated itself to protect the rights of all its ethnic minorities, amounting to about one third of its citizens. Besides guaranteeing individual rights, Poland also promised collective political and cultural rights under the National Minorities Treaty, but that promise was never kept. No single nationality ever enjoyed the autonomy which the treaty guaranteed. As for the Jews, attempts were made to deprive them of their individual rights, and they were denied their collective political and religious rights, as well as the government support of their institutions that the Minorities Treaty required.

Government regulations were introduced to exclude the Jews from certain occupations and industries which they themselves had originally developed. Jews became objects of harassment and violence, victims of boycotts and pogroms. Their access to universities—and thereby to professional careers—was limited by quota and their presence at the universities was discouraged by acts of terror committed by Polish students. In 1937 Polish professional associations of physicians, engineers, and architects adopted the so-called "Aryan Paragraph," borrowed from Nazi Germany's legislation, which barred Jews from those fields. The political actions designed to drive the Jews from the economy now aimed to drive them altogether from the country. The Endecja, having absorbed many ideas from the Third Reich, believed that by getting rid of the Jews, they would assure the eventual racial purity of the Polish state.[3]

That anti-Jewish attitude in Poland—with significant exceptions on the left—prevailed when in September 1939 Germany and the Soviet Union partitioned Poland for the fourth time in its history.

### The Anti-Semitic Heritage in Wartime Poland and After

The Germans used Poland as their gigantic laboratory for mass murder, not (as has sometimes been wrongly charged) because the Nazis counted on Polish anti-Semitism, but because that was where most of Europe's Jews were concentrated and where the Germans expected to settle for a long time. By early 1942 they had built six killing installations in Poland, where they murdered 5.5 million people, about 4 million of them Jews—nearly 3 million Polish Jews and a million Jews from elsewhere in Europe.

Within a year or even less after the German occupation, the Jews were separated from the Polish population and imprisoned in ghettos. The punishment for leaving the ghetto without authorization was death, and death was the punishment too for non-Jews who harbored Jews or otherwise aided them to escape.[4] Research conducted in Poland in the late 1960s indicated that a few hundred Poles were executed for helping Jews, while probably many thousands more helped, or tried to help.[5] Some Poles risked their lives for old friends. Others did so out of religious morality or a political commitment to equality and liberty. Many did so for money. But most of the 30 million Poles did nothing on behalf of the Jews, satisfied to observe how the Germans were now solving *their* "Jewish problem."

In September 1941 the commander of the Armia Krajowa, the Polish underground Home Army, reported to the Polish Government-in-Exile in London: "Please accept it as a fact that the overwhelming majority of the country is anti-Semitic . . . Anti-Semitism is widespread now." Three years later, after most of the Polish Jews had already been murdered, the head of the Polish underground organization advised his superiors in London to restrain their pro-Jewish statements because "the country does not like Jews."[6]

In a poem composed in Warsaw in 1943, Czesław Milosz indicted Polish indifference to the fate of the Jews. Titling the poem "Campo de Fiori," the Roman square where the Inquisitors burned to death the Italian philosopher Giordano Bruno as a heretic, Milosz compared Bruno's martyrdom amid an indifferent public to the martyrdom of the Polish Jews during the suppression of the Warsaw ghetto uprising:

> I was reminded of the Campo de' Fiori
> in Warsaw, near a merry-go-round,
> on a serene spring night
> by the sound of lively music.

The salvoes from the ghetto walls
were drowned in the lively tune
and couples soared
high in the serene sky.[7]

Those Jews who managed to flee into the Polish forests to join with underground forces fighting the Germans not only had to elude the implacable Germans forever hunting them, but also were compelled to do battle with the vicious anti-Semitism of the Polish partisans. Shortly after General Tadeusz Komorowski (Bor-Komorowski) took over as commander in chief of the Polish Home Army in the summer of 1943, he issued an order to his commanders to kill—his word was "liquidate"—the leaders of Soviet bands and other "robber gangs" which he claimed were marauding the countryside. The order explicitly referred to Jews: "Men and women—in particular Jewish women—participate in these attacks."[8] No doubt this order gave a cloak of legality to the murder of Jews by the Polish Home Army. Besides, right-wing military groups in Poland that had refused to recognize the Home Army's authority and were organized separately in the Narodowe Sily Zbrojne—NSZ (National Armed Forces)—accumulated an impressive record of murdering Jews who had escaped into the woods.[9] No one will ever know precisely how many hundreds of Jews were murdered by Polish partisans in the Polish forests and marshes.

When the war ended, about 70,000 Jewish survivors emerged from their hiding places in Poland. By the end of 1945 some 170,000 Polish Jews were repatriated from the Soviet Union. Of the 3.3 million Polish Jews, only some 240,000 were left in Poland, but they did not remain there long. Though the new Polish leaders promised that "in resurrected democratic Poland" there would be "no place for anti-Semitism," it was the Jews who found no place.

Jews who returned to claim their homes and property were greeted with terror, violence, even murder. After all, the experience of the German occupation had demonstrated to the Poles that Jews could be murdered with impunity. The Poles did not want the Jews back, even if they then amounted to less than one tenth of their prewar numbers. For the Poland emerging from the borders established by the Yalta Conference would be uniformly Polish and Catholic. The Russians had been given the Eastern lands of prewar Poland, with their concentrated Belorussian and Ukrainian populations who belonged to the Orthodox Church, while the millions of Germans living in Poland's newly acquired lands west to the Oder-Neisse line were sent back to Germany. At last within reach of their age-long ambition to have an integral national state, the Poles wanted to be rid also of the Jews.

From March 1945 to April 1946 more than 800 Jews were murdered in Poland, the ugliest pogrom occurring in Kielce on July 4, 1946, when nearly 50 Jews were killed by a mob backed up by Polish militiamen. Though the Polish regime tried and executed the murderers, the terror against Jews continued through all Poland. Finding no haven there, the Jews began a westward trek, through Czechoslovakia, into displaced-persons' camps in West Germany. By the end of 1946 some 150,000 Jews had departed from Poland, leaving behind no more than 90,000. A few thousand more left the next year, but early in 1948 the Polish authorities refused to issue passports without evidence of a written promise of a visa to a new country of settlement, thus virtually halting the exodus.[10]

## Poland: The Restive Soviet Satellite

Little by little the Communists in postwar Poland concentrated political power in their hands. By 1948 all opposition parties were erased from political life and all institutions were forced to conform to Communist doctrine and directives. The Communist party, which during the German occupation had operated under the name Polish Workers' party (Polska Partia Robotnicza—PPR), having swallowed the Polish Socialist party, now called itself the Polish United Workers' party (Polska Zjednoczona Partia Robotnicza—PZPR). By then politics in Poland had narrowed to a conflict between the nationalist Polish Communists, headed by Władysław Gomułka, who had been secretary-general of the PPR, and the so-called "Muscovites," who had spent the war years in the Soviet Union being trained to take over Poland's rule.

Poland's fate was settled after Yugoslavia opted for an independent Communist course and was expelled from the Cominform. Thenceforth Stalin no longer tolerated Gomułka's "Polish path to socialism," and the Moscow faction took over. (Though Gomułka confessed his sins and recanted, he was imprisoned.) In 1949 Stalin appointed Soviet Marshal Konstantin Rokossovsky as Polish Minister of Defense and commander in chief of Poland's armed forces, reducing Poland to the status of a mere Russian military outpost. Stalinism in Poland held powerful sway even beyond Stalin's death in March 1953.[11]

In this period also the Jewish parties and institutions were liquidated, only a bare handful of so-called communal and cultural groups remaining to operate under the party's vigilance. On September 1, 1949, the Ministry of Public Administration announced that Jews who wished to settle in Israel could register for emigration. A deadline of one year was set, later extended to the end of 1950. Nearly 30,000 Jews then quit Poland, leaving behind about 45,000. In 1951 emigration was once again halted.[12]

Khrushchev's speech in February 1956 released major tremors in Poland. A workers' strike in Poznań in June 1956 erupted into demonstrations and then, astonishingly, into an armed uprising. After two days of fighting that left 50 dead and hundreds wounded, the government brought in the army and the police to suppress the uprising, though it also tried to respond to the workers' demands. Gomułka, now released from prison, emerged as the spokesman for the liberal "revisionist" wing of the PZPR, the symbol of Poland's independent path to socialism. In October 1956, in the midst of a meeting of the party's Central Committee, the dramatic confrontation between the Muscovite and the revisionist factions reached a fearful climax. For three days Russian troops stood ready to attack Poland's mobilized armed forces. But the Russians yielded and at that Central Committee session Gomułka was elected the party's first secretary. The Stalinist contingent, including Marshal Rokossovsky, was ousted. Poland, it appeared, could now follow its own destiny, even if it still remained within the Communist sphere. The vigilance of the party and the police relaxed and Poland breathed with the promise of greater freedom that October.

But the changed climate in Poland did not improve the Jew-

ish situation. Since some Jewish Communists had been identified with the party's Stalinist wing and, still worse, with its
police apparatus, they became targets of public disapproval.
Because such disapproval could not be expressed in anti-Com-
munist terms, it was released in commonplace anti-Semitism.
Further, acting on Moscow's order, while publicly eschewing
anti-Semitism, Gomułka's new regime launched a purge of
Jews first from positions of top party leadership and then from
sensitive posts in the government and the army.[13]

In the summer of 1956 Poland had begun to ease its restrictions on Jewish emigration and by the end of 1957 about 30,000
Jews had left Poland. Meanwhile, under the terms of an agreement with the Soviet Union permitting Polish nationals to re-
turn home, an estimated 18,000 Polish Jews were repatriated,
some 6,000 of whom then emigrated to Israel. In 1958, new
regulations requiring some dollar payments in Poland slowed
down the exodus, but by 1960 only about 30,000 Jews remained in Poland.[14]

## The Tangled Web of Polish Historiography, 1944-1956

Writing Polish history has always been a sensitive undertaking,
for Polish history has been a tale of repeated failures and ad-
versity. Polish historians have sometimes explained Poland's
troubles in terms of the flaws and weaknesses of its own people
and their leaders and sometimes as a consequence of the rapac-
ity of its neighbors—the Germans and the Russians.[15] Either
way of writing Polish history has proved to be an exercise in
self-pity, self-flagellation, and self-justification. Polish historiographical problems become even more knotty with the tangle
of Polish-Jewish relations and more often than not these have
been solved by evasion and misdirection. Polish historians who
take notice of the Jews are likely to blame them for the anti-
Semitism directed against them or even to invent a tale of har-
mony between Poles and Jews.[16] And if these were not problems enough to discourage the Polish historians, they have
since 1948 been under the restraints of Communist censorship,
subject to the zigs and zags of the party line, the tugs and pulls
of party politics.

Like most peoples who had suffered under German occupation, the Poles set themselves the task of writing the history of
their experiences as soon as the war had ended. From the start,
history was to serve the ends of justice, and in the pursuit of
justice, the Poles began systematically to gather the documentary evidence needed to prosecute German war criminals. In
March 1945 the Polish Provisional Government established the
Central Commission to Investigate German Crimes in Poland
as an agency within the Ministry of Justice. The staff set to
work amassing a vast archival collection of documents, testimonies, memoirs, and photographs. In 1946 the commission
published the first volume of *German Crimes in Poland* (the
second appeared in 1947), containing substantial documentation on the murder of the Polish Jews as well as on the atrocities that the Germans committed against the Poles. In 1946 the
commission also began to publish a periodical bulletin of documentary materials. The commission's primary task was conceived to be the assembling and preparing of evidential data for
the trial of the major German war criminals before the International Military Tribunal at Nuremberg and for the numerous subsequent trials before the Supreme National Tribunal in
Poland.[17] The most notorious of the nearly 2,000 war criminals
whom Poland extradited from the Western occupation zones of
Germany and put on trial was Rudolf Hoess, commandant at
Auschwitz.[18]

Soon the Poles put many other governmental resources in
the service of documenting the Polish experience under German occupation. The surviving Polish Jews, in contrast, had no
such resources. Yet even in the misery of their ghetto existence
under SS rule, they had begun to compile the record of their
sufferings.[19] As early as the summer of 1944, a handful of Jewish historians, who had emerged from hiding or had returned
from the Soviet Union where some had been slave laborers,
founded a Jewish historical commission in Lublin. The most
eminent among them was Philip Friedman, whose reputation
as a historian—like that of his friend Emanuel Ringelblum—
had been established before the war. That commission sparked
the formation of others elsewhere in Poland. Their common
urgent purpose was to gather documents, testimonies, photographs, and all sorts of evidence about the life and death of the

Polish Jews under the German occupation to be used in the prosecution of war criminals and eventually as the basic sources for a history of Polish Jews during the war.

By the end of 1944, the several groups united as the Central Jewish Historical Commission, which found institutional support in the newly created Central Committee of Polish Jews, a representative coalition of all Jewish parties. In 1947, having already accumulated an archives, a library, and artifacts for a museum, the commission moved to Warsaw, changing its name to Żydowski Instytut Historyczny w Polsce—ŻIHwP (Jewish Historical Institute in Poland). The following year the Institute began publishing *Bleter far geshikhte*, a Yiddish journal of documentation and history. In its first few years, the Institute provided documentary evidence for the prosecution of nearly 2,000 war criminals. But as Stalinism intensified its grip on Poland and with the renewed possibility of emigration late in 1949, most of the Institute's founding scholars and staff members then chose to leave.[20]

At the Seventh Congress of Polish Historians in September 1948 it had become clear that the historians, like the rest of the population, would have to submit to the ideological imperatives of the PZPR and conform to the dictates of the Soviet Union. It was not enough that Polish historians were forced to interpret their past through the prism of historical materialism and to follow the party line; now they came under direct and official Soviet supervision, compelled to accept the instruction of Soviet historians in the writing of Polish history.[21] The existing Academy of Learning was replaced by a Soviet-style Polska Akademia Nauk (Polish Academy of Sciences) in 1950 and three years later an Institute of History was established under the Academy's aegis. One of its subdivisions was a Center for the History of Poland during the Second World War, later headed by Professor Czesław Madajczyk.

By and large Polish historiography withered away in those years of Stalinist scrutiny. Even the Central Commission to Investigate German Crimes in Poland ceased to publish its bulletin between 1951 to 1956. It was a time when many historians chose discretionary silence over political valor.

After the liquidation of the Central Committee of Polish Jews and the emigration of most staff members of the Jewish

Historical Institute, the Polish regime put the Institute under the supervision of the Ministry of Higher Education and Science and in September 1949 appointed Bernard Mark to be the new director. (Later the Institute was put under the control of the Polish Academy.) A Yiddish journalist from Warsaw, a lifelong Communist who had spent the war years in the Soviet Union, Mark had published a pamphlet in 1944 in Moscow in which he stretched historical truth to inflate the role of the Jewish Communists in the Warsaw ghetto uprising. Thenceforth, under his direction, the Jewish Historical Institute adhered to the party line, extolling Stalin, the Soviet Union, and the Polish Communist party.[22]

A consistently Stalinist view of the Jews in wartime Poland emerged in the Institute's publications. (A new Polish periodical, *Biuletyn Żydowskiego Instytutu Historycznego*, was launched in 1951, occasionally publishing the same material that had already appeared in the Yiddish journal.) The articles followed a crude scenario in which the Communists—Jews and Poles alike—were the heroes. The rest of the Jews—middle-class, Zionist, socialist—constituted the villains or, at best, the inert and passive victims of villainous leaders and misleaders. The members of the *Judenräte*, the Jewish councils which the Nazis imposed on the ghettos, drafted mainly from the middle-class Zionist parties, were depicted as willing collaborators of the Nazis. Armed resistance, as a historical theme, was given pride of place, an approach that reflected the prescribed approach in Soviet and Polish historiography. References to wartime Polish anti-Semitism were almost entirely eliminated, except to illustrate the reactionary character of right-wing Polish organizations that no longer existed. The Polish Government-in-Exile and its institutions inside Poland—Armia Krajowa (Home Army) and Delegatura Krajowa (Delegate for the Homeland), the top governing body of underground institutions in Poland, in liaison with the Polish Government-in-Exile—were rarely mentioned and if so, disparagingly.

In 1952 the Institute published a volume of Emanuel Ringelblum's notes kept in the Warsaw ghetto, found after the war.[23] It was demonstrably a politically bowdlerized version, for scholars who had been engaged in deciphering and annotating Ringelblum's manuscript had, when they left Poland in

1949, succeeded in taking with them copies of the original manuscript. Comparative analyses showed the tendentiousness of the Institute's version.[24] Ringelblum's references to incidents of anti-Semitism among Poles were deemphasized or eliminated. Individual acts of kindness to Jews by Poles were inflated to appear as acts performed by the Polish population as a whole. Many of Ringelblum's accounts of the social, cultural, and political activities of the Zionists and Bundists in the ghetto were altogether excised.

Communist bias permeated Mark's own books on resistance in the ghettos of Warsaw and Bialystok. Mark had expanded his 1944 pamphlet into a Yiddish history of the ghetto uprising which appeared in 1947. In 1953 he published a collection of documents in Yiddish on the uprising. In 1955 an enlarged and revised edition of the 1947 work appeared. His history of the Bialystok ghetto uprising was published in Yiddish in 1950 and in Polish in 1952.[25] These works brought to light much important documentation from the Institute's archives, but their value was vitiated by the author's political distortions. Mark presented the Communists in the PPR as those who had conceived, planned, and carried out the ghetto uprisings, while claiming that the Zionists and Bundists played only a secondary role, when the facts were just the reverse. Furthermore, he depicted the ghetto uprisings as part of the universal struggle for the liberation of Poland. His revisions of the various books' successive editions were politically determined, an attempt to keep up with the increasing Stalinization in Poland in those years.

In portraying the Soviet Union as the savior of the ghetto Jews, a claim that had no support in fact, Mark falsified, among others, a specific incident and his false version has since become a staple of Stalinist and Stalinoid versions of Warsaw ghetto history. On May 13, 1943, Soviet planes bombed Warsaw and dropped leaflets over the city. Mark described this bombing as a Soviet response to Polish Communist pleas for help to the ghetto. But the bombing and the leaflets had no relation whatsoever to the Jews in the ghetto or anywhere else. Nor was there any reliable evidence that the Polish Communists had ever requested Soviet aid on behalf of the Jews. As a matter of fact, by May 13, the uprising was nearly all extinguished and the Warsaw ghetto Jews were dead, dying, or deported to Treblinka.[26]

## The Holocaust in the Light of the Polish October

The Polish October of 1956 loosened the vise in which the party had held the country's intellectual life. The sluices of Polish historiography opened up, especially with regard to the history of the wartime occupation.[27] After the aridity of the Stalinist years came a torrent of productivity, with energies directed toward the renewed accumulation of source materials: documents, memoirs, eyewitness accounts, bibliographies, and readers' guides. Historical commissions proliferated in many government agencies and museums were created at Auschwitz (Oświęcim) and Majdanek.

Jewish subject matter remained the province of the Jewish Historical Institute, but some documents of major importance were published under Polish auspices, for instance, SS General Jürgen Stroop's report on the final destruction of the Warsaw ghetto and the first part of the chronicle of the Lodz ghetto.[28]

In 1958 the Institute for Western Affairs, a research institution devoted to the study of the newly acquired Polish territories, published an exemplary work of historical documentation as part of its ongoing series *Documenta Occupationis Teutonicae*. Edited by Karol Marian Pospieszalski, law professor at the Adam Mickiewicz University in Poznań and head of the Institute's research section on the German occupation, the two-volume work was a systematic documentary collection of German law in occupied Poland, enriched by Pospieszalski's "attempt at synthesis," in which he steered a nearly neutral course amid the political shoals of Communist historiography.[29]

Pospieszalski devoted close to one hundred pages to documents about the Jews and their destruction. His editorial tone was measured; the Jewish sources he cited were the least politicized available, with Mark notably absent. In a summary of the book's conclusions, Pospieszalski explicitly stated that "the priority task" the Germans had set themselves "was not the extermination of the Poles, but the complete extermination of the

Jews."[30] Had the Nazis remained in power, Pospieszalski surmised, they might also have undertaken to annihilate the Poles, but in historical actuality they had limited themselves to murdering the Polish elite. This historiographic assessment represented the fundamentally unbroken view in Poland since the war's end that the Jews were the only people destined to be entirely destroyed. It was a view that would not long prevail.

In a short history of Poland under the German occupation published in 1961, Janusz Gumkowski, director of the Central Commission to Investigate German Crimes, and a colleague gave fair coverage to the events up to and including the destruction of the Jews, even though their main focus was, understandably, on the history of the Poles. Yet the authors acknowledged that the Germans did not intend to murder the Poles, but had planned to deport about 80 to 85 percent of them to Western Siberia.[31]

One of Poland's most reputable historians, Franciszek Ryszka, reader in Modern History in the Polish Academy's Institute of History, wrote an elegant popular history of the Third Reich and its policies, in which he handled with finesse certain political embarrassments like the Soviet Union's complicity in Poland's partition.[32] His survey of Germany's anti-Jewish policies is fair, though without depth or thoroughness, and his closing remarks about the "exceptionally tragic afflictions of the Polish nation and of the Polish citizens of Jewish nationality"—a Communist neologism for the prewar epithet "Polish citizens of Mosaic faith"—suggest his distance, if not actual disinterest, with regard to the fate of the Jews in the Third Reich.[33]

In a study of the enslavement and murder of children under Nazi rule, Kiryl Sosnowski, a sociologist associated with the Institute for Western Affairs, gave particular attention to the Jewish children in Poland. He estimated that the Germans had murdered 1.2 million Jewish children under sixteen, and that barely 5,000 Jewish children survived. In view of the fact that some 2 million children in Poland were murdered (besides 200,000 Polish children kidnapped to the Third Reich to be "Aryanized") and that the Jewish children, once 10 percent of all living children in Poland, accounted for 60 percent of the murdered ones, Sosnowski concluded that all over Europe

"Jewish children suffered the most. They were doomed to die, no matter what the nationality of their parents."[34]

Resistance early became a theme of major political importance in Polish historiography. To be sure, in all European countries that endured the German occupation the subject and morality of resistance became a living political issue as well as the centerpiece of national history. The extent and effectiveness of resistance were usually overdrawn, not to falsify the record but to reinforce national pride and self-esteem. In the Soviet Union and its satellites, however, the treatment of resistance served political ends. The calculation was simple. If the Communist countries were, as their propaganda claimed, the vanguard of antifascist and anti-imperialist forces, then Communists must perforce have been the vanguard of anti-Nazi resistance.

In Poland the historiography of wartime resistance was a pursuit of state and party institutions. These included the Center for the History of Poland during the Second World War, within the Academy's Institute of History; the Institute for Party History, under the PZPR's Central Committee; and the Institute of Military History, with its section "History of the Armed Struggle under the Occupation" and its journal *Wojskowy Przegląd Historyczny*.[35]

Because it was politically sensitive, resistance as a theme of Polish history scarcely benefited from the relaxation of the Polish October. The party line remained virtually unchanged from the Stalinist years: the PPR and its military arm, the Gwardia Ludowa—GL (People's Guard)—were the only ones to resist the Germans, and they succeeded thanks to the help of the Soviet Union, the Red Army, and the Soviet partisan movement. The most ambitious work on resistance published in Poland was a collective history prepared under the auspices of the Institute of Military History, and it offered for the record a gargantuan inflation of the activities of the PPR, the GL, and its subsequent incarnation as the Armia Ludowa—AL (People's Army).[36] Though the Home Army had more than ten times the men of the GL-AL and though it carried out a greater number of resistance activities, its accomplishments in this book were minimized, relegated to mere footnotes, or altogether erased.

Relatively little space was accorded to the subject of Jewish resistance, but those events, including the formation of the Jewish Combat Organization and the Warsaw ghetto uprising, were described as Communist undertakings. The only non-Communist listed among the leaders of the Jewish resistance was Mordecai Anielewicz, commandant of the Jewish Combat Organization, but no one would know from text or context that he had been a Zionist or that the real leaders of the Jewish resistance had been Zionists and Bundists. Though excessive claims were made for combat assistance rendered to the Jews by the PPR and the GL, only two such incidents were recounted, whereas episodes of Home Army aid were merely compressed in two footnotes.[37] The facts are that Poles, both those in the Home Army and those in the People's Guard, carried out some dozen or so missions during the Warsaw ghetto uprising, including diversionary attacks on Germans and rescue operations of Jewish combatants. Communist sources were not at all likely to mention that several GL unit leaders were Jews passing as "Aryans" and that their participation in these forays could scarcely be characterized as help rendered by the Poles to the Jews.[38]

The Polish October of 1956 had a revivifying effect also on the Jewish Historical Institute. The freer atmosphere encouraged greater productivity. Staff members published several volumes of German documents on the murder of the Jews.[39] One staff member completed a historical account of Nazi policy leading to the annihilation of the Jews. It was a solid work of scholarship, if one makes allowances for the obligatory comments about the persistence of Nazism in West Germany and disregards the equally obligatory view that the Judenräte were "instruments of extermination of the Jews by Nazi hands."[40]

Institute researchers also ventured into areas which they had hitherto prudently avoided. A study of wartime Polish anti-Semitism, for instance, appeared in the Institute's Yiddish journal, its focus on an extreme right-wing organization whose wartime records had survived.[41] The author, of course, clearly distinguished between the good Poles who helped Jews and the bad ones who did not. The scenario was simple: the good Poles were the leftists. Yet despite its tendentiousness, this study, especially its extensive citation of the sources, was a valuable addition to Polish Jewish history.

Another study dealt with gentile-Jewish relations during the war primarily in Poland, but the implicit comparisons with the behavior of gentiles in Denmark, France, and Italy did not reflect great honor on the Poles. Nor did the authors shun the ugly aspects of Polish-Jewish wartime relations, so well documented in every survivor account and in the records of underground organizations—the extensive blackmailing of Jews in hiding by many Poles and the widespread Polish sport of bounty hunting, turning over to the German police those Jews in hiding who had run out of money to pay blackmail.[42] In no other country in Europe did such police informing and unsolicited cooperation with the SS assume the massive proportions they took on in Poland.

The Institute even tried to repair the damage it had committed earlier. Ringelblum's writings were republished in a new edition—the ghetto notes, now purportedly complete, and a second volume of his other writings, including a long monograph on Polish-Jewish relations during the occupation.[43] The editors acknowledged that the 1952 edition had been incomplete and deliberately selective, but even this edition did not meet Western standards. The Ringelblum monograph was bowdlerized and editorial liberties were taken with the original, all in the interests of minimizing Ringelblum's evidence of Polish wartime anti-Semitism.[44]

Mark too revised his history of the Warsaw ghetto uprising. A new Polish version appeared in 1959, and in 1963 a Yiddish volume appeared that combined a drastically revised version of the earlier history with a less politicized version of the documentary collection, the blatant Stalinism of the original now muted.[45] Mark still hewed to the party line, exaggerating the role of the Communists in the ghetto uprising, but his reference to the Soviet bombing of May 13, 1943, was now ambiguous.[46]

In sum, if we discount the political claims and distortions, knowing how to read texts written under political pressure, we can conclude that the Jewish Historical Institute accumulated an impressive record in the historiography of the war, notably in publishing documents retrieved from the ashes of the Holocaust.

## The Gathering Clouds

The promise of Gomułka's October 1956 that Poland could somehow pursue an independent path, permitting intellectual and political freedom, was soon aborted. New political realignments began to take shape after the ouster of the Muscovites. In the early 1960s a renewed struggle for power emerged within the party, with Gomułka now poised between two factions. On one side were the revisionists, his former comrades, demanding of him more liberty than he was prepared to grant. On the other side were the Polish nationalists, also his former comrades, headed by Mieczysław Moczar, a prewar Communist who had commanded a Communist partisan detachment in the Lublin/Kielce region during the occupation. In 1948 Moczar had been Deputy Minister of State Security, but was purged for his "rightist and nationalist deviation."[47] Gomułka in 1956 appointed him Deputy Minister of the Interior in charge of the secret police.

Noted for his ruthlessness as well as his anti-Semitism, Moczar soon became a powerful factor in Polish Communist politics. His faction, known as the "Partisans," appealed to the younger and more nationalistic Poles inside and outside the party. Moczar succeeded in building a mass base from among the war veterans and soon became the head of their 800,000-member organization Związek Bojowników o Wolność i Demokracje—ZBoWiD (Union of Fighters for Freedom and Democracy). Moczar found an invaluable ally in the unscrupulous Bolesław Piasecki, active in the prewar Obóz Narodowo-Radykalny—ONR, a fascist party closely patterned after the Nazis, especially in its racial anti-Semitism. During the war Piasecki first tried to collaborate with the Germans, then he tried to operate his own guerrilla movement. Arrested by the Soviet secret police in 1944, Piasecki saved his skin by proposing a scheme to split the Catholic Church in Poland and thus eventually bring about its disintegration. With

NKVD approval, Piasecki then formed the pseudo-Catholic organization PAX, becoming the Soviet Union's most reliable non-Communist in Poland.[48]

By the early 1960s the endemic Polish anti-Semitism whose public expression the liberal atmosphere of 1956 had somewhat inhibited began to surface again. One of contemporary Poland's most seminal thinkers, Adam Schaff—a philosopher of Marxism whose reputation had spread far beyond Eastern Europe and a member of the PZPR's Central Committee—confronted the persistence of anti-Semitism in Poland in an influential book published in 1965:

> Given our countries and their history, it is straining credulity to imagine that anti-Semitism disappeared overnight: it is not discreditable that it exists; what is discreditable is that it is not being combatted. This makes it all the more misguided to resort to the humbug of pretending, by invoking general principles, that the phenomenon does not exist since it is, by definition, impossible under socialism. The fallacy here is that this by no means follows logically from the definition of socialism (communism is another matter), and anyway there is no hiding the fact that the disease occurs, since it sometimes assumes all too widely visible forms. Thus, this kind of denial neither does us credit nor increases trust in us, and moreover, it certainly weakens our struggle for a just cause.[49]

Schaff's strictures found little resonance in Poland, for by that time the revisionists in the party were losing ground. The arena of the power struggle had shifted rightwards and the political conflict was now between Gomułka and the Partisans, while Poland's workers grew more restive because of high prices and economic hardship.

Israel's stunning victory in the Six Day War of June 1967, having inflamed the Soviet Union and its satellites by the defeat inflicted on their Arab clients, provided Gomułka with a good political opportunity to launch a vicious attack against the Polish Jews and thus to deflect antigovernment resentments. It was also a signal to party and public that he shared their anti-Jewish prejudices. Addressing the Sixth Congress of the Polish Trade Unions on June 19, 1967, Gomułka accused the Polish Jews of being a fifth column, "in favor of the aggressor, in favor of the wreckers of peace and imperialism."[50] Anti-Semitism reigned once more in Poland, now barely disguised as "anti-

Zionism" and legitimated by the highest government authority.

The Jews had already been forced to capitulate to Moczar's ZBoWiD in matters concerning the annual commemoration of the Warsaw ghetto rising. ZBoWiD had appropriated as its domain all activities concerning the wartime occupation and since 1963 had begun to dictate to the Jewish institutions how to commemorate the Warsaw ghetto uprising, deciding who the speakers should be and what they should say.[51]

The Jewish Historical Institute too felt the strong arm of the government, as it increasingly was isolated from Jewish cultural institutions abroad, was denied their publications, and was altogether put under strict censorship. The Institute was ordered to halt the microfilming of its holdings for Jewish research institutions in Israel and the United States and the staff was instructed to complete cataloguing the Institute's collections with all due speed. The State Controller's Office and other government agencies constantly monitored the Institute's activities and scrutinized its records, its mail, and its publications. Mark's illness in this period and his death in July 1966 heightened the Institute's precarious situation. After the Six Day War a sweeping campaign of abuse was directed against the Institute in both the general and academic press, presumably orchestrated by ZBoWiD. No newspaper or periodical afforded the Institute the right of reply in its own defense.[52]

### 1968: The Savagery of Anti-Semitism

Early in 1968 Adam Mickiewicz's classic drama *Dziady* opened in Warsaw. A play about tsarist oppression of Lithuanian Poland, its references to "the rascals sent to Poland from Moscow" brought demonstrative applause from the audiences. On January 30, 1968, the authorities banned all further performances. Protests by university students, writers, and intellectuals were followed by arrests and repression. On March 8, Warsaw students who had organized a demonstration "against censorship, arbitrary arrests, and suppression of freedom" were attacked by armed police and Communist party militia, beaten, and arrested. That brutality sparked rebelliousness all over Poland, though for two days neither the press nor the media mentioned the unrest. Then, on March 10, Piasecki's paper blamed the disturbances in Poland on the Jews, unloosing an anti-Semitic barrage which charged that "the Zionists in Poland intend to set intellectuals and youth at variance with the main requirements of patriotic responsibility for People's Poland." Overnight, it appeared, Moczar's people had succeeded in intimidating the top institutions of state and party and convincing them to blame the Jews for the turmoil in the country. A massive anti-Semitic witch-hunt was launched under the guise of "anti-Zionism."[53]

On March 19, 1968, Gomułka explained to party activists why "the slogan of struggle against Zionism" emerged. To defend himself—and Poland—against the accusation of anti-Semitism, he invented a new sociology, classifying Jews in three categories: those who regard Israel as their motherland, to whom he was ready to give exit papers; those who are "cosmopolitans," identifying themselves neither as Jews nor Poles, who should consequently "avoid fields of work in which national affirmation is essential"; and, finally, those for whom Poland is their only motherland.[54]

All over Poland a savage anti-Semitism was spewed from the press and the media. Jews were dismissed from businesses and public institutions. Purged from the party, they lost their jobs. Liberals and revisionists too were purged. Every ministry, every bureaucracy, every educational and cultural institution dismissed the Jews and liberals on its staff.

In June Andrzej Werblan, a member of the Central Committee's Science and Education Department, published a lengthy theoretical article, "On the Genesis of the Conflict," purportedly a historical analysis to explain the "Jewish problem" in Poland and in the Polish Communist party. Its thesis was that Jews were essentially alien elements in Poland and in the Communist movement.[55]

Werblan's article, followed by a flood of anonymous pamphlets demanding "a fight against revisionism and Zionism to the very end," was intended to help swing the balance of power from Gomułka to the Moczarites at the forthcoming party congress. But Gomułka's position was strengthened by an unexpected turn of events in Czechoslovakia.

A new government in Czechoslovakia under Alexander Dubček had been moving toward greater freedom and liberalization in economic affairs as in intellectual matters. But August 1968 was not like October 1956 in Poland. The Soviet Union sent its troops into Czechoslovakia, reinforced by units of the Warsaw Pact allies, including Poland's. Dubček's government was deposed; the liberal Communists were arrested. To justify its military intervention, the Soviet Union opportunistically labeled as "Zionism" and "revisionism" what had been the fundamental issues of democratization and freedom in Czechoslovakia.

Since Gomułka, in his pursuit of Poland's independent path to socialism, had managed to avoid that military confrontation which had now crushed the Czechs, his present accommodationist policy toward the Soviet Union seemed the better part of valor. The Soviet exploitation of anti-Semitism, on the other hand, reinforced the Moczarites. In July 1968 the Central Committee elected Moczar as an alternate member of the Politburo, though at the Fifth Party Congress in November, when Gomułka was reelected secretary general of the party, Moczar was denied a full seat. Gomułka remained in power until the end of 1970, when workers' riots in Gdańsk forced him out. Moczar then became a full member, but a year later was ousted and thereafter ZBoWiD declined as a political power.

But in the years from June 1967 through the end of 1970, the Jewish community of Poland was inexorably set on a course toward extinction. Emigration had resumed and by the end of 1969, barely 15,000 Jews remained in Poland; a year later, only 9,000 were left and each year thereafter the numbers shrank. The few Jewish institutions, like the Jewish Historical Institute, came under the direct administration of the Polish authorities.

## 1968: The Mockery of Historical Truth

The anti-Semitism of 1968 had an immediate and scandalous impact on Polish historiography with regard to the Jews, especially for the war years. Just a few weeks after the anti-Semitic

campaign had been launched, ZBoWiD took over the cere-
monies to mark the twenty-fifth anniversary of the Warsaw
ghetto uprising. The dedication of a Jewish pavilion at Auschwitz had been scheduled for April 20, a Saturday, the last day
of Passover. The authorities refused to reschedule the cere-
mony, which the Jews consequently boycotted, but the occasion served as a platform to condemn Israel's "aggression" in
the Middle East. Kazimierz Rusinek, Secretary-General of
ZBoWiD and Deputy Minister of Culture, attacked Jewish organizations outside Poland for having failed to come to the aid
of the Jews in the Warsaw ghetto.[56]

Moczar's Partisans and ZBoWiD moved in on some research
institutions in the purges of March and April 1968 on the
ground that previously these institutions had distorted the history of Polish-Jewish relations. For the Poles had been stung
by worldwide denunciation of Poland's anti-Semitic course.
Counterattacking, they responded that the Jews throughout
the world were lying about Poland and its treatment of the
Jews, now as in the past. Even Premier Józef Cyrankiewicz, in
a speech in the Sejm on April 10, 1968, delivered a savage attack against the "wave of anti-Polish slanders" which, he
charged, emanated from "Israel and the chauvinist Zionist circles in other countries, from the United States and from the
German Federal Republic."[57]

The major Polish encyclopedia, *Wielka Encyklopedia Pow-
szechna*, a target of the Partisans, was accused of having distorted the facts and statistics about victims of the Nazis, of
having exaggerated the number of Jewish victims and under-
stated the number of Polish victims. Its top editors were dismissed. Even more ominous for wartime historiography was
the purge within the Central Commission to Investigate Hitlerite Crimes in Poland, whose longtime director Janusz Gumkowski was ousted and replaced by one of his staff, Czesław
Pilichowski. Pilichowski, who had studied law, had belonged
to the same fascist ONR that had nurtured Piasecki. After the
war Pilichowski opportunistically joined the PPR, but was
soon expelled because of his ONR past. Nevertheless, after
1956, in the prevailing nationalist climate in Poland, he found a
place in the government bureaucracy, and after the Six Day
War he was readmitted to the Communist party.[58]

On April 22, 1968, at the height of the anti-Semitic agitation, the Central Commission to Investigate Hitlerite Crimes in Poland convened a plenary session to confirm the right-wing political and personnel takeover. Pilichowski laid down the new line, incorporated in resolutions unanimously adopted. The chief policy decision recommended that all institutional archives throughout Poland pertaining to German crimes during the occupation should be centralized within the Central Commission and that all research on the subject should be similarly centralized, a transparent attempt to preempt the subject matter and its source materials. Furthermore, the policy statement recommended that the Central Commission should stimulate research and publication "to rebut the slanderous campaign of lies published in the West, . . . especially with reference to accusations about the alleged participation of Poles in the annihilation of the Jewish population." The *Polish Encyclopedia* was singled out as an example of "highly irresponsible publications." The policy statement urged more extensive contacts with scholarly institutions abroad "in the light of the deficiencies and falsifications in a number of publications about the occupation and the Hitlerite crimes in Poland."[59]

As if this were not enough, a resolution was passed specifically addressed to the historiography of the Jews during the occupation, charging that "Zionist and neo-Nazi" propagandists were slandering the Poles with baseless accusations. Here is the full text of the resolution:

> In session during the twenty-fifth anniversary of the uprising of the Warsaw ghetto, we, the assembled members of the Plenary Session of the Central Commission to Investigate Hitlerite Crimes in Poland, representative of all strata of Polish society, scientific circles, researchers, participants in the resistance movement—express homage for the heroes of the armed action of resistance against the Hitlerite occupant, and recall the crime of genocide committed on Polish soil by the criminals and the common fate of those doomed to extermination, Poles and Polish citizens of Jewish origin.
>
> In the name of a mad racist theory, the Hitlerite Reich doomed the Polish nation and the Jewish population in Europe to extermination. The martyrdom and the struggle of the Polish Jews constitute a part of the history and the tragedy of the Polish state, and the losses of the Jewish population in Poland are an integral part of the general losses of Poland.

In accordance with the economic calculations of Hitlerite genocide, concentration camps and annihilation centers were built where the largest numbers of future victims were located. At present international Zionist centers, in partnership with the neo-Nazi groupings in the Federal Republic of Germany, have sounded false accusations, according to which Poland was chosen by the Hitlerites as an annihilation site for the Jews because the Polish nation is allegedly an anti-Semitic nation. This propagandist provocation and the unparalleled campaign of falsehood minister to the work of the neo-Hitlerite and neo-nationalist elements in the Federal Republic of Germany, who want to free of responsibility and punishment the Hitlerite criminals, those guilty, as far as the Polish nation is concerned, of genocide on Polish soil and to conceal the extent of the crimes committed by the Hitlerite Third Reich in Poland and in other European countries.

Zionist and neo-Nazi circles interested in strengthening the anti-Polish campaign count on the ignorance of Western societies about the extent of terror and of the criminal activities of the Hitlerite occupation on Polish soil. Poland was the only country in which the Hitlerites punished with death any help extended to Jews, in addition applying to the Poles the principle of collective responsibility and murdering entire Polish families, including their children, for hiding and helping the Jewish population. Despite this, the Poles rendered assistance to those doomed to annihilation, the Polish citizens of Jewish origin and Jews of other European countries. This was assistance rendered both spontaneously by the Polish population and by organized aid through the Council to Aid Jews (RPŻ). Thanks to this assistance, which cost the lives of many thousand Poles, over 100,000 Jews survived on Polish soil.

In the time of the war and the Hitlerite occupation the Polish nation fulfilled its human responsibility with honor. The truth about the posture of the Polish nation is documented in the lives of those thousands of Jews who survived the time of the crematoria thanks to the sacrifices of the Poles.

Expressing outrage and protest at the lies of the Zionist and neo-Nazi anti-Polish campaigns, the Plenary Session of the Central Commission to Investigate Hitlerite Crimes in Poland turns to the populations of all countries and especially to those who themselves had the opportunity to benefit from the aid which Poles rendered to them, with an appeal to counteract those falsehoods which serve only to deflect attention from the prosecution and just punishment of the Hitlerite criminals guilty of genocide and of those criminals who even now in the aggressive war against Vietnam and in the Arab lands illegally seized by Israel commit crimes against humanity and war crimes.[60]

A torrent of material then poured from the Polish presses, presumably orchestrated by ZBoWiD, Pilichowski, and their cohorts. Journalists, historians, and pseudohistorians were conscripted in this campaign. They rewrote history and in doing so vilified the murdered Jewish victims of the Third Reich and the surviving Jews as well, with Israel and the "Zionists" serving as the ostensible targets. In May and June three scurrilous pamphlets by Tadeusz Walichnowski were released which accused the Jews of slandering Poland while collaborating with the Nazis and neo-Nazis.[61] A political journalist with a Ph.D. from the Copernicus University at Toruń, Walichnowski is today director of Poland's State Archives, the post no doubt a reward for political services. Some years earlier Walichnowski had headed a department in the Ministry of Interior, specializing in racial genealogies, which determined who was Jewish and consequently ineligible for government employment. His political muscle and facile pen have won him academic status as well.[62]

To mark the twenty-fifth anniversary of the Warsaw ghetto uprising, Wacław Poterański prepared an entirely new version of the pamphlet he had written five years earlier, this one sponsored by ZBoWiD's so-called Central Historical Commission, probably created to give a scholarly facade to crude political propaganda. An exceptional exercise in historical falsification, this pamphlet was also published in English and other European languages for distribution abroad.[63] The Jews in prewar Poland were described as separatist, bourgeois, and reactionary. Except for the Communists among them, the Jews during the German occupation were depicted as passive and collaborationist. Poterański altogether denied the existence of anti-Semitism in prewar Poland: "the vast majority of the Polish people had nothing to do with anti-Semitism and viewed the Jews in Poland as their fellow-citizens." Polish aid to the Jews and Polish self-sacrifice on their behalf were contrasted with Jewish passivity. Furthermore, the persecutions that the Poles suffered under the Germans, in Poterański's view, "eclipsed" the persecutions of the Jews.[64] Poterański is today director of the Central Archives in Poland's Ministry of Internal Affairs.

Still more extreme in its claims about the help that the Poles rendered to the Jews under the German occupation was a pamphlet by Tadeusz Bednarczyk.[65] Issued in an edition of 40,000 copies, the pamphlet illustrated the remarkable convergence of the Polish right and left in dealing with Polish-Jewish relations. Presumably distilling a lengthy unpublished manuscript of his wartime reminiscences,[66] Bednarczyk wrote of his experience as a member of a rightist underground military organization, Organizacja Wojskowa—Korpus Bezpieczeństwa (Military Organization—Security Corps), which had in fact given considerable help to the Zionist-Revisionist military resistance organization Żydowski Związek Wojskowy (Jewish Military Union). Bednarczyk claimed that he served as liaison between the KB and the ŻZW, presumably because his work as tax collector for the authorities frequently brought him into the ghetto, where he supervised workshops producing goods for the Germans.[67]

If one could give credence to Bednarczyk's claims, all the wartime Polish organizations devoted themselves heart and soul to helping the Jews, and the Polish military underground provided them lavishly with arms, fought side by side with them, and then brought them to safety. Without offering any evidence, Bednarczyk claimed that about 3 million Poles were involved in efforts to aid Jews, that for these efforts some 50,000 Poles were killed by the Germans or sent to labor camps. In 1943–44, according to Bednarczyk, Poles gave refuge to about 30,000 Jews in Warsaw and 300,000 throughout Poland. Bednarczyk's anti-Jewish prejudices expressed themselves in the accusation that Jewish organizations in the West refused to send money to aid their fellow Jews and thereby facilitated the German murder of the Jews. Furthermore, in repudiating the evidence of Polish prewar and wartime anti-Semitism, Bednarczyk turned his defense of the Poles into an assault on the Jews. He accused the Jews in the Warsaw ghetto of having had more traitors and collaborators among them than the Poles had ever had.[68]

A similar confluence between left and right showed itself in the warm reception the Polish authorities gave to the writings of Władysław Bartoszewski, who—in contrast to Bednarczyk and the others cited—actually rendered great help to the Jews during the war. Now a professor at the Catholic University in

Lublin, Bartoszewski had been deputy chief of the Jewish Section of the Delegatura's internal affairs department from 1942 to 1944 and one of the founders of the Rada Pomocy Żydom—RPŻ (Council to Aid Jews). Using his own records of Polish wartime assistance to Jews as a base, Bartoszewski began in 1963 to gather more data through polls and questionnaires. With an associate, he compiled a massive collection of anecdotal material describing how Poles helped to hide Jews during the war and otherwise rendered assistance to them.[69] The book happened to come out just at the start of the Polish regime's anti-Semitic campaign in 1967 and even though it was a truthful book, documenting actual incidents of aid to Jews by the Polish Home Army, the Delegatura, and Catholic Church groups, without magnifying the role of the Communists or vilifying the Jews, the Polish authorities welcomed the book as a vindication of their own partisan views. In 1969, when the writing of anti-Semitic revisionist history of Polish-Jewish relations had become a minor industry, a second and enlarged edition of Bartoszewski's book was issued. That same year, the emigré Poles in London published it in an English translation and the Home Army Circle in Great Britain awarded it a prize.[70]

In 1970 Bartoszewski, in a new book, attempted a more systematic account of Polish wartime help to the Jews, going beyond the mere compilation of anecdotal material, but his rudimentary and frail interpretive framework still depended on the same documentary sources.[71] Understandably, Bartoszewski's books, despite their clearly apologetic character, have been warmly received by Poles both in Poland and in their forced exile abroad because these books serve to redeem Polish honor. But they do not answer fundamental historiographical questions, for Bartoszewski's anecdotal materials are only one side of the story. These data must be reconciled with the massive and impressive documentation of prewar and wartime anti-Semitism among the Polish population and in the Home Army. Indeed, it can be shown that many of the Poles whom the Germans murdered because they were protecting Jews had been betrayed by their bounty-hunting fellow Poles.

The ultimate staggering claim of Polish aid to the Jews was made in what seemed to be a sober sociopolitical study by Eugeniusz Duraczyński, a historian of the younger generation who was obviously trained in Marxist historiography. Since anti-Nazi resistance was, according to Duraczyński, logically the province of the Communist-led proletariat, the Jews, having been primarily artisans, tradesmen, and professionals in prewar Poland, could not have played a significant role in the resistance movement. Consequently, Duraczyński argued, the Warsaw ghetto uprising was accomplished mainly by Poles: "The Jewish population, first imprisoned in ghettos and later exterminated in a body, neither participated in principle in the Polish resistance nor organized a resistance movement of its own (the uprising in the Warsaw ghetto in the spring of 1943 was the exploit of barely a few hundred Jewish combatants armed and supported by the Polish resistance)."[72]

This academic falsification of history reflected the contemporary political scene. At the twenty-seventh anniversary commemoration of the Warsaw ghetto uprising, the battle of the Warsaw ghetto was described as "primarily a Polish battle," and a ZBoWiD orator hyperbolized that "thousands of Poles spilled their blood and sacrificed their lives in defense of the Jewish population."[73]

## History Done, Redone, and Undone

In 1970, the first major work of historical synthesis on the Nazi occupation of Poland was published.[74] It was the consummate product of Polish national communism, written by Czesław Madajczyk, who was awarded a doctorate in 1954 by Poland's most conformist Communist institution of higher learning—Instytucja Nauk Społecznych KC PZPR, the Institute of Social Science of the Central Committee of the PZPR. This was one of several institutions of higher learning that the Communist party established in Poland to train its students in the methods of Communist scholarship. Madajczyk's doctoral dissertation was on "bourgeois landowners' agrarian reform in the years 1918–1939." Shortly after its completion, he began to concentrate on the German occupation of Poland, publishing several monographic studies. He has since preempted this field and occupies a leading position in the Institute of History of the Polish Academy of Sciences.

Completed at the height of the 1968 anti-Semitic campaign, Madajczyk's history reflects the political imperatives of the times. This was as true in small matters—the obligatory compliments to Gomułka and a particularly sycophantic one to Moczar (which would, no doubt, have to be removed in any future edition)—as in large ones, including the treatment of the fate of the Jews in German-occupied Poland.

Madajczyk's fundamental thesis was that the Germans intended "the biological destruction of the Polish population," a thesis consciously calculated to downgrade the murder of the Polish Jews, while inflating the Polish losses. This *Tendenz* showed itself in Madajczyk's enumeration of six methods by which, he argued, the Germans undertook to destroy the Poles. The listing submerged to the point of near disappearance the destruction of the Jews. Here is Madajczyk's listing, unchanged:

1. Annihilation of the Polish leadership;
2. Annihilation of persons regarded as enemies of the Reich;
3. Murdering categories of undesirables: antisocials, Jews, Poles of Jewish origin, Gypsies, the incurably sick and mentally ill (the so-called "euthanasia" program), one fifth of the Polish deportees from the Zamość region (Himmler's abortive attempt to deport the Poles and resettle the area with Germans);
4. Reprisals against persons engaged in resistance;
5. Limiting food rations to a level sufficient only to maintain the capacity to work;
6. Plans to reduce procreation among the Polish population by separating the sexes and postponing marriages.[75]

But Madajczyk's thesis was not quite correct. To be sure, the Germans intended to destroy the Polish state and to reduce its population to a state of peonage. The Poles were to be consigned to a reservation. Polish nationhood, the Polish language, and Polish culture were to be extirpated, a fate intended also for the Russians and other Slavic peoples. But the Poles were not destined, in the Nazi scheme of things, to biological destruction. Instead they were to suffer restrictions on their biological growth, an unhappy fate, yet to be distinguished from destruction.

Of course the German occupation of Poland was relentlessly harsh. Tens of thousands of Poles were murdered, their political rights destroyed, their culture suppressed. Subjected to hunger (though never to the starvation inflicted upon the Jews) and to forced labor (though never obligatory as upon the Jews), the Poles suffered egregiously. Still, German plans for Poland's ultimate enslavement were never fully implemented. Even the attempt to resettle Zamość in November 1942 was abandoned because of the exigencies of war (the turnabout on the Eastern front which led to the German defeat at Stalingrad) and the priorities of murdering the Jews (the need for German manpower and rolling stock).[76]

Madajczyk's thesis had originated in the anti-Semitic campaign of 1968 but had never before been given sanctuary in Polish historiography. Now he had rewritten history in accordance with the party line, magnifying Polish losses so as to discredit the claim of the Jews as the primary victims of Nazi Germany. At the same time, Madajczyk managed to appeal to the Polish nationalist romantic tradition. For his thesis of Poland's martyrdom evoked an image of nineteenth-century Polish messianism in its subliminal depiction of Poland once again as the Christ of the nations, bearing the cross of sufferings for all the European nations that endured the German occupation during the Second World War. Thus Madajczyk succeeded in joining doctrinaire Communism with Polish nationalism.

In addition to many passages scattered throughout both volumes of his work, Madajczyk devoted two chapters entirely to the Jews: "Outline of the Situation of the Jewish Population" and "The Final Solution." These provided a barely adequate account of the Jewish experience in Poland under German occupation—ghettoization, pauperization, hunger, disease, forced labor, terror, violence, and, finally, total annihilation. Madajczyk's somewhat Olympian style kept his account dry, though the occasional citations from documents and survivor accounts infused some drama into the writing. Negative comments about Jews and Jewish behavior appeared with some frequency. These Madajczyk supported by citations from Jewish sources, most frequently from documents and studies published in the *Biuletyn* of the Jewish Historical Institute during the Stalinist period.

Madajczyk's portrait of prewar Polish Jewry highlighted certain invidious characteristics among some subgroups in the Jewish community with astringent correctness, yet the whole portrait was an ugly caricature. His analysis of Jewish socio-economic structure served to condemn the Jewish community for its "bourgeois character," while the religiosity of the Orthodox subcommunity was adduced as evidence of Jewish passivity, that is, reliance on God rather than on themselves.[77] Madajczyk leveled the charge of passivity against the Jews several times. In one passage he accused Chaim Rumkowski, head of the Judenrat in Lodz, and the Jews in the Lodz ghetto of having chosen (as if it were a matter of choice) an "unworthy death," presumably as contrasted with the "worthy death" that armed resistance to the Germans would have given them.[78] That accusation comes with little grace from a Pole whose people offered no armed resistance to the Germans until August 1944, and only because they then fully expected the Red Army to come to their aid and prevent their slaughter by superior German forces.

It is instructive to track down the sources for one incident Madajczyk recounted to illustrate Jewish passivity. He described a meeting, which General Stefan Rowecki purportedly convened, of commanders of the Home Army, shortly after the Germans began to deport some 300,000 Jews from the Warsaw ghetto to Treblinka. Rowecki proposed to offer military aid to the Jews and to inform them that the Home Army would be prepared to coordinate military action with theirs. According to this account, liaison was established between the ghetto leaders and the Home Army, but the Jews rejected the proposal to fight. Madajczyk gave as the source for this incident Raul Hilberg, *The Destruction of the European Jews,* a work by an American political scientist, who is Jewish.[79]

But Hilberg's account was an almost verbatim extract from a wartime memoir by Rowecki's successor, General Tadeusz Bor-Komorowski, *The Secret Army,*[80] and was in fact a totally invented episode (though Hilberg failed to recognize it as such), fabricated after the war to deflect Jewish accusations against the Home Army for having given so little aid to the embattled ghetto Jews. The military liaison to which Bor-Komorowski referred had not yet come into existence; it was set up in late November 1942. Besides, there is a body of documentation to prove that General Rowecki was the least likely person to volunteer military aid to the Jews.[81] Madajczyk should have been familiar with this material and should, in any case, have tried to verify the story. But politics transcended scholarship, for it served him to use the false story, relying on a Jewish source to defame the Jews, instead of on the unacceptable Home Army source. Similarly, when Madajczyk accused the ghetto Jews of collaboration with the Germans in bringing about the destruction of their own people, Madajczyk cited as his authorities Hannah Arendt's controversial *Eichmann in Jerusalem* and Hilberg again.[82]

Almost every argument that had surfaced in 1968 against the Jews found its way into Madajczyk's work. Thus, while admitting that some Poles had indeed betrayed Jews in hiding, Madajczyk went on the offensive, echoing Bednarczyk, and argued that the plague of informers and scoundrels was more widespread among the ghetto Jews than among the Poles.[83] As for the statistics of Jewish losses, Madajczyk followed the position laid down by Pilichowski and the now official Polish line: the statistics of Jewish losses were subsumed under the statistics of Polish losses.

### The End of a Millennial History

In June 1968, whole sections of the archival collections of the Jewish Historical Institute were removed and transferred to various regional archives. Archives pertaining to the Lodz ghetto, for instance, were deposited in state archives in Lodz. The intention may have been to remove the Jewish records from the Institute's custody and thereby prevent the staff from making copies of documents to send to Jewish depositories abroad. It may also have been intended to restrict access to materials that would not support claims about unstinting Polish wartime aid to the Jews.[84]

The Institute now faced a new accusation. Its staff members were charged with having doctored documents found at Auschwitz because they had been "actuated by the feeling of a

wrongly conceived national solidarity."[85] The politically motivated charge concerned the transcription and translation from
Yiddish of a diary found in 1962 which had been written by a
member of the Sonderkommando at Auschwitz. The State
Museum had requested the Jewish Historical Institute to decipher and translate this badly charred, crumbling manuscript of
unnumbered pages. Two Institute staff members somehow
succeeded in deciphering and translating the pages they had
been given—not the entire text, it later turned out—which
they then published in the *Biuletyn*, actually just at the height
of the anti-Semitic campaign of 1968.[86]

The diary described the Sonderkommando's plans for an uprising in Auschwitz. Its author criticized the Polish and Russian camp prisoners for not supporting the Jews in this ven-
ture. The Institute staff members, sensitive to the prevailing
political climate, suggested in their commentary that the diarist
may have been mistaken in his judgment, but that was what
was in the document. The authorities of the State Museum,
however, were dissatisfied. They accused the translators of
"undue Jewish nationalism" for intimating that the Polish and
Russian prisoners at Auschwitz had been motivated by anti-
Jewish feelings. In the Museum's subsequently published text
of this diary, Jews share the blame with the Poles and Russians
for not having carried out the resistance action.

The strict surveillance under which the regime kept the Jewish Historical Institute and the atmosphere of public censure
that engulfed it hastened the departure of many staff members
from the Institute and from Poland altogether. The Institute's
activity soon ground to a halt. Books ceased to be published,
*Bleter far geshikhte* closed down in 1970. The *Biuletyn* continued to appear, its sparse contents supplemented by compila-
tions of anecdotal accounts of Polish wartime aid to the Jews.
These were for the most part raw materials, affidavits, eyewitness reports, memoirs, presented without analysis or historical
context.[87]

In December 1971, a former secretary of the Polish Communist party circulated a letter among members of the Party Congress which accused Gomułka of having used "anti-Zionism"
as a cover-up for anti-Semitism.[88] But that document had little

resonance inside the party or out. To all intents and purposes, the Jewish community and its institutions had been liquidated, the Polish Communists having themselves put the finishing touches to the Final Solution of the Jewish Question which the Germans had so efficiently accomplished for them.

Although history has no meaning, we can
give it a meaning.

KARL POPPER

# THE PERSPECTIVE OF CATASTROPHE:

# THE HOLOCAUST IN

# JEWISH HISTORY

In December 1941, when the German police entered the Riga
ghetto to round up the old and sick Jews, Simon Dubnow, the
venerable Jewish historian, was said to have called out as he
was being taken away: "Brothers, write down everything you
see and hear. Keep a record of it all." Everywhere in Europe,
despite the terror of German rule, Jews did in fact keep records
of their ordeals. In some ghettos of Poland, record keeping became a Jewish communal enterprise designed to document
every aspect of the hitherto unimagined and unimaginable experiences to which the Jews were exposed under the Nazis.[1]
The chroniclers and archival custodians even made plans to
safeguard these records and ensure their survival when it appeared that the record keepers themselves would not survive.
Thanks to their foresight and self-sacrifice, many posthumous
records have come down to us.

The quintessential people of history, the Jews originated the
idea of the God of history and they produced a written record
of the past at least four centuries before Herodotus, whom the
Western Christian world called "the father of history." The
earliest Jewish records, the Five Books of Moses, resound with
the word z'chor, elaborating the concept of memory and remembrance, the stuff out of which history is constituted. The

Bible exhorted the Jews to "remember what Amalek did unto thee." In times of recurrent persecution throughout the course of Jewish history, that injunction has retained its authority. In modern times, Jews came to believe also in the moral force of their history, in the compelling power which the history of Jewish sufferings and martyrdom could exercise on non-Jews and thereby purge them of their Jew-hatred.[2]

Under the Nazis the Jews everywhere felt the urgency of history, the imperative to remember Amalek. They also had another energizing motive which persuaded them to risk their lives by keeping written records of their terrible and terrifying experiences: they hoped for justice after the war's end and for revenge. They were determined to preserve a record of evidence that would convict the Third Reich not only before the bar of history, but also before a judicial tribunal which would punish the guilty for their inhuman crimes. The historical record was thus to serve as the bill of indictment, the testimony and evidence, even the argument.

## The Survivor as Chronicler

The drive to create a body of admissible evidence against the Third Reich intensified that sense of moral obligation among the survivors to chronicle the history of their sufferings. In Poland, the first Jewish historical committee for this end was established in Lublin in 1944.[3] In France, the Centre de Documentation Juive Contemporaine, which had operated clandestinely in Grenoble since 1943, continued its activities in Paris after the liberation. In 1945, surviving Jews in the displaced-persons' camps in Germany, Austria, and Italy formed historical committees to collect testimonies, eyewitness accounts, memoirs, and other kinds of historical documentation.[4] They were loosely coordinated by the Central Historical Commission in Munich, which had been established by the Central Committee of Liberated Jews in 1945. This commission published a journal for several years and provided evidence and witnesses for the German war-crimes trials at Nuremberg.[5] When the displaced-persons' camps were later disbanded and their inmates had emigrated, the accumulated records were transferred to Israel and were eventually acquired by Yad Vashem.

Elsewhere in Europe—in Italy, Bulgaria, Yugoslavia, and Rumania, for instance—local Jewish communities set up commissions to document the murder of the Jews in their cities and countries and to publish historical accounts based on those documentary materials.

Yad Vashem—the Martyrs' and Heroes' Remembrance Authority—was established in Jerusalem by an act of the Israel Knesset in 1953.* Funded from moneys paid by the Federal Republic of Germany as collective indemnity to the Jews, Yad Vashem received a mandate from the Knesset consisting of two related but not always compatible functions. It was authorized to document the destruction of the Jews and also their resistance, and it was charged additionally with the responsibility of commemorating the martyrs and heroes of that destruction.[6] To fulfill this dual mandate, Yad Vashem established a library and an archive, launched an extensive program to publish the documentation that it had undertaken to accumulate, and fostered a variety of activities in Israel and in Jewish communities elsewhere in the world to mark the annual observance of the Holocaust and commemorate it in other ways.

In its early years, Yad Vashem was staffed exclusively by survivors who had themselves experienced the German occupation, some of them having previously been with the Jewish Historical Institute in Poland. Few had been trained as historians, but all had been imbued with a persistent tradition of folk participation in East European Jewish historiography that went back to the nineteenth century.[7]

Critical study of East European Jewish history began late, in the last decade of the previous century, when Simon Dubnow decided to devote his life to the history of the Jews in Russia and Poland. Dubnow's first step was to collect basic raw data, those primary source materials which are the building blocks

---

* Its name is taken from Isaiah 56:5:

> Even unto them will I give in My House
> And within My walls a monument and a memorial [*yad vashem*]
> Better than sons and daughters;
> I will give them an everlasting memorial
> That shall not be cut off.

of history, and then to construct from them a vast chronology of events in Russian Jewish history, all preparatory to the task of writing critical history. To compensate for the lack of national or municipal Jewish archives, Dubnow started a movement for what may be described as "folk" archives. He sparked an extraordinary popular movement among thousands of Jews in the Tsarist empire—university students as well as plain folk—who, following his guidance and instruction in *Voskhod*, a Russian Jewish periodical, accumulated for him great numbers of documentary sources. Dubnow's historiographical efforts, which coincided with the rise of secular national and socialist movements among East European Jews, succeeded in making plain people aware of the national uses of history and of coopting them to the great national enterprise of producing modern Jewish history.

The Dubnovian tradition was transmitted to the YIVO Institute for Jewish Research in interwar Poland and to other East European Jewish institutions. It proved especially serviceable for a community whose access to universities was limited by a system of *numerus clausus*, and whose religious tradition anyway discouraged university training. At the same time, under Western influences, a handful of Polish Jews turned to Jewish history as an academic discipline, applying to it the professional skills and methodologies in which they had been trained at their universities. Jewish historiography was becoming professionalized as several notable historians appeared in Poland to stand alongside Dubnow—Meir Bałaban and Ignacy Schipper, to name the two outstanding figures—as well as many promising ones.[8] But the Second World War and the subsequent murder of the European Jews cut off further development of Jewish historiography and cut down the historians.

Disabled by an arrested historiographical tradition and by a critical deficiency of professional historians, Yad Vashem for much of its existence has devoted itself largely to collecting raw data, mostly gathered by and from the plain people. That emphasis in its early years was justified by the pressing need—so long as survivors could still recall their experiences with the sense of freshly remembered pain and a passion for accurate detail—to fill out, augment, and enrich the substantive sources for the history of the Holocaust. Yad Vashem's publications too have been primarily documentary in character. That continued and continuing concentration on accumulating source materials is both a strength and a weakness. The weakness calls to mind Lord Acton's advice in 1895 to his students at Cambridge: "The main thing to learn," he told them, "is not the art of accumulating material, but the sublimer art of investigating it, of discerning truth from falsehood and certainty from doubt."[9]

Yad Vashem's historiographical predicament can be largely explained by the fact that its work has been in the hands of survivors who are chroniclers rather than historians. Many survivors who have preempted the field of Holocaust historiography believe that their experiences qualify them better than persons who have only book-learned skills. In this, they share the outlook of the ancient Greek historians who held that history could be written only by those who experienced it. The Greeks were the first advocates of contemporary history, rejecting the possibility that history could be written about the past. They were also the first to develop the use of oral evidence, that is, the testimony of people who experienced the happenings of contemporary history.

Thus survivor-chroniclers can claim that they are following a venerable historiographic tradition. Holocaust survivors have, to be sure, lived through experiences beyond the conception of most men and women, and those extraordinary experiences have deepened their understanding and broadened the range of their vision. Still, survivor-chroniclers can seldom transmit more than their individual circumscribed experiences, however harrowing, however extraordinary; they can seldom transcend their own suffering and bereavement.[10] For few survivors had an overview of events beyond their immediate experience. Few held responsible positions in official or underground institutions in ghettos or camps, and consequently only a few were party to making the critical decisions that affected the fate of their fellow-Jews. Survivor-chroniclers, caught up in the whirlwind of history, were so buffeted by its winds that they could not chart the storm's course, measure its velocity, assess the damage it wrought.

Long after Thucydides, who had no use for documents, historians have studied documents as the major source and resource in writing history. They have developed a variety of skills to evaluate these documents for accuracy and veracity. They have learned to test the documents for subjectivity and bias. In our time history is seldom written on the basis of oral evidence alone or on the uncorroborated testimony of eyewitnesses. Holocaust survivors who aspire to write history rather than a chronicle must have, despite the authority of their own experience, recourse to documents, and they must subject those documents, even their own accounts, to the rigors of critical historical method.

Furthermore, writing history requires a different perspective from writing a chronicle and demands a distance that only the remove of time or space can provide. For most Jews, historians as well as chroniclers, survivors of the Holocaust as well as those who lived through it in safety or were born after it, the Holocaust remains their central experience—a trauma, a nightmare, an obsession. As Salo W. Baron observed in 1960, a mere fifteen years after the war's end: "a generation that has gone through that extraordinary traumatic experience cannot completely divorce itself from its own painful recollections and look upon the Holocaust from an Archimedean standpoint outside its own turbulent arena."[11] In our time, distance in writing the history of the Holocaust can be achieved only by an act of will, by the imposition of discipline over self.

### Martyrdom and Resistance

The mass of oral testimonies and written chronicles of the survivors' experiences constituted a contemporary equivalent of those medieval martyrologies describing the persecutions visited upon the Jews during the Crusades. But the depiction of the Jews as suffering martyrs under the Nazis was soon challenged by a segment of survivors: those who had participated in the resistance movements in the ghettos and had fought with the partisans. For the most part, they had been associated with left-wing political parties and youth movements, Zionist and non-Zionist, before the outbreak of the war.

Long before the Second World War and even before the First World War, the young Jews who streamed into the secular radical movements that transformed traditional Jewish society in Eastern Europe had committed themselves to changing the status of Jews as a powerless pariah people. They opted either for a revolutionary transformation of their oppressive political condition or for Jewish statehood which would make Jews like other nations. Such socialist and socialist-Zionist ideas and ideologies continued to permeate the youth of East European Jewry between the two wars, imbuing them with both radical and national fervor and directing their energies toward realizing an ideal Jewish existence in the future, though often they lavished contempt on the Jews of the past and present.

Such young people, still in their teens when they were imprisoned in the ghettos of Poland and Lithuania, fantasized about armed resistance against the Germans. They gave a new meaning to the Biblical phrase for martyrdom "like sheep to the slaughter," turning it into a derogatory epithet for the ghetto Jews whom they accused of going unresistingly to death.[12] After the war, the survivors of the resistance movements, especially those who settled in Israel, were among the first to contest the martyrological approach to Holocaust history. For one thing, they needed to justify their parties and their ideologies, especially in Israel, where a generation of sabras disparaged the European Jews even more than the survivor-resisters had once done themselves.[13] But beyond self-interest, they wished also to transform the image of Jews as only suffering victims, as only passive objects of German destructiveness. They wanted to rectify the historical account, balancing the record of suffering with a record of active heroism. Thenceforth, the story of Jewish resistance as told by its participant survivors, became exalted and magnified. It was portrayed as individually ennobling and socially purifying; it became a vindication of Zionist ideology and leftist politics.[14]

That rhetorical debate among the survivors about resistance and passivity was soon taken up by two Jewish historians who, in time, were to produce some of the fundamental historical studies of the Holocaust. One was Philip Friedman (1901–1960), who had managed to survive the German occupation in hiding in his native Lwów. The other was Isaiah Trunk, who had spent the war years as a slave laborer in the

Soviet Union. Both men had completed their professional training in Poland before the war and had established their credentials as academic historians. Right after the war's end, Friedman had been a founder of the Jewish Historical Institute in Poland; Trunk was for a short time a staff member there. Both eventually settled in the United States, having decided, or the course of their lives having decided for them, to devote themselves to writing about the murder of the European Jews during the Second World War.

Friedman's and Trunk's earliest essays on resistance were published in Yiddish political journals.[15] Each, in his own way, addressed himself to objective problems—the prevailing wartime conditions; the extensiveness and terror of the German occupation; the support systems available to resistance movements by the Western powers and by the Soviet Union, as contrasted with the resources available to the Jewish underground; the varieties of resistance among Jews and non-Jews and options other than armed action. Both historians considered the subject with the requisite coolness, though hardly with disinterest. Still, those essays had little resonance, perhaps because of the obscurity of the journals in which they appeared, but more likely because the subject matter was still too traumatic for historical consideration. Furthermore, in the early 1950s, the Jewish scholarly community professionally interested in these matters was far too small for fruitful discussion.

In the next decade, the controversy about Jewish resistance and passivity erupted beyond the familiar circles of the Yiddish and Hebrew press. The chief polemicists now were not participants of the underground movements, but American scholars whose proficiency was not in Jewish studies and whose training was not in history. They lacked altogether that necessary empathy with which a historian reconstructs a period of the past, an empathy even more necessary to understand that terrible period of the Holocaust. In their works, these writers charged the murdered European Jews with passivity under German terror and attributed the failure of the Jews to prevail over the Germans not to lack of Jewish resources, but to ingrained Jewish psychology and to age-old Jewish cultural traditions.[16]

The subsequent bitter polemics were no longer confined to Yiddish and Hebrew periodicals, but spilled over into the general press, where the frequent repetition of the charges that the Jews by their passivity were culpable of their own deaths eventually hardened into the semblance of received truth and became a confident commonplace among those who knew nothing else of the history of the Holocaust. The charges against the Jews were as perverse as those leveled 150 years earlier against the Russian soldiers slaughtered in Napoleon's invasion of 1812. To these accusations Tolstoy had responded in *War and Peace* and his views are apposite also for the debate on Jewish resistance: "The Russian soldiers did all that could or ought to have been done to attain an end worthy of the people, and half of them died doing it. They are not to blame because other Russians, sitting in warm rooms at home, proposed that they should do the impossible."

In the early sixties, when Friedman's and Trunk's essays had been all but forgotten, new essays and books appeared which undertook to refute the ugly charges of Jewish passivity. They did so not by engaging in angry polemics, but by offering historical evidence and critical analysis.[17]

In 1968, to mark the twenty-fifth anniversary of the Warsaw ghetto uprising, Yad Vashem convened a conference on Jewish resistance.[18] Nearly all the participants who read papers were survivors, most of them Israelis. Many were associated with Israel's political parties and were veterans of leftist Zionist movements. It was their political and ideological outlook that animated the conference. While some of the papers met the test of professionalism, many did not.

To begin with, the meaning of resistance was strained beyond its usual meaning. The most widely accepted definition of resistance that was postulated at the conference was not of resistance as an auxiliary form of warfare, but rather as a process familiar in medicine or physics: resistance as the ability of an organism to withstand disease or as an opposing or retarding force to motion and energy. The logic was simple: since the Germans were determined to destroy all Jews, whatever Jews did to thwart that end and survive could justifiably be defined as resistance. Probably the most strained presentation was one which claimed that telling jokes against Hitler was a form of resistance: "If you do not possess the physical force to over-throw him, there is no more effective way to fight a dictator than to make a laughingstock of him."[19]

What emerged from the conference was a glorification of resistance as an ultimate value, rather than a historiographic assessment of the possibilities of resistance, of the costs of resistance, and of the effectiveness of resistance. The apologetics were so glaring not because the Jewish historical record in this regard was too scanty (it is no worse than that of other nations and peoples), but because the place of resistance—among Jews as well as among all occupied European people—was inflated beyond historical reality and sanctified. In part this was a function of Zionist ideology; in part, of a modern sensibility which values activism and misunderstands the heroism of martyrdom. Since that conference, resistance has been the subject of several popular and scholarly studies conceived and written from the point of view that holds resistance to be an ultimate value.[20]

The debate on resistance among Jewish historians suggests comparison with the debate on slavery among American historians.[21] Both subjects, no matter how professionally and objectively treated, touch charged feelings of group identity and self-esteem that affect the historian and his readers. In the historiography of slavery and of the Holocaust, the extent of resistance becomes a matter not only of historical truth but also of group pride. History becomes tinged with apologetics. In dealing with either subject the historian must work out a reconciliation between two counteractive forces that operated on the individuals as well as on their own inner conflicts. The slavery debate seeks to resolve the dilemma: how did the harsh brutalizing system of slavery affect the slaves' capacities to withstand its terrible impact and what did they derive from their culture and traditions to sustain their endurance against the system or to spark their energy to resist it? Obviously, the more brutalizing the system, the weaker the individual's ability to resist.

The dilemma in writing Holocaust history is comparable. To what extent was resistance possible, given the overpowering might of German military forces and the savage terror of the SS? To what extent could the Jews offer significant resistance, given the physical conditions of their incarceration and oppression and the political conditions of their powerlessness? The answer to the first question determines in great part the answer to the second question.

The slavery debate generated new methodology and further research, but the resistance debate has been less productive. The field of Jewish historians is smaller. The more fundamental reason, however, for the thinness is that the subject of Jewish resistance is still too close to trauma and too close to ideology.

## Judenrat: The Charge of Collaboration

Even more intractable emotionally and historiographically is the problem of the *Judenräte*, the Jewish councils that the Germans established to help them administer the ghettos of Eastern Europe. The very word *Judenrat* has come to offend the ear. It conjures up nightmarish images of evil Jewish leaders, collaborating with the Germans, betraying millions of Jews into the gas chambers, while they saved their own and their kin's lives. The diabolization of the Judenrat has paralleled the apotheosis of resistance in survivor historiography and its impact on Jewish consciousness has been devastating.

The historiographic problem of the Judenrat originates in its anomalous historical position in the ghettos. In its first stages, the Judenrat was usually composed of administrative officials who had before the war been associated with the local Jewish community organization, the *kehillah*. The normal tensions between an administrative bureaucracy, especially in countries without democratic traditions, and its constituency became even more exacerbated in the ghettos because of the conditions of privation which the Germans had imposed. Food distribution, housing allocations, health and sanitation, forced labor, tax collections—services upon which all ghetto existence was premised—were within the purview of the Judenrat. Given the Judenrat's pitifully shrunken resources, the lack of available options, and the conventional abuses that thrive everywhere in petty officialdom, it was to be expected that in most ghettos the officials of the Judenräte would be set on a collision course with the population.[22]

In many ghettos—there were notable exceptions—the Jews regarded the officials of the Judenräte with dislike, distrust, and sometimes contempt. That hostility was fanned even more by the excessive rhetoric of the leftist underground press. Still, no member of the Judenrat was ever chosen as a target for assassination in the ghettos, though the resistance groups carried out a considerable number of death sentences against members of the Jewish police who had behaved with exceptional brutality or against Jews who worked as informers for the Gestapo.

After the war's end, survivors in the displaced-persons' camps in Germany, Austria, and Italy, established courts of honor before which they tried a few Judenrat officials and many members of ghetto police forces or concentration-camp kapos (foremen of labor squads). Each defendant was tried and judged on his own acts, in accordance with standards set for the prosecution's presentation of sufficient evidence and for the defendant's rights, including appeal. In Israel, under the Nazis' and Nazi Collaborators' (Punishment) Law, enacted in 1950, some ghetto policemen and camp kapos—though no Judenrat members—were brought to trial. The paucity of cases against Judenrat officials suggests that only a small proportion survived and that there was no evidence, or insufficient evidence, on which to bring charges against them.

The one exception was the case of Rudolf Kastner, a Zionist official in Budapest, who had been accused in Israel, where he was living after the war, of collaboration with the Nazis. The proceedings, which originated as a libel case, riveted public opinion in Israel from 1954 to 1957, for it combined Zionist party politics with moral issues and judicial matters.[23] The lower court ruled that Kastner had collaborated with the Nazis and acted in bad faith with regard to the Hungarian Jews, but the Israeli Supreme Court, hearing the appeal, overturned that decision by a split vote.

The moral issues and the political partisanship that agitated survivors on the question of the Judenrat had produced, by the early 1960s, more than two hundred essays and articles in Yiddish, Hebrew, and Polish. Published in journals and in the

spate of commemorative volumes issued about destroyed Jewish communities, these accounts were highly subjective, fil-
tered through the memory of anger, colored by personal prejudice. At that time critical historical writing about the Judenrat
was rare, amounting to perhaps a handful of short studies—
portraits of three demagogues who headed Judenräte and one
path-breaking methodological study by Philip Friedman.[24]
This essay, a model of historical scholarship, spelled out every
aspect of the subject that needed to be investigated—the origins of the Judenrat members, their social and political back-
grounds, the composition of the Judenräte and the continuing
process of elimination and replacement of their officials and
staff, the administrative functions, jurisdiction of authority and
limits of power, class conflict, moral dilemmas, and the con-
stant dynamics of change as the situation of the Jews continued
to deteriorate and as the Germans abandoned their makeshift
policy of ghettoization to proceed to their final solution of outright mass murder.

None of this research had been done when Hannah Arendt
published her book on the Eichmann trial, in which she made
the monstrous and altogether unfounded charge that "wherever Jews lived, there were recognized Jewish leaders, and this
leadership, almost without exception, cooperated in one way or
another, for one reason or another, with the Nazis."[25] Relying
for the most part upon secondary sources, some of them lamen-
tably ill-informed about the Judenräte, Miss Arendt made unsupported accusations of Jewish collaboration with the Nazis
that far outdistanced any charges ever leveled by survivors,
even by the sloganizing left, which abused the Judenräte as the
symbolic representation of the Zionist bourgeoisie. Furthermore, her account was written in a tone that Gershom Scholem, eminent Jewish scholar and an old friend of hers, characterized in a letter to her as "heartless, frequently almost
sneering and malicious."[26]

*Eichmann in Jerusalem* was in no sense a work of objective
historical research, as one critic pointed out,[27] but rather a
moral tract, whose discussion of good and evil and individual
responsibility was directed not so much to understanding the
past as to sounding an alarm for the future. What was additionally perplexing was Miss Arendt's failure to give considera-

tion to a subject of relevant and fundamental concern, particularly to a political philosopher: the limits of freedom and the operation of necessity under conditions of extreme persecution. Such a discussion might have yielded more understanding of the moral predicament in which the officials of the Judenräte found themselves.

*Eichmann in Jerusalem* reversed the normal progression of historical scholarship. Instead of beginning with research and investigation and following with analysis and finally conclusions, Miss Arendt began with grand generalizations and sweeping moral judgments. At the time she was writing, no study of any single Judenrat had been completed, no biography of any individual associated with the Judenrat had been written. Only fragmentary bits and pieces, which had not even been cumulated for a modest historical synthesis, existed.

Not even a handful of essential documents had then been published or were in the process of being published. Only the minute-books of the Judenräte of Bialystok and Lublin and the diary of Adam Czerniaków, head of the Warsaw Judenrat, were available.[28] Issued in Hebrew, with the accompanying originals in Yiddish and Polish, languages unfamiliar to many modern historians, those documents were and still are not sufficiently used as basic source materials to study the operations of the Judenrat.[29] At about that time, too, Isaiah Trunk's Yiddish monograph on the Lodz ghetto appeared,[30] enriched by the inclusion of documents from the extensive archival collections on the Lodz ghetto which he used for his research. Rather than writing narrative history, Trunk used a sociological approach to portray the Lodz ghetto and all the institutions of the Judenrat as they operated under German orders and in relation to the ghetto population.

One beneficial effect of Arendt's *Eichmann in Jerusalem* was that it prompted Yad Vashem and the YIVO Institute for Jewish Research to sponsor further historical research on the Judenrat. The first serious work to appear, following the journalistic torrent in response to Arendt, was a book-length rebuttal by Jacob Robinson, a specialist in international law, then coordinator of Holocaust research projects of Yad Vashem and YIVO.[31] It focused narrowly on Arendt's mistakes in facts, misreadings of texts, and misinterpretations of events.

Nearly a decade passed before Trunk's magisterial study *Judenrat* appeared, a work which received the National Book Award. Declaring that he did not intend to pronounce judgment, but wished instead to "probe deep into the entire complex topic,"[32] Trunk gathered together in this book an overwhelming historical record about the Judenräte in Eastern Europe, which is descriptive and documentary rather than analytic. No truly critical history of the Judenrat can ever be written without reliance on this book.

Relatively little other research on the Judenrat was subsequently produced.[33] Nor was there any noticeable acceleration of scholarly publication in other areas of history dealing with the Holocaust. Several serviceable monographs on the fate of the Jews in individual countries and documentary collections have appeared,[34] but even now no definitive work about any one ghetto, any one community, or any one country has been produced.

The shock of the Holocaust probably accounts for the paucity of historical research about it. Some Jewish historians, under the impact of the Holocaust, have turned instead to the study of anti-Semitism in the distant as well as the recent past, in Germany and elsewhere in Europe.[35] Perhaps in another generation, when the suppurating wounds which the Holocaust inflicted on all Jews will have closed, it will be possible for Jews to confront Holocaust history.

## The Perspective of Jewish History

Trauma has had its own history as the Jewish response to disaster and destruction. Though the Jewish tradition exhorts Jews to "remember what Amalek did," there is also a countertradition. Jews had written their history and accounts of their origins back to the obscurest reaches of man's memory, yet the writing of Jewish history came to an abrupt halt with the destruction of the Second Temple in 70 C.E.

The Temple's destruction convulsed the course of Jewish history and ruptured the course of Jewish historiography. Except for Josephus, whom the Jews considered a traitor, no Jewish account was produced about the events leading up to and encompassing the destruction of the Second Temple and no coherent historiographic explanation was offered for those events. A generation later, Simon ben Gamaliel, who lived through the Hadrianic persecutions, said: "We too cherish the memory of our troubles, but what are we to do? For they are so numerous that if we came to write them down, we would not be able to do so." Furthermore: "The dead flesh in a living person does not feel the scalpel."[36] Thus the Talmud commented on the futility of historical explanation at a time of despair and trauma.

In the Middle Ages, the persecutions which the Jews suffered during the Crusades restored their historic consciousness and a new form of Jewish historiography emerged with the genre of the chronicle. These naive chronicles of the persecutions rendered with pathos the Jews' sufferings and their ultimate agony as martyrs for Judaism. The idealization of martyrdom particularly distinguished *Sefer Yosifon*, a tenth-century Hebrew account of the destruction of the Second Temple. As the most widely read book of Jewish history for many centuries, *Sefer Yosifon* nourished that collective Jewish historic consciousness which Salo Baron characterized with asperity as "the lachrymose conception of Jewish history."

Eventually the naive medieval chronicler gave way to the critical historian, but the persisting pattern of persecution and suffering in Jewish history determined the perspective of the historians. Heinrich Graetz, who dominated nineteenth-century Jewish historiography, and Dubnow, who bestrode the first half of the twentieth century, both placed suffering and martyrdom at the heart of the millennial Jewish historic experience. But alongside the history of suffering they conceived also of a history of Jewish creativity and of Jewish vitality that defied persecution and survived it.

Since the days of Graetz and Dubnow, Jewish historians have refrained from espousing wide-ranging constructs about the nature of Jewish history. Under the prevailing influence of positivism and the paramountcy of empiricism, historians have ceased to offer metaphysical or metahistorical speculations about the course of Jewish history and the destiny of the Jews. Even though the destruction of the European Jews during the

Second World War eclipsed all previous disasters in Jewish history and may have imperiled the future of the Jewish people, Jewish historians have avoided theorizing about the Holocaust in the perspective of Jewish history, leaving such reflections to the philosophers and the theologians. Occasionally an Israeli historian looks at the Holocaust through the Zionist prism, concluding that the Holocaust was a vindication in history of Zionist doctrine and a confirmation of the State of Israel as a historic necessity; but such doctrinal or dogmatic views are the exception.

It may well be premature to expect any appraisal, however speculative, of the place of the Holocaust in the millennial span of Jewish history. Jewish historians are still too preoccupied with the building blocks and the scaffolding of the historical structure to be able to see it in the landscape of historical time. They are still too close to the events. They are still mourning the loss of their past.

The first law for the historian is that he shall never dare utter an untruth. The second is that he suppress nothing that is true.

CICERO

# AFTERWORD

From the evidence offered in this book on one subject—the destruction of the European Jews during the Second World War—it appears that writing objective history is a consummation desired more often than attained. Even nowadays, when scholars pride themselves on the advanced skills of their craft, historians do not always turn out to be reliable guides to the recovery of the past. The obstacles to writing objective history reside within the historian himself and sometimes in the society in which he lives.

One of the fundamental elements that mold the historian's personal identity is the sense of belongingness to a people, a nation, a country. More than 2,000 years ago, Polybius conceded as a regrettable necessity "that historians must show some partiality to their own countries."[1] Nevertheless, he cautioned against writing untruths in behalf of one's country. While Polybius's methodological strictures are no longer the criteria used in modern historiography, this particular advice still retains its moral energy.

Every people has used its history to justify itself in its own eyes and in the eyes of the world and every people has enlisted its historians to that end. History has traditionally been a partisan or an accessory of national policy. When nationalism became a driving force in nineteenth-century politics among peoples striving for nationhood as well as among those who had already achieved it, history was called on to shape national consciousness and historians were called on to provide the shaping materials. Rousseau advocated patriotic education to rear the nation's children to love of country. Inculcation of knowledge of their country, of its traditions and history, would make them "honest citizens and good patriots." Michelet and Guizot, each in his own way, used history to extol France for its intellectual and political traditions and achievements. Treitschke and Ranke, for their part, put their craft at the service of the German *Machtstaat*. Nikolai Mikhailovich Karamazin, Russia's first national historian, glorified imperial Russia even over the grandeur that had been the Roman Empire.[2]

Among the Czechs, the Serbs, and the host of nationalities submerged in the Hapsburg, Ottoman, and Tsarist empires, the poets and the historians became the chief molders of national identity. They articulated their people's aspirations for liberty and independence. They used history as an adjunct of politics. Jewish historians too, like Graetz and Dubnow, imbued their histories with a powerful sense of the unity of the Jewish people through time and space. In a time of accelerating anti-Semitism, they used history as comfort and consolation, impressing upon their Jewish readers their belief in the continuing viability and creativity of Jewish religious, cultural, and communal traditions. Everywhere, in the words of John Morley, "the historian has been the hearth at which the soul of the country has been kept alive."[3]

Nowadays, in countries where historians are free to pursue any historical investigation that interests them, they are less likely to make their work a validation of national policy or a passionate statement of patriotism. The war in Vietnam definitively effected such a change in the United States; the Algerian war did so in France. In Germany the impact of the Third Reich on historians loosened the traditional ties between them and the state. Nevertheless, though professional historians are nowadays more detached than their predecessors, they are still bound by ties to their country and their people, perhaps especially when they take their country to task for its moral shortcomings in war and peace. For attachment to one's roots is an abiding element of the personality and the historian is not exempt from such attachment.

National identity is not the only factor that shapes the historian's personality. "It is astonishing," Herbert Butterfield noted in his critique of the liberal bias in British historiography, "to what extent the historian has been Protestant, progressive, and whig, and the very model of the 19th century gentleman."[4] Another English historian has advised readers to "study the historian before you begin to study the facts."[5] For besides the ties that bind him to his people and his nation, the historian retains ties of love and faithfulness to his religion, his language, his family, his class. His home, his upbringing, his education have inculcated in him beliefs and values that govern his thoughts and his acts. This complexity of subjective elements affects the kind of history he writes, the choices he makes in subject matter, the intensity of his involvement in the events of the past he is constructing, the sympathies or antipathies he holds for certain historic figures. These subjective elements may, to be sure, provide the very qualities that endow the historian's work with character, distinctiveness, and vitality. Yet they have the capacity also to implant bias and prejudice in the historian's conceptions, to warp his historical judgment, to cause him to distort the events of the past and to misrepresent the men and women who took part in them, or altogether to overlook them.

The responsible historian, conscious of his predilections, his indifferences, and his dislikes, conscientious about his self-imposed mission to construct the past as it was, strives to offset his subjectivity. To compensate for the inadequacy of his experience and the limits of his vision which create the pitfalls of subjectivity, he relies on the discipline of his craft, on the methodology of writing critical history. The historian's craft obliges him to rigorous readings of documents, fair selections of significant data, and honest deliberation. It compels him to divest himself of bias, though not of empathy. The responsible historian knows that, like unthinking devotion, commitment to dogma interferes with the pursuit of historical truth. By distinguishing between "apologetic" history and "conscientious" history—Lord Acton's distinctions—the historian can attain his goal of writing objective history.

History is a discipline dedicated to the recovery of the past from the black pit of oblivion. To fulfill this task the historian must pursue truth. This historical truth is not, of course, truth in the sense of eternal verity, absolute and unqualified. The pursuit of truth in writing history entails the obligation to construct the past with the utmost accuracy, without misreading the documents, without misrepresenting the events of the past, without falsification. The historian's task is often to uncover and expose fraud and deceit as it existed in the past and in written history, to bring to light suppressed facts and documents, to lay bare documentary forgeries, to strip away the accumulated overlays of myth and legend upon the past. "The morality of historians," said Lord Acton, "consists of those things which affect veracity."[6]

The authoritarian and totalitarian societies that flourish in our time have suffered no dearth of historians who have been willing to subvert their craft in the service of political dogma. In the Soviet Union and in Poland, as this book has shown, there is a sufficiency of historians who are prepared to falsify history in their national interest. Those who do so convincingly are well rewarded, but those who write history with moral integrity and with respect for professional standards have been punished. Aleksandr Solzhenitsyn's *Gulag Archipelago* testifies to the fact that gathering historical documentation in the Soviet Union is a sacrificial enterprise and that the even more challenging task of using that documentation for a truthful historical account of slave labor in the Soviet Union is practically a suicidal enterprise.

Lying in history can also take more devious forms than the outright falsifications or obliterations of the past that characterize Communist or Nazi historiography. In his search for explanations to account for how things came to pass, in his investigation of causes and effects, the historian assigns historical responsibility for the events of the past. This aspect of writing history, like other stages of historical scholarship, demands intellectual integrity as well as methodological rigor. In times long past, chroniclers used to attribute responsibility for the course of human events to the wheel of fortune or the hand of God. In more sophisticated times, historians have found more sophisticated substitutes for the *deus ex machina*. Under the influence of German historicism and then of Marxist historical materialism, as we have seen, historians assigned responsibility for certain events not to the men of history who acted, governed, and legislated, who made war and peace, who conspired and revolted, who agitated and educated, who tyrannized and murdered, but rather to "vast impersonal forces," beyond direct human responsibility. The phrase, which is T. S. Eliot's, has been used by Sir Isaiah Berlin as an epigraph to his classic essay "Historical Inevitability."[7]

By attributing historical responsibility to the medieval mind, the Renaissance spirit, the Industrial Revolution, mass culture, secularism, or inevitability, some historians have managed to evade the attribution of human responsibility for the occurrence of historic events. But the Renaissance spirit was, after all, created by individuals and that spirit, once it became a historical phenomenon and a cultural presence, could act as a historic agent only in relation to human beings. The historian who assigns causal responsibility to those "vast impersonal forces" rather than to the movers and shakers who made events happen has abdicated his professional obligation, for if he cannot locate the human factor in explaining historical events, he cannot then decipher the import of those events. History is at bottom an account of what men did and achieved, and the historian's task is to untangle that meshwork of human character, behavior, and motive whose intertwining creates the very material of history.

Morality in history has less to do with the historian's judgments about the actors in his historical drama and more to do with the historian's ethics in dealing with his historical data. "The morality of history-writing," according to G. J. Renier, "is exclusively methodological."[8] To maintain his intellectual integrity the historian is required to discipline his biases, though not to divest himself of his values. To preserve his intellectual honesty, the historian must apply the same kind of skepticism with which he regards all historical sources to whatever religious or political dogma claims his allegiance.

NOTES    INDEX

# NOTES

## 1. Thinking About the Six Million: Facts, Figures, Perspectives

1. Karl Shapiro, "Elegy for a Dead Soldier," *Selected Poems* (New York: Vintage, 1973), p. 105.

2. No sources cite the same statistics; discrepancies exist among all figures. Cf. "Great Patriotic War of the Soviet Union of 1941–45,"*Great Soviet Encyclopedia: A Translation of the Third Edition* (New York: Macmillan, 1974), vol. 4; "World Wars," *Encyclopedia Britannica.*

3. Szymon Datner, *Crimes Against POWS: Responsibility of the Wehrmacht* (Warsaw: Zachodnia Agencja Prasowa, 1964), esp. pp. 218–227; Hans-Adolf Jacobsen, "The Kommissarbefehl and the Mass Executions of Soviet Russian Prisoners of War," in Helmut Krausnick et al., *Anatomy of the SS State* (New York: Walker, 1968), p. 531.

4. Jan Szafranski, "Poland's Losses in World War II," *1939–1945: War Losses in Poland*, Studies and Monographs (Poznań: Zachodnia Agencja Prasowa, 1960), esp. pp. 44–49.

5. Central Commission for the Investigation of German Crimes in Poland, *German Crimes in Poland*, 2 (Warsaw, 1947), 49–50.

6. Henri Michel, *The Second World War* (New York: Praeger, 1975), pp. 781–782.

7. Central Commission for the Investigation of German Crimes in Poland, *German Crimes in Poland*, 1 (Warsaw, 1946), esp. 45. For the variety of reasons that brought people to Auschwitz see Bernd Naumann, *Auschwitz: A Report on the Proceedings Against Robert Karl Ludwig Mulka and Others Before the Court at Frankfurt* (London: Pall Mall, 1966). For an excellent critical analysis of available statistics on concentration camp population, turnover, and mortality see Joseph Billig, *Les Camps de Concentration dans L'Economie du Reich Hitlérien* (Paris: Presses Universitaires de France, 1973), pp. 68–99.

8. For an exposition of racial anti-Semitism in National Socialist ideology and practice see Lucy S. Dawidowicz, *The War Against the Jews, 1933–1945* (New York: Holt, Rinehart & Winston, 1975), esp. pp. 3–22, 56–60, 63–69, 130–166.

149

9. Ota Kraus and Erich Kulka, *The Death Factory: Document on Auschwitz* (Oxford: Pergamon Press, 1966), pp. 205–206.

10. H[elmut] Kr[ausnick], "Denkschrift Himmlers über die Behandlung der Fremdvölkischen im Osten," *Vierteljahrshefte für Zeitgeschichte,* 5 (1957), 197. For Himmler's speech, October 4, 1943, see Lucy S. Dawidowicz, ed., *A Holocaust Reader* (New York: Behrman House, 1976), pp. 131–132.

11. The most reliable source about the fate of the Gypsies under the Nazis is Donald Kenrick and Grattan Puxon, *The Destiny of Europe's Gypsies* (London: Chatto Heineman for Sussex University Press, 1972), esp. pp. 83–99, 144–149, and the statistics on pp. 183–184.

12. For statistics on the European Jews killed see Dawidowicz, *The War Against the Jews*, pp. 402–403.

13. See William Styron, "Auschwitz's Message," *New York Times,* June 25, 1974, and his essay "Hell Reconsidered, " *New York Review of Books,* June 29, 1978, which appeared, in somewhat different form, as an introduction to the paperback edition of Richard L. Rubenstein, *The Cunning of History* (New York: Harper Torchbook, 1978). See also Kurt Vonnegut, Jr., *Slaughterhouse-Five* (New York: Dell, 1971), p. 96, where he provides an indiscriminate list of victims of the Nazi state: "Jews and Gypsies, and fairies and communists, and other enemies of the State."

14. Karl Jaspers and Rudolf Augstein, "The Criminal State and German Responsibility: A Dialogue," *Commentary,* 41 (February 1966), 35.

15. Vladimir Nabokov, interviewed by Herbert Gold, in George Plimpton, ed., *Writers at Work: The Paris Review Interviews,* 4th ser. (New York: Penguin, 1977), pp. 101–102. I am indebted to Norma Rosen for this reference.

16. Vonnegut, *Slaughterhouse-Five*, p. 101 et passim. See also Gabriel Habib, "A Statement," in Eva Fleischner, ed., *Auschwitz: Beginning of a New Era? Reflections on the Holocaust* (New York: Ktav, 1977): "The drama of Auschwitz should not be separated from the drama of World War II. Decisions such as those to bomb Dresden, or the annihilation of Hiroshima, along with the more recent massacre of the Vietnamese, can only be characterized as the same madness on the part of the industrialized nations" (p. 417).

Everyone has his favorite disaster. Thus Louis Morton, a specialist in American military and diplomatic history, wrote on the siege of Leningrad: "No incident of World War II, with the possible exception of the gas chambers of Auschwitz and Belsen, can compare in human suffering to the epic defense of Leningrad." "World War II: A Survey of Recent Writings," *American Historical Review,* 75 (December 1970), 1993.

17. See Chapter 2 for a discussion of Irving's *Hitler's War.*

Vonnegut's choice of historical sources may be more deliberate than would appear, for he chose to flaunt his own German ancestry in *Slaughterhouse-Five,* describing himself on the title page as "a fourth-generation German-American." That statement of identity in that book assumes the defiance of a political statement. Even in World War II, Vonnegut appears to be saying, to have been a German was no worse morally than to have been an American, for in his view, it was more reprehensible to have bombed Dresden than to have murdered 6 million European Jews.

18. Bernard Lazare, *Job's Dungheap* (New York: Schocken Books, 1948), p. 68.

19. Karl Jaspers, *The Origin and Goal of History* (New Haven: Yale University Press, 1953), p. 149.

## 2. The Eye of the Beholder: The Holocaust According to English and American Historians

1. See Geoffrey Barraclough, "Farewell to Hitler," *New York Review of Books*, April 3, 1975, p. 11. See also Leonard Krieger, "Nazism: Highway or Byway?" *Central European History*, 11 (March 1978), 3–22. He concludes: "the unforgettable evil that [the Nazis] did—this is their legacy to all mankind."

2. For critical reviews of college and high school texts see Henry Friedlander, *On the Holocaust: A Critique of the Treatment of the Holocaust in History Textbooks Accompanied by an Annotated Bibliography* (New York: Anti-Defamation League, 1972); Gerd Korman, "Silence in the American Textbooks," in Livia Rothkirchen, ed., *Yad Vashem Studies on the European Jewish Catastrophe and Resistance*, 8 (Jerusalem, 1970), 183–202; Korman, "The Holocaust in American Historical Writing," *Societas*, 2 (Summer 1972), 251–270; Gerald Krefetz, "Nazism: The Textbook Treatment," *Congress Bi-Weekly*, 28 (November 13, 1961), 5–7; Lloyd Marcus, *The Treatment of Minorities in Secondary School Textbooks* (New York: Anti-Defamation League, 1961); Michael B. Kane, *Minorities in Textbooks: A Study of Their Treatment in Social Studies Texts* (New York/Chicago: Anti-Defamation League/Quadrangle Books, 1970).

Some inadequate texts in this regard are Wallace K. Ferguson and Geoffrey Brunn, *A Survey of European Civilization*, 4th ed. (Boston: Houghton Mifflin, 1969); Gordon A. Craig, *Europe Since 1815*, 3rd ed. (New York: Holt, Rinehart and Winston, 1971); Felix Gilbert, *The End of the European Era* (New York: W. W. Norton, 1970).

For a comparable review of French textbooks see Bernhard Blumenkranz, "How Holocaust History Is (Not) Taught: Shortcomings of French Textbooks," *Patterns of Prejudice* (London), 9 (May–June 1975), 8–12. For a personal view of the failure of American schools to teach about the Holocaust see Susan Jacoby, "Susan, What's *Kristallnacht?*" *Present Tense* (Autumn 1978), p. 64.

3. G. Barraclough, *The Origins of Modern Germany* (Oxford: Basil Blackwell, 1966), p. 455. First published in 1946, this book is still in print in both hardcover and paperback editions.

4. John A. Garraty and Peter Gay, eds., *The Columbia History of the World* (New York: Harper & Row, 1972). The passages referred to appear on pp. 1054, 1055, 1065, 1068. Two examples of errors: Hitler is described as

"a former Austrian house painter" and the SS, which was the Nazi party's security force, is characterized as "Hitler's elite corps within the army."

5. R. R. Palmer and Joel Colton, *A History of the Modern World*, 5th ed. (New York: Knopf, 1978).

6. Koppel S. Pinson, *Modern Germany: Its History and Civilization*, 2d ed. (New York: Macmillan, 1968).

7. Gordon A. Craig, *Germany: 1866–1945* (New York: Oxford University Press, 1978).

8. Arnaldo Momigliano, "The Swathes and the Tunnels," *Times Literary Supplement*, September 22, 1978, p. 1054.

9. See Henry Cord Meyer, *Five Images of Germany: Half a Century of American Views on German History*, 2d ed. (Washington, D.C.: American Historical Association, 1960).

10. See Miriam Yardeni, "Tefisot hadoshot shel toldot am yisrael aharei ha-hurban bereshit tenuat ha-haskala—Basnage ve-Bayle," *Proceedings of the Sixth World Congress of Jewish Studies* (Jerusalem, 1973), pp. 179–184.

11. Hannah Adams, *A Dictionary of All Religions and Religious Denominations, Jewish, Heathen, Mahometan, and Christian, Ancient and Modern*, 4th ed. (Boston: James Eastburn and Co., 1817), p. 376.

12. Leopold Ranke, *Deutsche Geschichte im Zeitalter der Reformation* (Berlin: Duncker und Humblot, 1842–1847). Volume 1 contains three references (pp. 211, 235, 273), one describing peasant attacks against Jews and two dealing with the attempts of the Dominicans to introduce the Inquisition in Germany and the controversy involving Johann Reuchlin. Volume 6 contains one reference (p. 64) to the persecution of Jews as a consequence of their role as usurers.

13. Theodor Mommsen, *The History of Rome*, translated with the author's sanction and additions by William P. Dickenson (New York: Charles Scribner's Sons, 1891), 4:643.

14. Gavin I. Langmuir, "Majority History and Post-Biblical Jews," *Journal of the History of Ideas*, 27 (July-September 1966), 343–364.

15. John Higham, with Leonard Krieger and Felix Gilbert, *History* (Englewood Cliffs, N.J.: Prentice-Hall, 1965).

16. Quoted in Robert Allen Skotheim, *American Intellectual Histories and Historians* (Princeton, N.J.: Princeton University Press, 1966), p. 22. Cf. Lord Acton: "Ideas which, in religion and in politics, are truths, in history are forces."

17. The following selection of scholarly works, most of them issued by university presses, are characteristic of this approach.

Oron J. Hale, *The Captive Press in the Third Reich* (Princeton, N.J.: Princeton University Press, 1964), a workmanlike study of the operations of the publishing industry in Nazi Germany, which gives scarcely any attention to the substance of what was permitted to be published and what was suppressed. The author's tone-deafness to the function of ideas and propaganda and his insensitivity to anti-Semitism are evident throughout, and most distressingly in the choice of his title for Chapter 5: "The Final Solution—The Amann Ordinances," which deals not with the murder of the

Jews, for which "The Final Solution" was the code name, but with the elimination of privately owned newspapers and/or their takeover by the Nazi party in 1935-36.

Edward L. Homze, *Foreign Labor in Nazi Germany* (Princeton, N.J.: Princeton University Press, 1967), a useful factual compendium about foreign labor in Germany. Its five-page discussion on "The 'Untermensch' Philosophy in Action" is quite inadequate as philosophic underpinning.

Robert J. O'Neill, *The German Army and the Nazi Party, 1933-1939* (New York: James H. Heineman, 1966), an analysis of the relations between the army and the Nazi party, in which the traditional anti-Semitism of the German military is scanted and the ideological *Gleichschaltung* of the German armed forces is only occasionally mentioned. The emphasis tends to be on military matters rather than political ones.

Dietrich Orlow, *The History of the Nazi Party: 1919-1933* (Pittsburgh, Pa.: University of Pittsburgh Press, 1969); *The History of the Nazi Party: 1933-1945* (Pittsburgh, Pa.: University of Pittsburgh Press, 1973). The first volume contains a bare half dozen references to anti-Semitism, notwithstanding its centrality in the party's ideology and operations; the second volume touches inadequately on the Nazi party's involvement in anti-Jewish activity (the boycott of April 1933, the Nuremberg laws, the anti-Jewish street violence, *Kristallnacht*, and the murder of the Jews). In his postscript, Orlow concludes that "in practice, the Nazis failed in all but the most gruesome of their goals, the extermination of the European Jews" (p. 486). But Orlow never investigated why this was so.

George H. Stein, *The Waffen SS: Hitler's Elite Guard at War, 1939-1945* (Ithaca, N.Y.: Cornell University Press, 1966), a competent institutional history of the Waffen SS, from which the reader will not learn that the SS was permeated with racist anti-Semitism and that all its divisions participated in the murder of the Jews. When Stein does mention the mass murders, he refers to the victims not specifically as Jews, but as "people" (see esp. p.263). Relying on the memoirs of a single American Marine, Stein manages to equate the racial attitudes of the whole Marine Corps toward the Japanese with those of Himmler toward the Slavic *Untermenschen* (p. 128), *poshlost* with vengeance.

James J. Weingartner, *Hitler's Guard: The Story of the Leibstandarte SS Adolf Hitler, 1933-1945* (Carbondale, Ill.: Southern Illinois University Press, 1974), an unremarkable study which devotes a mere half dozen pages to ideological indoctrination among the SS men and officers. It generally belittles the role of ideas and beliefs in attracting men to the SS and the Leibstandarte particularly, stressing instead nonideological factors like the freebooter spirit. Weingartner makes no attempt to analyze the dynamic influence of anti-Semitism on the attitudes and actions of the men in the SS.

18. See my review of Mosse in *Commentary* 66 (December 1978), 86–88. Mosse has made a seminal contribution to our understanding of German nationalism and National Socialism. *The Crisis of German Ideology: Intellectual Origins of the Third Reich* (New York: Grosset & Dunlap, 1964) is the most innovative of his works; the rest have flowed logically from his basic

concern with the etiology of nationalist and Nazi ideas. *Nazi Culture* (New York: Grosset & Dunlap, 1966) is a well-edited collection of source materials which illuminate the intellectual and cultural life of Hitler's Germany. *Germans & Jews* (New York: Grosset & Dunlap, 1970) consists of seven essays on as many aspects of German history, covering "the Right, the Left, and the search of a 'Third Force' in pre-Nazi Germany." This was followed by *The Nationalization of the Masses: Political Symbolism and Mass Movements in Germany from the Napoleonic Wars Through the Third Reich* (New York: Howard Fertig, 1975). His most recent book, *Toward the Final Solution: A History of European Racism* (New York: Howard Fertig, 1978), will probably be the definitive work on this subject for years to come.

19. Fritz R. Stern's first book on German history, *The Politics of Cultural Despair: A Study of the Rise of the Germanic Ideology* (Berkeley/Los Angeles, Cal.: University of California Press, 1961; 1974), combines close meticulous scholarship with penetrating synthesis, his brilliant writing a match to his original thinking. His latest book, *Gold and Iron: Bismarck, Bleichröder, and the Building of the German Empire* (New York: Knopf, 1977), is an extraordinary accomplishment of historical scholarship. It is unique in the attention that it gives to the place of Jews (and anti-Semitism) in German society and in German historiography.

20. Fritz Stern, *The Failure of Illiberalism: Essays on the Political Culture of Modern Germany* (New York: Knopf, 1972), p. xi. Other scholars in this group include:

Alexander Dallin, whose primary field of study is the Soviet Union, but who has to his credit one of the finest books on Nazi Germany, *German Rule in Russia, 1941–1945: A Study of Occupation Policies* (New York: St. Martin's Press, 1957).

Walter Laqueur, whose *Young Germany: A History of the German Youth Movement* (London: Routledge & K. Paul, 1962) presents an original analysis of the ideas and ideologies of the German youth movements that served as a feeding ground for the spread of nationalism and Nazism. His *Russia and Germany: A Century of Conflict* (Boston: Little, Brown, 1965) describes the cultural relations between Russia and Germany since the mid-nineteenth century, showing the penetration of Russian reactionary and anti-Semitic ideas into the German orbit and eventually into National Socialist ideology.

Guenter Lewy, a political scientist whose study *The Catholic Church and Nazi Germany* (New York: McGraw-Hill, 1964) is still the finest historical work we have on this subject.

Peter G. J. Pulzer, the author of *The Rise of Political Anti-Semitism in Germany and Austria* (New York: Wiley, 1964), a standard work whose only serious competition is Paul W. Massing, *Rehearsal for Destruction: A Study of Political Anti-Semitism in Imperial Germany* (New York: Harper, 1949), now regrettably out of print.

Gerhard L. Weinberg, who discovered the manuscript of Hitler's unpublished "second book," the sequel to *Mein Kampf,* and who delineated the ideological foundation of racism and anti-Semitism in National Socialism as a prior condition to understanding the more conventional aspects of Nazi diplomacy in *The Foreign Policy of Hitler's Germany: Diplomatic Revolution in Europe, 1933-36* (Chicago: University of Chicago Press, 1970).

John Lukacs, whose book *The Last European War: September 1939/December 1941* (Garden City, N.Y.: Anchor Press/Doubleday, 1976) is something of an anomaly. Born and raised in Hungary, Lukacs became an American citizen in 1953. His book, which deals extensively with Jews and anti-Semitism and which regards Hitler's obsession with the Jews as one of his two principal beliefs, nevertheless cannot be regarded as the product of an American historian, for it is thoroughly the work of a politically conservative and religiously committed Hungarian. Appalled by the murder of the Jews, which he believes has since made it impossible for anyone to avow an anti-Semitic position, Lukacs argues that the murder of the Jews is the only evidence to sustain the claim that Hitler and Nazism were more criminal than Stalin and Communism.

21. Harold J. Gordon, Jr., *Hitler and the Beer Hall Putsch* (Princeton, N.J.: Princeton University Press, 1972), is an excellent treatment of the *Putsch*, including analyses of the interplay between ideology and power politics.

Norman Rich's two-volume work *Hitler's War Aims* is an excellent work on National Socialist diplomacy, integrating his discussion of ideology and anti-Semitism into the whole treatment. The first volume, subtitled *Ideology, the Nazi State, and the Course of Expansion* (New York: W. W. Norton, 1973), devotes major attention to Nazi ideology in terms of power and expansion. The second, subtitled *The Establishment of the New Order* (New York: W. W. Norton, 1974), includes a discussion of the fate of the Jews in those countries that came under Hitler's rule and influence.

Bradley F. Smith, *Heinrich Himmler: A Nazi in the Making, 1900-1926* (Stanford, Cal.: Hoover Institution Press, 1971), is a first-class study that is attentive to the development of Himmler's ideas and the intellectual influences at work upon him.

Andrew Gladding Whiteside, *Austrian National Socialism Before 1918* (The Hague: Martinus Nijhoff, 1962), offers a good analysis of a proto-Nazi movement from the perspective of the Czech-German nationality conflict within the Hapsburg Empire.

Barbara Miller Lane and Leila J. Rupp, eds., *Nazi Ideology Before 1933: A Documentation* (Austin, Texas: University of Texas Press, 1978), appears naive in the authors' "discovery" of the importance of ideology for an understanding of the history of the Nazi movement and its state.

Charles W. Sydnor, Jr., *Soldiers of Destruction: The SS Death's Head Division, 1933-1945* (Princeton, N.J.: Princeton University Press, 1977), underscores the centrality of ideological indoctrination in this SS division.

22. Alan Bullock, *Hitler: A Study in Tyranny,* rev. ed. (New York: Harper & Row, 1964).

23. Ibid., pp. 406-407, 313, 279.

24. See also Alan Bullock, "Hitler and the Origins of the Second World War," in E. M. Robertson, ed., *The Origins of the Second World War: His-*

*torical Interpretation* (London: Macmillan/St. Martin's Press, 1971), esp. pp. 118–121. Here Lord Bullock confuses the driving force of Hitler's ideas with his will power, as if will alone were an autonomous force, operating without mental guidance and the motivating drive of a system of beliefs.

25. A. J. P. Taylor, *The Course of German History: A Survey of the Development of Germany since 1815* (New York: Capricorn Books, 1962), p. 10.

26. A. J. P. Taylor, *The Origins of the Second World War* (New York: Atheneum, 1964), p. 71. This book sparked enormous controversy. Most reviews and criticisms are cited in W. H. Dray, "Concepts of Causation in A. J. P. Taylor's Account of the Origins of the Second World War," *History and Theory: Studies in the Philosophy of History,* 17 (1978), 149–174.

27. Ibid., p. 70.

28. A. J. P. Taylor, "The Fuehrer as Mohican," *The Observer,* June 12, 1977.

29. *Hitler's Secret Conversations, 1941–1944* (New York: Farrar, Straus and Young, 1953), p. viii.

30. H. R. Trevor-Roper, *The Last Days of Hitler,* 3d ed. (New York/London: Collier Macmillan, 1962), p. 239.

31. Nigel Nicolson, ed., *Harold Nicolson's Diaries and Letters, 1939–1945* (London: Collins, 1967), p. 268. Cf. Anthony Eden, *The Memoirs of Anthony Eden, Earl of Avon: The Reckoning* (Boston: Houghton Mifflin, 1965), p. 415.

32. J. P. Stern, *Hitler: The Führer and the People* (Berkeley/Los Angeles, Cal.: University of California Press, 1975), p. 15.

33. Robert Payne, *The Life and Death of Adolf Hitler* (New York: Praeger, 1973); John Toland, *Adolf Hitler* (New York: Doubleday, 1976).

34. David Irving, *Hitler's War* (New York: Viking, 1977). Irving's work has been described as "revisionist," but the label is improperly applied. Irving is merely an apologist for Hitler and deserves no consideration as a historian, revisionist or otherwise.

35. His first book, *The Destruction of Dresden* (London: W. Kimber, 1963), caused a sensation by its accusation that the Anglo-American raids on Dresden in February 1945 constituted a major war atrocity. Irving's book, which exaggerated threefold the number of deaths that actually occurred and made unfounded charges about Allied actions, has since been refuted. Two of his later books, *Accident: The Death of General Sikorski* (London: W. Kimber, 1967) and *The Destruction of Convoy PQ 17* (New York: Simon and Schuster, 1969), prompted legal action. Irving lost both cases and had to pay damages and costs of about £45,000 in the libel suit on *Convoy PQ 17.*

36. Irving, *Hitler's War,* pp. xi, xiv.

37. Ibid., p. 332; Himmler's handwritten notes appear on p. 505 and are here reproduced from the National Archives Microfilm Publication T84, Roll 26. I wish to acknowledge the help of Dr. Fred Grubel, director of the Leo Baeck Institute, in deciphering the script and its meaning. Nearly every reviewer who considered Irving's "evidence" tried to explain this document. No one thought to look at the item in its entirety. Martin Broszat comes up

with a very convoluted but unconvincing explanation. "Hitler und die Genesis der 'Endlösung,' " *Vierteljahrshefte für Zeitgeschichte,* 25 (October 1977), 739-775.

38. Walter C. Langer, *The Mind of Adolf Hitler: The Secret Wartime Report* (New York: Basic Books, 1972).

39. For critiques see Robert G. L. Waite, "Afterword," in Langer, *Mind of Adolf Hitler,* pp. 215-238, esp. 229-235; Hans W. Gatzke, "Hitler and Psychohistory," *American Historical Review,* 78 (April 1973), 394-401; Robert Coles, "Shrinking History—Part Two," *New York Review of Books,* March 8, 1973, esp. pp. 25-26.

40. Rudolph Binion, *Hitler among the Germans* (New York: Elsevier, 1976).

41. Lest it be thought that I am unfairly presenting Binion's arguments, here are two excerpts from his text: "[Hitler's] anti-Semitism was his reaction against his guilt for his mother's agony of 1907 following Bloch's ministration that he prompted. That reaction, long repressed, was released by a gas poisoning reminiscent of his mother's agony—a reminder of traumatic intensity that impelled him to relive the unassimilated experience behind it" (p. 35).

"The specific terms of the mission—to undo and reverse Germany's defeat—did not cover her traumatic business as they did his. But the Providence that conferred that mission was, transparently, his nursing mother: the version he authorized even had him receiving the mission in a nurse's arms. And the mission left the way open for a second mode of fulfillment, this one suited to his experience of his nursing mother rather than his dying mother" (p. 86).

42. Robert G. L. Waite, *The Psychopathic God Adolf Hitler* (New York: Basic Books, 1977). My paraphrase was not intended as burlesque. Here is Waite's text: "His decision to seize Austria in the *Anschluss* (annexation) of 1938 provides a particularly vivid illustration of the connection between private feelings and foreign relations. Of course it is true there were other reasons for the *Anschluss,* but since they have been set forth in many books, they need no emphasis here.

"We have seen that in Hitler's imagery his mother was identified with Germany . . . As he loved her as the racially pure Motherland, so he hated the bureaucratic, racially mixed Austria, which he associated with his bureaucratic and racially suspect father . . . To his mind, the 'debauched' Austrian dynasty—exactly like his father—had defiled and 'betrayed' Germany again and again" (p. 389).

43. Ernst L. Freud, ed., *The Letters of Sigmund Freud and Arnold Zweig* (London: Hogarth/Institute of Psycho-Analysis, 1970), p. 78.

44. Norman Cohn, *The Pursuit of the Millennium: Revolutionary Messianism in Medieval and Reformation Europe and Its Bearing on Modern Totalitarian Movements,* rev. ed. (New York: Harper, 1961).

45. Norman Cohn, *Warrant for Genocide: The Myth of the Jewish World Conspiracy and the Protocols of the Elders of Zion* (New York: Harper & Row, 1969).

46. Gershom Scholem, *Sabbatai Sevi: The Mystical Messiah, 1626–1676,* Bollingen Series XCIII (Princeton, N.J.: Princeton University Press, 1973), p. xii.

47. See Lucy S. Dawidowicz, "Can Anti-Semitism Be Measured?" in *The Jewish Presence: Essays on Identity and History* (New York: Holt, Rinehart and Winston, 1977), pp. 193–194.

### 3. The Shadow of the Past: German Historians Confront National Socialism

1. Friedrich Meinecke, *The German Catastrophe: Reflections and Recollections* (Boston: Beacon Press, 1950), pp. 53, 86. The German original, *Die deutsche Katastrophe: Betrachtungen und Erinnerungen,* was first published in 1946.

2. Gerhard Ritter, *The German Resistance: Carl Goerdeler's Struggle against Tyranny* (London: George Allen & Unwin, 1958), p. 13. The German original, *Carl Goerdeler und die deutsche Widerstandsbewegung,* appeared in 1954.

3. Quoted in Ludwig Dehio, *Germany and World Politics in the Twentieth Century* (New York: W. W. Norton, 1967), p. 54. The historian was Otto Hintze, coeditor with Friedrich Meinecke, Hermann Oncken, and Hermann Schumacher of *Deutschland und der Weltkrieg,* the collection of essays cited.

4. The definitive work on German historiography is Georg G. Iggers, *The German Conception of History: The National Tradition of Historical Thought from Herder to the Present* (Middletown, Conn.: Wesleyan University Press, 1968). Also useful is Iggers, *New Directions in European Historiography* (Middletown, Conn.: Wesleyan University Press, 1975).

5. Meinecke, *The German Catastrophe,* p. 25.

6. Dehio, *Germany and World Politics,* pp. 23–24, 70–71.

7. See the excellent study by Bernd Faulenbach, "Deutsche Geschichtswissenschaft zwischen Kaiserreich und NS-Diktatur," in Bernd Faulenbach, ed., *Geschichtswissenschaft in Deutschland: Traditionelle Positionen und gegenwärtigen Aufgaben* (Munich: Verlag C. H. Beck, 1974), pp. 66–85. See also Fritz K. Ringer, *The Decline of the German Mandarins: The German Academic Community 1890–1933* (Cambridge, Mass.: Harvard University Press, 1969), and Fritz Stern, *The Failure of Illiberalism: Essays on the Political Culture of Modern Germany* (New York: Knopf, 1972), pp. 22–23.

8. Faulenbach, "Deutsche Geschichtswissenschaft," p. 69. The German is more succinct: "Ich bleibe, der Vergangenheit zugewandt, Herzensmonarchist und werde, der Zukunft zugewandt, Vernunftrepublikaner."

9. Dehio, *Germany and World Politics,* pp. 65–66; Iggers, *New Directions,* p. 85; Faulenbach, "Deutsche Geschichtswissenschaft," pp. 72–73. See also Hans Rothfels, "Die Geschichtswissenschaft in den dreissiger Jahren," in Andreas Flitner, ed., *Deutsches Geistesleben und Nationalsozialismus*

(Tübingen: Rainer Wunderlich Verlag Hermann Leins, 1965), esp. pp. 93–97.

10. Hans Liebeschütz, *Das Judentum im deutschen Geschichtsbild von Hegel bis Max Weber* (Tübingen: J. C. B. Mohr [Paul Siebeck], 1967), pp. vii, 159, 163, 185, 190, et passim. See also Werner Jochmann, "The Jews and German Society in the Imperial Era: Opening Address at the Session on German-Jewish History, Thirtieth Congress of German Historians, on 3rd October 1974," *Leo Baeck Institute Year Book XX* (London: Secker & Warburg, 1975), pp. 5–11, and Fritz Stern, *Gold and Iron: Bismarck, Bleichröder, and the Building of the German Empire* (New York: Knopf, 1977), p. xix. In addition, see Chapter 2.

11. Ringer, *Decline of the German Mandarins*, pp. 436–437, 439, 444.

12. Karl Ferdinand Werner, *Das NS-Geschichtsbild und die deutsche Geschichtswissenschaft* (Stuttgart: Kohlhammer, 1967), pp. 41ff, 97, et passim. See also Werner, "Die deutsche Historiographie unter Hitler," in Faulenbach, ed., *Geschichtswissenschaft*, pp. 86–96.

13. Heinz Gollwitzer, "Karl Alexander von Müller 1882–1964: Ein Nachruf," *Historische Zeitschrift*, 205 (1967), 295–322.

14. Werner, *Das NS-Geschichtsbild*, pp. 71ff. Even Meinecke found much to admire in Hitler's regime. After Germany invaded and conquered France, Meinecke wrote to a friend: "Joy, admiration and above all pride in this Army dominate me too ... It was after all amazing and perhaps the greatest positive achievement of the Third Reich to have built from scratch such an armed force of millions in four years and to have developed it for such achievements." (Ibid., p. 104.)

15. Georg G. Iggers, "Die deutschen Historiker in der Emigration," in Faulenbach, ed., *Geschichtswissenschaft*, pp. 97–111.

16. The definitive work on the Nazi takeover of the historical profession, on which I have relied for this section, is Helmut Heiber, *Walter Frank und sein Reichsinstitut für Geschichte des neuen Deutschlands* (Stuttgart: Deutsche Verlags-Anstalt, 1966), a massive volume of 1274 pages. See also Max Weinreich, *Hitler's Professors* (New York: Yiddish Scientific Institute/Yivo, 1946), esp. pp. 45–58.

17. "Ansprache von Prof. Karl Alexander von Müller: Die Kundgebung zur Eröffnung der Forschungsabteilung Judenfrage des Reichsinstituts für Geschichte des neuen Deutschlands," *Forschungen zur Judenfrage*, 1 (Hamburg: Hanseatische Verlagsanstalt, 1937), 12. When one considers Müller's long involvement, however lukewarm, with the Reichsinstitut, and especially its *Forschungsabteil Judenfrage*, it is astonishing that Heinz Gollwitzer in his eulogy of Müller (see n. 13 above) made no reference to this aspect of Müller's career.

18. Heiber, *Walter Frank*, pp. 454, 468–471, et passim; Weinreich, *Hitler's Professors*, p. 54.

19. Gerhard Ritter, "Deutsche Geschichtswissenschaft im 20. Jahrhundert," *Geschichte in Wissenschaft und Unterricht*, 1 (June 1950), 129–130.

20. Heiber, *Walter Frank*, p. 1061; Weinreich, *Hitler's Professors*, p. 104.

These collections, or their remnants, were found after the German defeat and, under the auspices of the Allies, returned to their rightful owners.

21. Ralf Dahrendorf, *Society and Democracy in Germany* (New York: Doubleday, 1969), pp. 365-366. The German original, *Gesellschaft und Demokratie in Deutschland,* was published in Munich in 1965.

22. Golo Mann, *The History of Germany Since 1789* (New York: Praeger, 1968), p. 482.

23. Thomas Mann, *Doctor Faustus: The Life of the German Composer Adrian Leverkühn As Told by a Friend* (New York: Random House, 1971), p. 482. The speaker is the narrator Serenus Zeitblom.

24. Carl Becker, *Detachment and the Writing of History: Essays and Letters of Carl L. Becker,* ed. Phil L. Snyder (Ithaca, N.Y.: Cornell University Press, 1958), p. 26. The citation is from the lead essay which was first published in 1910.

25. It is a particular irony that mostly German Jewish emigrés elaborated the theories of universal fascism (Italy and Nazi Germany as similar political phenomena) and of totalitarianism (Nazi Germany and the Soviet Union as two aspects of the same political development). The most notable were Franz Neumann, *Behemoth: The Structure and Practice of National Socialism, 1933-1944* (New York: Oxford University Press, 1944), and Hannah Arendt, *The Origins of Totalitarianism* (New York: Meridian, 1958). Nowadays the concept of a generic fascism is widely questioned among historians, and the idea of a universal totalitarianism, once enthusiastically hailed, is discounted by both historians and political scientists. See Walter Laqueur, ed., *Fascism: A Reader's Guide: Analyses, Interpretations, Bibliography* (Berkeley/Los Angeles, Cal.: University of California Press, 1976). Of special interest with regard to National Socialism is Wolfgang Sauer, "National Socialism: Totalitarianism or Fascism?" *American Historical Review,* 73 (December 1967), 404-424; Gilbert Allardyce, "What Fascism Is Not: Thoughts on the Deflation of a Concept," *American Historical Review,* 84 (April 1979), 367-398.

26. Meinecke, *The German Catastrophe,* p. 70. Subsequent references in the text to this work are to be found on pp. 93, 95-96, 15, 32.

27. For a thorough discussion see Pinchas E. Rosenblüth, "Friedrich Meineckes Anschauung über Juden und Judentum," *Bulletin des Leo Baeck Instituts,* 15 (1976), 96-123. Also instructive is Robert A. Pois, *Friedrich Meinecke and German Politics in the Twentieth Century* (Berkeley/Los Angeles, Cal.: University of California Press, 1972), esp. pp. 105-113, 123, 139-140.

28. Gerhard Ritter, *Europa und die deutsche Frage: Betrachtungen über die geschichtliche Eigenart des deutschen Staatsdenkens,* was first published in Munich in 1948. A revised and expanded version appeared there in 1962 and was issued in English as *The German Problem: Basic Questions of German Political Life, Past and Present* (Columbus, Ohio: Ohio State University Press, 1965).

29. Ibid., p. 50. Subsequent quotations in the text are to be found on pp. 195, 118-119, 221.

30. Hans Rothfels, *The German Opposition to Hitler: An Appraisal*, rev. ed. (Chicago: Henry Regnery, 1962), esp. pp. 24, 41, 152–160.

31. An excellent study on the state of East German historiography dealing with the Nazi era is Konrad Kwiet, "Historians of the German Democratic Republic on Antisemitism and Persecution," *Leo Baeck Institute Year Book XXI* (London: Secker & Warburg, 1976), pp. 173–198.

32. Institut für Zeitgeschichte, *Informationsbericht*, Munich, February 1953 (unpaged, mimeographed). See also Robert Koehl, "Zeitgeschichte and the New German Conservatism," *Journal of Central European Affairs*, 20 (July 1960), 131–135.

33. Hans Rothfels, "Zeitgeschichte als Aufgabe," *Vierteljahrshefte für Zeitgeschichte*, 1 (January 1953), 8.

34. See Iggers, *German Conception of History*, p. 265; Koehl, "Zeitgeschichte," p. 135.

35. Fritz Fischer, *Griff nach der Weltmacht* (Düsseldorf: Droste Verlag, 1961), published in English as *Germany's Aims in the First World War* (New York: W. W. Norton, 1967).

36. Ibid., p. xxii. Fischer was not quite the first postwar historian to argue for the continuity of German history into the Nazi era. Ludwig Dehio, in his major work *Gleichgewicht oder Hegemonie* (Krefeld: Scherpe-Verlage, 1948), published in English as *The Precarious Balance: Four Centuries of the European Power Struggle* (New York: Knopf, 1962), traced the evolution of German foreign policy through the centuries. Perhaps because his presentation, abstract and philosophical, was not integrated with questions of domestic policy and national values, Dehio's work had relatively little impact on German public opinion.

37. Fischer, *Griff nach der Weltmacht*, pp. 7, 141–143.

38. Quoted by Fischer in his *World Power or Decline: The Controversy Over Germany's Aims in the First World War* (New York: W. W. Norton, 1974), p. 95, published originally as *Weltmacht oder Niedergang* (Frankfurt-am-Main: Europäische Verlagsanstalt, 1965). See also Fritz Stern's "German Historians and the War: Fischer and His Critics," in his *The Failure of Illiberalism*.

39. Fischer, *World Power or Decline*, p. viii.

40. An excellent discussion on general developments is Iggers, *New Directions*, pp. 80–122.

41. Karl Dietrich Bracher, *The German Dictatorship: The Origins, Structures, and Effects of National Socialism* (New York: Praeger, 1970), published originally as *Die deutsche Diktatur: Entstehung, Struktur, Folgen des Nationalsozialismus* (Cologne/Berlin: Kiepenheuer & Witsch, 1969). The quotations that follow are found on pp. xii and 501.

42. Since the publication of *Die deutsche Dikatur*, some German historians have undertaken to write about Jews in Germany (e.g., Reinhard Rürup) and about anti-Semitism (e.g., Thomas Nipperdey).

## 4. Palimpsest History: Erasing the Holocaust in the USSR

1. Since I do not read Russian, I had to rely in good measure on secondary sources. But some Soviet historical works have been translated under the auspices of the Soviet government into English and other European languages. These translations are not always complete and do not always include the original scholarly apparatus. Nevertheless, for the purposes of my work, they appear to suffice. *The Current Digest of the Soviet Press*, published weekly by the American Association for the Advancement of Slavic Studies and issued since 1949, has been an invaluable resource. It has followed the ups and downs of Soviet historiography over the years, as reflected in the Soviet press and in Soviet historical journals. Critical analysis of Soviet historiography does not, of course, exist in the Soviet Union. English, German, and American historians who specialize in Soviet history have produced interesting studies that map the zigs and zags of the party line as reflected in Soviet historical writings. Many people helped me with Russian texts and shared their insights, among them Dina Abramowicz, Szymon Dawidowicz, Maurice Friedberg, William Korey, Aleksandr M. Nekrich.

2. "Soviet Historical Sciences at a New Stage of Development" [in Russian], *Voprosy istorii*, 6 (August 1960), 3–18; complete text in *Current Digest of the Soviet Press*, 12 (November 2, 1960), 6–14. In the rare periods of liberalization, a few daring historians have suggested that the prevailing orthodoxy is not necessarily the correct way of arriving at historical truth. See Arthur P. Mendel, "Current Soviet Theory of History: New Trends or Old," *American Historical Review*, 72 (October 1966), 50–73.

3. Roy A. Medvedev, *Let History Judge: The Origins and Consequences of Stalinism* (New York: Knopf, 1972), p. 223. See also C. E. Black, ed., *Rewriting Russian History: Soviet Interpretations of Russia's Past* (New York: Praeger, 1956), pp. 12–16.

4. George Orwell, *1984* (New York: Harcourt, Brace, 1949), pp. 40–41, 35.

5. Bertram D. Wolfe, "Party Histories from Lenin to Khrushchev," in John Keep and Liliana Brisby, eds., *Contemporary History in the Soviet Mirror* (New York: Praeger, 1964), p. 49.

6. Alexander Dallin, "Recent Soviet Historiography," in Abraham Brumberg, ed., *Russia under Khrushchev: An Anthology from Problems of Communism* (New York: Praeger, 1972), p. 478.

7. Wolfe, "Party Histories," p. 43.

8. The definitive work about Soviet historiography on the Second World War up to the Khrushchev era is Matthew P. Gallagher, *The Soviet History of World War II: Myths, Memoirs, and Realities* (New York: Praeger, 1963). See also Gallagher, "Trends in Soviet Historiography of the Second World War," in Keep and Brisby, eds., *Contemporary History*, pp. 222–242.

9. Konstantin F. Shteppa, *Russian Historians and the Soviet State* (New Brunswick, N.J.: Rutgers State University, 1962), p. 229.

10. Compare this passage from "The Party Central Committee Resolution 'On the Tasks of Party Propaganda in Present-Day Conditions' and

Historical Science," which appeared in *Voprosy istorii*, 6 (June 1960), 3–9. The English version appeared in *Current Digest of the Soviet Press*, 12 (August 31, 1960), 8–10: "Historical science must make its contribution to the disclosure of socialism's advantages over a capitalism that is on its last legs; it must skillfully propagandize the outstanding achievements of our compatriots in all fields of social life, to the end of educating Soviet people in a spirit of socialist patriotism, national pride and proletarian internationalism."

11. P. Zhilin, *The Second World War and Our Time* (Moscow: USSR Academy of Sciences, 1978), p. 118. See also Kurt Marko, "History and the Historians," *Survey*, 56 (July 1965), 71–82.

12. For an evaluation of a collection of documents on French-Soviet relations during the war published by the Ministry for Foreign Affairs in 1959 see Alfred J. Rieber, *American Historical Review*, 66 (April 1961), 794–795.

13. *Istoriia Velikoi Otechestvennoi voiny Sovetskovo Soyuza 1941–1945* [The History of the Great Patriotic War of the Soviet Union], 6 vols. (Moscow: Military Publishing House of the Ministry of Defense of the USSR, 1960–1965). See reviews in *American Historical Review*, 67 (October 1961), 137–138; 72 (July 1967), 1452–1453.

14. *Current Digest of the Soviet Press*, 12 (November 2, 1960), 9.

15. Kenneth A. Kerst, "CPSU History Re-Revised," *Problems of Communism*, 26 (May–June 1977), 17–32; James Douglas, "Stalin in the Second World War," *Survey*, 17 (Autumn 1971), 179–187.

16. Aleksandr M. Nekrich, *The Punished Peoples: The Deportation and Fate of Soviet Minorities at the End of the Second World War* (New York: W. W. Norton, 1978), pp. ix–x.

17. Zhilin, *Second World War*, pp. 118–121. For a review of several volumes see William J. Spahr, *American Historical Review*, 82 (October 1977), 1027.

18. For a review of several volumes of recent Soviet works about the Second World War see Earl F. Ziemke, *American Historical Review*, 81 (June 1976), 637–639; Arthur E. Adams, on a history of Soviet foreign policy, *American Historical Review*, 74 (December 1968), 675–676, and 75 (December 1969), 550–551; John A. Armstrong, on studies of military history, *American Historical Review*, 80 (April 1975), 443–444.

Selected Soviet histories are translated into English and disseminated as propaganda. See Vsevolod Klokov, *History-Making Exploit* (Kiev: Politvidav Ukraini, 1975), and I. K. Koblyakov, *USSR: For Peace Against Aggression 1933–1941* (Moscow: Progress Publishers, 1976).

19. Koblyakov, *USSR*, p. 237.

20. See Walter Laqueur, *Russia and Germany: A Century of Conflict* (Boston: Little, Brown, 1965), pp. 196–251.

21. "Great Patriotic War of the Soviet Union of 1941–45," *Great Soviet Encyclopedia: A Translation of the Third Edition* (New York: Macmillan, 1974), 4:333.

22. Klokov, *History-Making Exploit*, p. 15. See also pp. 45–47, which

refer to Nazi enslavement of the occupied people and the mass murders at Auschwitz and Maidanek without once mentioning the Jews.

23. Solomon M. Schwarz, *The Jews in the Soviet Union* (Syracuse: Syracuse University Press, 1951), pp. 309–350: Lukasz Hirszowicz, ed., "The Soviet Union and the Jews during World War II: British Foreign Office Documents," *Soviet Jewish Affairs*, 3 (1963), 104–119, esp. 115, 118–119.

24. For more see Lucy S. Dawidowicz, *The War Against the Jews, 1933–1945* (New York: Holt, Rinehart & Winston, 1975), pp. 120–128, 397–403. See also Wila Orbach, "The Destruction of the Jews in the Nazi-Occupied Territories of the USSR," *Soviet Jewish Affairs*, 6 (1976), 14–51.

25. See Stroop's report in International Military Tribunal, *Trial of the Major War Criminals Before the International Military Tribunal: Official Text* (Blue Series), 26, which gives the names of members of the Trawniki foreign-guard battalion on pp. 629–631. See also John A. Armstrong, "Collaboration in World War II: The Integral Nationalist Variant in Eastern Europe," *Journal of Modern History*, 40 (September 1968), 396–410.

26. Abram Tertz [Andrei Sinyavsky], *A Voice from the Chorus* (New York: Bantam, 1978), pp. 131–132.

27. Ben-Cion Pinchuk, "Soviet Media on the Fate of the Jews in Nazi-Occupied Territory (1939–1941)," in Livia Rothkirchen, ed., *Yad Vashem Studies*, 11 (Jerusalem: Yad Vashem, 1976), 221–233.

28. The Jewish Anti-Fascist Committee was established in an atmosphere of conspiracy, intrigue, and murder. For the background see Schwarz, *Jews in the Soviet Union*, pp. 201–205, and Lucy S. Dawidowicz, "Two of Stalin's Victims," *Commentary*, 12 (December 1951), 614–616.

29. Yehoshua A. Gilboa, *The Black Years of Soviet Jewry, 1939–1953* (Boston: Little, Brown, 1971), pp. 38–41, 72–73.

30. Ilya Ehrenburg, *Merder fun felker: Materialn vegn di retsikhes fun di daytche farkhaper in di tsaytvaylik okupirte sovetishe rayonen* (Moscow: Emes, 1944).

31. *The Black Book: The Nazi Crime Against the Jewish People* (New York: Jewish Black Book Committee, 1946). Albert Einstein had written a preface which the Soviet authorities rejected; the book appeared without it. For some passages see Gilboa, *The Black Years*, pp. 75–76.

The Russian typescript, with an introduction by Vasilii Grossman, survived and is now in the possession of Yad Vashem Archives, Jerusalem. A copy is available in New York in the Library of the Yivo Institute of Jewish Research.

32. "Dekn dem khyoiv farn land un folk," *Eynikayt*, no. 149 (399), December 14, 1946, p. 3. My attention was called to this editorial by a reference in Bernard J. Choseed, "Jews in Soviet Literature," in Ernest J. Simmons, ed., *Through the Glass of Soviet Literature: Views of Russian Society* (New York: Columbia University Press, 1953), p. 143.

33. Shteppa, *Russian Historians*, pp. 209–210, 229–231, 234ff; Schwarz, *Jews in the Soviet Union*, p. 210.

34. Daniel Fish, "The Jews in Syllabuses of World and Russian History:

What Soviet School Children Read about Jewish History," *Soviet Jewish Affairs*, 8 (1978); William Korey, *The Soviet Cage: Anti-Semitism in Russia* (New York: Viking, 1973), pp. 86–89, 90–97. See also "The Great Patriotic War in the Soviet Union, 1941–45" [in Russian], *Great Soviet Encyclopedia*, 2d ed. (Moscow, 1951), p. 191, which speaks of losses of life and property of Soviet inhabitants, but never mentions Jews.

35. See V. V. Kurasova, ed., *Vsemirnaia Istoria*, 10 (Moscow: Publishing House of Socio-Economic Literature "Mysl," 1965), 299–300. See also the entry "Warsaw Uprising of 1943," *Great Soviet Encyclopedia*, 3d ed., 4:670.

36. See John Armstrong's review, *American Historical Review*, 79 (February 1974), 193–194.

37. A. Anatoli (Kuznetsov), *Babi Yar: A Document in the Form of a Novel* (New York: Farrar, Straus and Giroux, 1970), p. 470.

38. "Monument at Baby Yar" [in Russian], *Pravda*, June 23, 1976; condensed text in *Current Digest of the Soviet Press*, 28 (July 21, 1976), 27.

In 1978, *Heavy Sand*, a novel by Anatoli Rybakov, appeared in three installments in a Soviet literary journal. A fictional account of a Jewish family in a ghetto in a Ukrainian town, the novel is a minimally accurate portrayal of the Jewish experience. But it also follows the newest Soviet line in depicting some Jews as collaborators of the Nazis.

39. Masha Rolnik, *Ikh muz dertseyln* (Moscow/Warsaw: Novosti/Yidish Bukh, 1965).

40. Ibid., pp. 115–117. For an account of those events as they really happened see Dawidowicz, *The War Against the Jews*, pp. 326–327.

41. V. Bolshakov, "Anti-Sovietism Is the Zionists' Profession" [in Russian], *Pravda*, February 18 and 19, 1971; complete text in *Current Digest of the Soviet Press*, 23 (March 16, 1971), 1–4. An enlarged version of these articles was published as a separate pamphlet in Russian and also in an English edition as *Anti-Communism, The Main Line of Zionism* (Moscow: Novosti, 1972).

42. William Korey, "Making Anti-Semitism Respectable," *Moment*, 4 (December 1978), 27–30.

43. Ibid. See also William Korey, "Anti-Zionism in the USSR," *Problems of Communism*, 27 (November-December 1978), 63–69.

44. Institute of Jewish Affairs, *Soviet Antisemitic Propaganda: Evidence from Books, Press and Radio* (London: Institute of Jewish Affairs, 1978), pp. 69, 70, 75. All italics were in the original. For further illustrations see Baruch A. Hazan, *Soviet Propaganda: A Case Study of the Middle East Conflict* (New York: John Wiley, 1975), pp. 151–164.

## *5. Appropriating the Holocaust: Polish Historical Revisionism*

For help with Polish materials, I wish to express my indebtedness to Dina Abramowicz, Lucjan Dobroszycki, Mark Nowogrodzki, Isaiah Trunk, and Marek Web.

1. Quoted from Robert H. Lord, *The Second Partition of Poland*, in

Hans Kohn, *The Idea of Nationalism: A Study in Its Origins and Background* (New York: Macmillan, 1961), p. 520. See also Herbert H. Kaplan, *The First Partition of Poland* (New York: Columbia University Press, 1962), pp. 182–189.

2. See W. F. Reddaway et al., eds., *The Cambridge History of Poland: From Augustus II to Pilsudski (1697–1935)* (Cambridge: Cambridge University Press, 1941), pp. 320–321, 324–331. O. Halecki, *A History of Poland*, rev. ed. (London: J. M. Dent & Sons, 1961), pp. 242ff; Bernard Ziffer, *Poland: History and Historians: Three Bibliographical Essays* (New York: Mid-European Studies Center [of the National Committee for a Free Europe], 1952), pp. 18–19; Roman Dyboski, *Poland in World Civilization* (New York: J. M. Barrett Corp., 1950), pp. 13–15, 91–95; Abraham G. Duker, "Adam Mickiewicz's Anti-Jewish Period: Studies in 'The Books of the Polish Nation and of the Polish Pilgrimage,' " in *Salo Wittmayer Baron Jubilee Volume* (Jerusalem: American Academy for Jewish Research, 1975), pp. 311–343.

3. See Pawel Korzec, "Antisemitism in Poland as an Intellectual, Social and Political Movement," in Joshua A. Fishman, ed., *Studies on Polish Jewry, 1919–1939: The Interplay of Social, Economic and Political Factors in the Struggle of a Minority for Its Existence* (New York: YIVO Institute for Jewish Research, 1974), pp. 12*–104*. Also in the same volume, Isaiah Trunk, "Der ekonomisher antisemitizm in poyln tsvishn di tsvey velt-milkhomes," pp. 3–99; Leonard Rowe, "Jewish Self-Defense: A Response to Violence," pp. 105*–149*; Zosa Szajkowski, "Western Jewish Aid and Intercession for Polish Jewry, 1919–1939," pp. 150*–241*. Other useful sources include Leon Brandes, "Der rekhtlekher matzev fun di yidn in poyln tsvishn beyde velt-milkhomes," *YIVO-Bleter*, 42 (1962), 147–186; Simon Segal, *The New Poland and the Jews* (New York: Lee Furman, 1938); Bernard D. Weinryb, "Poland," in Peter Meyer et al., *The Jews in the Soviet Satellites* (Syracuse: Syracuse University Press, 1953), pp. 207–225; Celia Heller, *On the Edge of Destruction: Jews of Poland Between the Two World Wars* (New York: Columbia University Press, 1977). *Yidishe ekonomik*, a journal edited by Jacob Lestchinsky and published by the Yiddish Scientific Institute's Section for Economics and Statistics in Warsaw, 1937–1939, contains valuable data on the consequences of Poland's discriminatory policies on the living standards of the Polish Jews. Also, the annual reviews on Poland in the *American Jewish Year Book* contain much documentary material for those who do not read Yiddish or Polish.

4. For the text of this regulation see Lucy S. Dawidowicz, ed., *A Holocaust Reader* (New York: Behrman House, 1976), pp. 67–68. Polish historians and polemicists argue that the Germans applied the death penalty to persons helping Jews only in Poland. That appears to be true, but in other countries the Germans applied other kinds of severe punishment which in fact entailed death. In the Netherlands, for instance, the Nazis decreed that non-Jews helping Jews would have their property confiscated and that they would be sent to concentration camps. Raul Hilberg, *The Destruction of the European Jews* (Chicago: Quadrangle, 1961), p. 376.

5. See Szymon Datner, *Las sprawiedliwych: Karta z dziejów ratownictwa Żydów w okupowanej Polsce* (Warsaw: Książka i Wiedza, 1968); Stanisław Wroński and Maria Zwolakowa, eds., *Polacy i Żydzi 1939–1945* (Warsaw: Książka i Wiedza, 1971).

6. Quoted in Jan Tomasz Gross, *Polish Society under German Occupation: The Generalgouvernement, 1939–1945* (Princeton, N.J.: Princeton University Press, 1979), pp. 184–185. See also the memorandum sent to the London Government-in-Exile by Roman Knoll, head of the Foreign Affairs Commission of the Delegatura, in Emmanuel Ringelblum, *Polish-Jewish Relations During the Second World War* (Jerusalem: Yad Vashem, 1974), pp. 256–258. For an example of the statements on the murder of the Jews issued by the Polish Government-in-Exile see Republic of Poland, Ministry of Foreign Affairs, *The Mass Extermination of Jews in German Occupied Poland: Note Addressed to the Governments of the United Nations on December 10th, 1942, and Other Documents* (London: Hutchinson & Co., n.d.).

7. The poem first appeared in *Z Otchłani: Poezje*, a 24-page collection of poems about the ghetto issued clandestinely in Warsaw in 1944 by the underground Jewish National Committee (ŻNK). The translation of the quoted stanza is my own.

8. The text of the order appears in Reuben Ainsztein, *Jewish Resistance in Nazi-Occupied Eastern Europe* (London: Paul Elek, 1974), p. 405. For more on the Home Army's attitude toward the Jews see the memorandum submitted to Stanisław Mikołajczyk, Prime Minister of the Polish Government-in-Exile, by Dr. Ignacy Schwarzbart, August 29, 1944, in Ringelblum, *Polish-Jewish Relations*, pp. 258–266.

9. Stefan Korbonski, *The Polish Underground State: A Guide to the Underground, 1939–1945*, East European Monograph Series XXXIX (Boulder, Colo.: East European Quarterly, 1978), pp. 104–109. See also Moshe Kahanowitz, "Why No Separate Jewish Partisan Movement Was Established During World War II," *Yad Vashem Studies*, 1 (1957), 153–167.

10. See surveys on Poland in *American Jewish Year Book*, vols. 47–49 (New York: The American Jewish Committee/The Jewish Publication Society of America, 1945–1948); Weinryb, "Poland," pp. 247–257.

11. M. K. Dziewanowski, *Poland in the Twentieth Century* (New York: Columbia University Press, 1977), pp. 162–175.

12. Weinryb, "Poland," pp. 299–313; Leon Shapiro, "Poland," *American Jewish Year Book*, vols. 50–52 (1948–1951).

13. "USSR and the Politics of Polish Antisemitism, 1956–1968," *Soviet Jewish Affairs*, 1 (June 1971), 19–21; Paul Lendvai, "Poland: The Party and the Jews," *Commentary*, 46 (September 1968), 56–59; Lucjan Blit, ed., *The Anti-Jewish Campaign in Present-Day Poland: Facts, Documents, Press Reports* (London: Institute of Jewish Affairs, 1968), pp. 8–10; Dziewanowski, *Poland*, pp. 176–186; Czesław Milosz, "Anti-Semitism in Poland," *Problems of Communism*, 6 (May–June 1957), 35–40.

14. Leon Shapiro, "Poland," *American Jewish Year Book*, vols. 58–61 (1957–1960).

15. See Antoni Mączak, "The Style and Method of History," *Polish Per-*

*spectives*, 16 (July–August 1973), 12–17; Franciszek Ryszka, "Poland: Some Recent Revaluations," *Journal of Contemporary History*, 2 (1967), 107–123. Professor Ryszka, in a book on contemporary German historians, carefully delineated the problem in an impersonal way: "Historiography has a political quality. The political determinants of the historian's work are all the more evident when he is dealing with the most recent past." *Polish Perspectives*, 12 (March 1969), 72.

16. Pawel Korzec (see n. 3 above) cites two emigré writers who blame the Jews for the persecution they suffered. One is the historian W. Poból-Malinowski, whose history of modern Poland, *Najnowsza historia polityczna Polski 1864–1945*, 2d ed., 2 vols. (London: B. Swiderski, 1963–1967), contains hostile references to the Jews. The other is W. T. Drymmer, author of a memoir on the "Jewish question" in Poland, 1935–1939, published in *Zeszyty historyczne*, 13 (Paris, 1968).

Even the *Cambridge History of Poland* is not free of hostile or contemptuous passages about the Jews (Wł. Konopczyński, pp. 36, 42; St. Estreicher, pp. 434, 457). The inadequate treatment of anti-Semitism is evident throughout and most dramatically in the failure to mention its central role following the election to the Polish presidency of Gabriel Narutowicz and his assassination in 1922 (pp. 576–577).

Halecki, *History of Poland*, manages in three sentences to blame the Jews for the presence of Polish anti-Semitism and then to minimize its existence (p. 297). Hans Roos, *A History of Modern Poland From the Foundations of the State in the First World War to the Present Day* (London: Eyre & Spottiswood, 1966), just barely refers to anti-Semitism in interwar Poland. Dyboski is unpleasantly anti-Jewish, accusing the Jews of atheism, Communism, and disloyalty, and describing them as "not only politically indigestible, but economically and socially unbearable for the Polish people" (p. 59). In *History of Poland*, ed. Aleksander Gieysztor (Warsaw: PWN—Polish Scientific Publishers, 1968), the chapter by H. Wereszycki on "Poland, 1918–1939" refers lightly to anti-Semitism (p. 701), and in the conclusion S. Kiewiewicz writes: "Millions of Poles were killed by the Nazis; the overwhelming part of Polish Jews were the victims of this extermination" (p. 712).

Probably the most astonishing reference to Poland's treatment of Jews and other national minorities appears in Jan Ostaszewski, ed., *Modern Poland Between East and West* (London: Polish School of Political and Social Science, 1971). In an editorial addendum to a chapter on independent Poland, he writes of "the satisfactory solution of the minorities' question as one of Poland's serious attainments in the interwar period" (p. 31). Thus, history becomes a means of obliterating the past.

17. In the early 1950s the commission made a fine political distinction, no doubt to appease the East Germans, by changing the word "German" in its name to "Hitlerite." The commission's Polish name presently reads: Główna Komisja Badania Zbrodni Hitlerowskich w Polsce, now officially rendered as The High Commission for the Investigation of Nazi Crimes in Poland. For an institutional survey prepared on the occasion of the commission's

thirtieth anniversary see Czesław Pilichowski, "Badanie i ściganie zbrodni hitlerowskich w latach 1945-1975," *Biuletyn Głównej Komisji Badania Zbrodni Hitlerowskich w Polsce*, 26 (1975), iii–xv. See also Zyg. Mankowski, "L'Historiographie polonaise consacrée à la politique de l'occupant et à la résistance en Pologne," *Revue d'histoire de la deuxième guerre mondiale*, 78 (April 1970), 68–69; Jerzy Topolski, "Developpement des études historiques en Pologne," in Andrzej Wyczanski, ed., *La Pologne au XIIIe Congrès International des Sciences Historiques à Moscou*, part 1 (Warsaw: PWN—Polish Scientific Publishers, 1970), p. 60.

18. While in a Polish prison awaiting trial, Hoess wrote his autobiography, one of the most important documents of the Nazi era. It was first published in a Polish translation in 1951. The original German text appeared in Germany in 1958. The English translation from the German original, entitled *Commandant of Auschwitz: The Autobiography of Rudolf Hoess*, appeared in 1960.

19. See Dawidowicz, ed., *A Holocaust Reader*, pp. 4–9.

20. For a politically prudent review of the Institute's history from 1944 to 1979 see Maurycy Horn, "Żydowski Instytut Historyczny w Polsce w latach 1944-1949," *Biuletyn Żydowskiego Instytutu Historycznego w Polsce*, no. 109 (January–March 1979), 3–15; "Szkic z przeszłości Żydowskiego Instytutu Historycznego w Polsce (1949-1966)," no. 110 (April–June 1979), 3–19; "Działalność Żydowskiego Instytutu Historycznego w Polsce w latach 1967-1979," no. 111 (July–September 1979), 7–20.

For a description of the Institute's holdings in its library, archives, and museum in the mid-1960s see Abraham Wein, "The Jewish Historical Institute in Warsaw," *Yad Vashem Studies*, 8 (Jerusalem, 1970), 203–213.

21. Elizabeth Valkenier, "Soviet Impact on Polish Post-War Historiography, 1946-1950," *Journal of Central European Affairs*, 11 (January 1952), 373–396. See also Richard Breyer, "Die polnische Millenium-Diskussion zwischen Geschichtswissenschaft und Ideologie," in Richard Breyer, ed., *Probleme der Wissenschaft im heutigen Polen* (Marburg/Lahn: J. G. Herder-Institute, 1968), 85–104.

22. One example comes from an article about the Communist party in Poland in the mid-thirties: "The Communist Party of Poland unmasked nationalism and anti-Semitism as the perfidious instruments of capitalist exploitation, teaching the working class the principles of proletarian internationalism." T. Berenstein, "KPP w walce z pogromami antyżydowskimi w latach 1935-1937," *Biuletyn ŻIH*, 15-16 (July–December 1955), 3–74.

23. Emanuel Ringelblum, *Notitsn fun varshever geto* (Warsaw: Yidish bukh, 1952). Portions of the text had already appeared in *Bleter far geshikhte* and were published also in a Polish translation in *Biuletyn ŻIH* (1951-1955).

24. Joseph Kermisz, "In varshever geto," *YIVO-bleter*, 37 (New York: Yiddish Scientific Institute-YIVO, 1953), 282–296; an English version of this article in *YIVO Annual of Jewish Social Science*, 8 (New York, 1953), 289–301; Nachman Blumental, "Di yerushe fun Emanuel Ringelblum," *Di goldene keyt*, 15 (Tel Aviv, 1953), 235–242. The English version, *Notes*

*from the Warsaw Ghetto: The Journal of Emmanuel Ringelblum* (New York: McGraw-Hill, 1958), was translated by Jacob Sloan from the mutilated 1952 Yiddish version.

25. B. Mark, *Dos bukh fun gvure: Oyfshtand fun varshever geto* (Lodz: Dos naye lebn, 1947); *Dokumentn un materialn vegn oyfshtand in varshever geto* (Warsaw: Yidish bukh for the Jewish Historical Institute, 1953); *Der oyfshtand in varshever geto* (Warsaw: Yidish bukh for the Jewish Historical Institute, 1955); *Powstanie w getcie warszawskim* (Warsaw: Jewish Historical Institute, 1953); a second enlarged edition with the same title appeared in 1954; *Der oyfshtand in bialistoker geto* (Warsaw: Jewish Historical Institute, 1950); *Ruch oporu w getcie białostockim: Samobrona—zagłada—powstanie* (Warsaw: Jewish Historical Institute, 1952).

26. Numerous articles protesting Mark's falsification of Jewish history appeared in the Yiddish and Hebrew press, many by founding members of the Jewish Historical Institute then in Israel or the United States. Perhaps the most substantial was Philip Friedman, "A shpogl naye oystaytchung fun varshever geto-oyfshtand," *Tsukunft*, 59 (1954), 162–167. For a detailed critical rebuttal of Mark's claims about the Soviet bombing based on new historical evidence see Reuben Ainsztein, *The Warsaw Ghetto Revolt* (New York: Holocaust Library, 1979), pp. 223–227. This is a revised and expanded version of a section of his larger earlier work already cited, *Jewish Resistance in Nazi-Occupied Eastern Europe*.

27. Elizabeth K. Valkenier, "Sovietization and Liberalization in Polish Postwar Historiography," *Journal of Central European Affairs*, 19 (1959–1960), 149–173.

28. The Stroop report, edited and annotated by J. Gumkowski and K. Leszczyński, appeared in the *Biuletyn Głównej Komisji Badania Zbrodni Hitlerowskich w Polsce*, 11 (1960), 113–209. Only the first volume of the Lodz ghetto chronicle was ever published: Danuta Dąbrowska and Lucjan Dobroszycki, *Kronika getta łódzkiego* (Lodz: Wydawnictwo Łódzkie, 1965). Further publication was halted with the drastic change in political climate after 1967.

29. Karol Marian Pospieszalski, *Hitlerowskie "prawo" okupacyjne w Polsce: Wybór dokumentów i próba syntezy*, 2 vols. (Poznań: Instytut Zachodni, 1958).

30. K. M. Pospieszalski, "Nazi Terror in Poland, 1939–1945," *Polish Western Affairs*, 5 (1964), 65–91.

31. Janusz Gumkowski and Kazimierz Leszczyński, *Poland Under Nazi Occupation* (Warsaw: Polonia Publishing House, 1961). For comments on the fate of Jews and Poles compared see pp. 16–17.

32. Franciszek Ryszka, *Noc i mgła: Niemcy w okresie hitlerowskim* (Wrocław: Zakład Narodowy im. Ossolińskich-Wydawnictwo, 1962). See p. 292 for the reference to the Soviet Union.

33. Ibid., p. 403.

34. Kiryl Sosnowski, *Dziecko w systemie hitlerowskim* (Poznań: Zachodnia Agencja Prasowa, 1962). An English version, *The Tragedy of Children under Nazi Rule*, was issued the same year by the same publisher,

containing material that does not appear in the Polish text (e.g., pp. 82–83). The references to the Jewish children appear on pp. 70–73, 187. Sosnowski's work contrasts with later publications on children in wartime Poland, which practically overlook Jewish children altogether. See "Children and Genocide," *Polish Perspectives* (Warsaw), 22 (July–August 1979), 9–15.

35. See Andrzej Zahorski, "L'historiographie militaire polonaise au cours des années 1944–1960," *Acta Poloniae Historica*, 6 (1962), 89–117.

36. Ernest Wiśniewski, ed., *Wojna wyzwoleńcza narodu polskiego w latach 1939–1945*, vol. 1: *Węzłowe problemy*, vol. 2: *Szkice i schematy* (Warsaw: Publishing House of the Ministry of National Defense, 1963).

37. Ibid., pp. 257, 287–288. For data about the Warsaw ghetto uprising, Wiśniewski used Mark and Wacław Poterański, *Walka warszawskiego getta* (Warsaw: Zarząd Główny ZBoWiD, 1963), a shamelessly political pamphlet whose subsequent incarnations are discussed later in this chapter.

38. For more details of these episodes see Korbonski, *The Polish Underground State*, pp. 130–135; Ainsztein, *The Warsaw Ghetto Revolt*, pp. 110–125, 134–136, 149–151.

39. T. Berenstein, A. Eisenbach, A. Rutkowski, eds., *Eksterminacja Żydów na ziemiach polskich w okresie okupacji hitlerowskiej: Zbiór dokumentów* (Warsaw: Jewish Historical Institute, 1957).

40. Artur Eisenbach, *Hitlerowska polityka zagłady Żydów* (Warsaw: Książka i Wiedza, 1961). In English see his "Operation Reinhard: Mass Extermination of the Jewish Population in Poland," *Polish Western Affairs*, 3 (1962).

41. A. Wein, "Di anti-yidishe tetigkeyt fun dem 'Antik' in der tsayt fun der daytchisher okupatsye," *Bleter far geshikhte*, 12 (1959), 119–143.

42. T. Berenstein and A. Rutkowski, "Vegn ratevn yidn durkh polyakn beys der hitler-okupatsye," *Bleter far geshikhte*, 14 (1961), 65–104. A revised version which glossed over the negative aspects was published in book form in Polish as *Pomoc Żydom w Polsce 1939–1945* and in an English version for export, *Assistance to the Jews in Poland, 1939–1945* (Warsaw: Polonia Publishing House, 1963).

43. Emanuel Ringelblum, *Ksovim fun geto*, vol. 1: *Togbukh fun varshever geto 1939–1942* (Warsaw: Yidish bukh, 1961); vol. 2: *Notitsn un ophandlungen (1942–1943)* (Warsaw: Yidish bukh, 1963).

44. Joseph Kermish, "Emmanuel Ringelblum's Notes Hitherto Unpublished," *Yad Vashem Studies*, 7 (Jerusalem, 1968), 173–183. See also Kermish's introduction to Ringelblum, *Polish-Jewish Relations*, p. xxxii. This critical edition of Ringelblum's complete manuscript, massively annotated by Kermish and Shmuel Krakowski, was republished in New York under Howard Fertig's imprint.

45. Ber Mark, *Walka i zagłada warszawskiego getta* (Warsaw: Ministry of National Defense, 1959); *Der oyfshtand in varshever geto: Naye dergantste oyflage un dokumentn-zamlung* (Warsaw: Yidish bukh, 1963).

46. An abridged English version of Mark's narrative and a selection of documents, translated from the 1963 Yiddish version, was published as *Uprising in the Warsaw Ghetto* (New York: Schocken Books, 1975). The fal-

sified account of the Soviet bombing appears on pp. 80–81. The political se-
lectivity of this abridgement exacerbated the bias of the original version. A
chapter of Mark's 1963 version appears in Yuri Suhl, ed., *They Fought Back:
The Story of Jewish Resistance in Nazi Europe* (New York: Crown Publishers, 1967), an altogether tendentious work which follows the orthodox
Communist position on resistance.

47. Paul Lendvai, *Anti-Semitism Without Jews: Communist Eastern Europe* (Garden City, N.Y.: Doubleday, 1971), pp. 227–228.

48. Korbonski, *The Polish Underground State*, pp. 108–109.

49. Adam Schaff, *Marksizm a jednostka ludzka* (Warsaw: Panstwowe
Wydawnictwo Naukowe, 1965), translated into English as *Marxism and the
Human Individual* (New York: McGraw-Hill, 1968). This quotation ap-
pears on p. 224 of the English edition; the entire passage dealing with anti-
Semitism can be found on pp. 223–225.

50. Władysław Gomulka, "A New Threat to World Peace," *Polish Reports* (Warsaw), no. 8 (67), 1967, p. 15.

51. Michal Mirski and Hersh Smolar, "Commemoration of the Warsaw
Ghetto Uprising: Reminiscences," *Soviet Jewish Affairs*, 3 (1973), 98–103.

52. Wein, "The Jewish Historical Institute," pp. 212–213. On Oct. 12,
1979, when Mr. Wein was in New York, I interviewed him about the events
of 1968 as they affected the Jewish Historical Institute. The tape of that interview is in my possession.

53. Dziewanowski, *Poland*, pp. 187–205; Blit, ed., *The Anti-Jewish Campaign*, pp. 11–25; Lendvai, *Anti-Semitism Without Jews*, pp. 89–137.

54. *Polish Reports*, no. 4 (74), 1968.

55. S. J. Roth, "The Theory of Polish Communist Antisemitism," *Bulletin on Soviet Jewish Affairs* (London), no. 2 (July 1968), 1–12.

56. Leon Shapiro, "Poland," *American Jewish Year Book*, 70 (1969),
400.

57. *Polish Reports*, no. 5 (75), 1968.

58. Simon Wiesenthal, *Anti-Jewish Agitation in Poland* (*Prewar Fascists
and Nazi Collaborators in Unity of Action with Antisemites from the
Ranks of the Polish Communist Party*): *A Documentary Report* (Bonn
[1969]), p. 16.

59. "Uchwała: Plenum Głównej Komisji Badania Zbrodni Hitlerowskich
w Polsce w Sprawie Kierunków Działania," supplement to Czesław Pilichowski, "Działalność Głównej Komisji i Okręgowych Komisji Badania
Zbrodni Hitlerowskich w Polsce w 1967 r.," *Biuletyn GKBZHwP*, 18
(1968), 178–180.

60. "Rezolucja: Plenum Głównej Komisji Badania Zbrodni Hitlerowskich
w Polsce," *Biuletyn GKBZHwP*, 18 (1968), 180–181.

Pilichowski himself wrote three articles in the Warsaw daily, *Trybuna
Ludu* (May 23, 25, and 26, 1968), which purported to give the "truth" about
Jewish and Polish wartime losses, the aid that the Poles rendered to Jews, the
collaboration of Jews themselves in the murder of their own people, and the
"Zionist" and "neo-Nazi" falsifications about the Poles and especially about
"traditional Polish anti-Semitism."

A more elaborate version of some of these points, including the statistics of Jewish and Polish losses, appeared in Pilichowski's introduction to an encyclopedic handbook about Nazi camps on Polish soil. See Czesław Pilichowski et al., eds., *Obozy hitlerowskie na ziemiach polskich 1939-1945: Informator encyklopedyczny* (Warsaw: Państwowe Wydawnictwo Naukowe, 1979), esp. pp. 22-24 and 85-86 for statistics and pp. 60-67 for his discussion of the Jews.

61. Tadeusz Walichnowski, *Izrael-NRF a Polska* (Warsaw: Wydawnictwo Interpress, 1968). Chapter 3, "Antypolska akcja ruchu syjonistycznego jako część składowa kampanii rehabilitowania NRF" (pp. 50-71), concentrates on showing how Jews have "defamed" Poland by speaking of Polish anti-Semitism, whereas some Jews themselves, so he claims, collaborated with the Gestapo. Among the books that he cites as offering such slanderous and unfounded charges about Polish anti-Semitism are Chaim Kaplan's Warsaw ghetto diary and a German translation of Isaac Bashevis Singer, *The Slave*, a novel about a Jew in seventeenth-century Poland.

Fifty thousand copies of this 84-page pamphlet were published. At the height of the anti-Jewish campaign of 1968, Walichnowski also produced a series of pamphlets entitled "Doktryna Syjonizmu" (*Syjonizm a państwo Żydowskie, Organizacje i działacze Syjonistyczni, Syjonizm a NRF*), published in Katowice, the first two in an edition of 20,000 copies each, and the third in 30,000 copies.

For illustrations of the articles that flooded the popular and even the academic press see Wojciech Sulewski, "Against Resignation—For Survival Through Fight," *Contemporary Poland* (Warsaw: Interpress), 2 (April 1968), 30-35; Stanisław Okęcki, "O fałszowaniu historii przez syjonistów," *Wojskowy Przegląd Historyczny* (Warsaw), 13 (1968), 458-463.

62. Lendvai, *Anti-Semitism Without Jews*, p. 108. In 1971 Walichnowski participated in a conference organized by the Historical Institute of Polish-Soviet Relations of the Polish Academy of Sciences and then edited its proceedings on behalf of the Academy. *Konsekwencje polityczne klęski III Rzeszy w Europie środkowej i południowo-wschodniej* (Warsaw: Książka i Wiedza, 1971). A collection of his essays, published in 1973, received a respectful review in *Polish Western Affairs*, 14 (1973), 331-332.

63. Wacław Poterański, *Warszawskie getto: w 25-lecie walki zbrojnej w getcie w 1943 r.*, 2d enl. ed. (Warsaw: Książka i Wiedza, 1968). The English version appeared as *The Warsaw Ghetto: On the 25th Anniversary of the Armed Uprising in 1943* (Warsaw: Interpress, 1968), without indicating the existence of a previous version. See n. 37 above for reference to the 1963 edition.

64. Ibid., pp. 9, 14-15, 21, 23-28, 34, 50-55.

65. Tadeusz Bednarczyk, *Walka i pomoc: OW-KB a organizacja ruchu oporu w getcie warszawskim* (Warsaw: Iskry, 1968).

66. References to the unpublished manuscript appeared in Czesław Madajczyk, *Polityka III Rzeszy w okupowanej Polsce*, a work discussed later in this chapter. Entitled "Getto warszawskie i ludzie, jakimi ich znałem (wspomnienia 1939-1945)," Bednarczyk's manuscript was identified as a

typescript in the possession of the publishing institute of PAX, Boleslaw Piasecki's unsavory organization. Madajczyk made no reference to Bednarczyk's pamphlet.

67. No independent corroboration of Bednarczyk's claims of his involvement with the ŻZW has appeared in any Revisionist literature. The only wartime reference to him, I have been told, is in a still unpublished portion of Ringelblum's ghetto notes, which mentions a certain Bednarczyk as a man who squeezed money out of ghetto Jews, no doubt an allusion to his function as tax collector.

68. Bednarczyk, *Walka i pomoc*, pp. 30–34, 52–55, 56–57, 58–66. Though he appears not to have had published anything in the past ten years, Bednarczyk apparently regards himself as an expert on the history of the Warsaw ghetto. In 1978, at a conference sponsored by the Jewish Historical Institute to mark the thirty-fifth anniversary of the Warsaw ghetto uprising, Bednarczyk participated in the discussion, objecting to the inadequacy of the presentations about Polish aid to the Jews. He later wrote a letter to the editor, *Kwartalnik Historyczny*, 86 (1979), 565–569, setting forth his views, since he was dissatisfied with the reports of the meeting that had appeared in an earlier issue of the journal, 85 (1978), 1097–1101.

One more point should be made for the record with regard to materials in *Walka i pomoc*, and presumably in the unpublished memoirs. Bednarczyk described a clandestine meeting in January 1940 between leaders of the OW-KB and Adam Czerniaków, head of the Warsaw ghetto Judenrat, regarding Jewish armed resistance and the possibility of coopting Czerniaków himself to that effort. According to Bednarczyk, Czerniaków expressed his personal interest in such an undertaking but held that the Jews should follow an accommodationist policy vis-à-vis the Germans. No evidence to corroborate this unlikely story has ever been offered. Nevertheless, Professor Madajczyk used it. The Jewish Historical Institute's edition of Czerniaków's diary (*BŻIH*, 83–84 [1972]) cites Madajczyk's reference to Bednarczyk, but does not substantiate the story, which must be regarded as entirely fictional.

69. Władysław Bartoszewski and Zofia Lewinówna, eds., *Ten jest z ojczyzny mojej: Polacy z pomocą Żydom 1939-1945* (Cracow: Wydawnictwo "Znak," 1967).

70. Władysław Bartoszewski and Sofia Lewin, *Righteous Among the Nations: How Poles Helped the Jews, 1939-1945* (London: Earlscourt Publishers Ltd., 1969).

71. Władysław Bartoszewski, *The Blood Shed Unites Us* (*Pages from the History of Help to the Jews in Occupied Poland*) (Warsaw: Interpress, 1970). See Wroński and Zwolakowa, eds., *Polacy i Żydzi 1939-1945*, a far more tendentious compilation of memoirs, documents, and photographs, compiled between 1968 and 1970 by ZBoWiD and the Central Commission to Investigate Hitlerite Crimes.

72. Eugeniusz Duraczyński, "Struktura społeczno-polityczna podziemia antyhitlerowskiego w Polsce," *Miesięcznik Literacki* (Warsaw), 5 (February 1970), 90–98. The identical study was published also as "La structure

sociale et politique de la résistance anti-Hitlérienne en Pologne (1939–1944)," *Revue d'histoire de la deuxième guerre mondiale*, 78 (April 1970), 47–66. The quotation appears on p. 52.

73. Quoted in Leon Shapiro, "Poland," *American Jewish Year Book*, 72 (1971), 414. See also Krzysztof Dunin-Wąsowicz, *La résistance polonaise et l'insurrection du ghetto de Varsovie* (Warsaw: Polish Academy of Science, Scientific Center in Paris, 1974). The documentation of this paper read at an international conference in Paris in 1973 is less than impressive: fourteen footnotes in all, four citing Bartoszewski and two Poterański.

74. Czesław Madajczyk, *Polityka III Rzeszy w okupowanej Polsce*, 2 vols. (Warsaw: Państwowe Wydawnictwo Naukowe, 1970).

75. Ibid., 2:369–370.

76. For more on Germany's Polish policy see Martin Broszat, *National-sozialistische Polenpolitik 1939–1945* (Stuttgart: Deutsche Verlags-Anstalt, 1961), esp. pp. 19–28. See also Norman Rich, *Hitler's War Aims: The Establishment of the New Order* (New York: W. W. Norton, 1974), 2:68–105.

77. Madajczyk, *Polityka III Rzeszy*, 2:215–216.

78. Ibid., p. 311.

79. Ibid., p. 320.

80. Hilberg, *The Destruction of the European Jews*, pp. 319–320.

81. For detailed scholarly refutations of this passage in Bor-Komorowski see the extended notes by Joseph Kermish and Shmuel Krakowski in Ringelblum, *Polish-Jewish Relations*, pp. 161–164, and also Ainsztein, *Jewish Resistance*, pp. 584–588. For a brief account of the actual course of events between the Jewish underground movement and the Home Army see Lucy S. Dawidowicz, *The War Against the Jews, 1933–1945* (New York: Holt, Rinehart & Winston, 1975), pp. 318–320.

82. Madajczyk, *Polityka III Rzeszy*, pp. 339–340.

83. Ibid., pp. 335–336. For more on Madajczyk's bias see Shmuel Krakowski, "Policy of the Third Reich in Conquered Poland," *Yad Vashem Studies*, 9 (1973), 225–245.

84. Wein, "The Jewish Historical Institute," p. 213. It is also possible dispersal of these archives to regional collections prevented their falling into Pilichowski's hands. See the transcript of an interview with Dr. Stefan Krakowski in the Oral History Collection of the Institute of Contemporary Jewry of the Hebrew University, Jerusalem.

85. Jadwiga Bezwińska and Danuta Czech, eds., *Amidst a Nightmare of Crime: Manuscripts of Members of the Sonderkommando* (Oświęcim: State Museum, 1973), p. 9; the quotation comes from the editors' preface.

86. Zelman Lewental, "Pamiętnik członka sonderkommando Auschwitz II," *Biuletyn ŻIH*, nos. 65–66 (January–June 1968), 211–233.

87. See Szymon Datner, "Relacje o pomocy Żydom z czasie okupacji hitlerowskiej," *Biuletyn ŻIH*, nos. 71–72 (July–December 1969), 229–236.

88. Leon Shapiro, "Poland," *American Jewish Year Book*, 73 (1972), 546–548.

## 6. The Perspective of Catastrophe: The Holocaust in Jewish History

1. For a description of the archives accumulated in ghettos and camps see Lucy S. Dawidowicz, ed., *A Holocaust Reader* (New York: Behrman House, 1976), pp. 4–9.

2. See Simon Dubnow's essay "Jewish History: An Essay in the Philosophy of History," first published in 1893: "When, in days to come, the curtain rises upon the touching tragedy of Jewish history, revealing it to the astonished eye of a modern generation, then, perhaps, hearts will be attuned to tenderness and on the ruins of national hostility will be enthroned mutual love, growing out of mutual understanding and mutual esteem." Simon Dubnow, *Nationalism and History: Essays on Old and New Judaism*, ed. Koppel S. Pinson (Philadelphia: Jewish Publication Society of America, 1958), pp. 270–271.

3. See Chapter 5 for an account of the origin of the Jewish Historical Institute in Poland.

4. See Philip Friedman, "European Jewish Research on the Recent Jewish Catastrophe in 1939–1945," *Proceedings of the American Academy for Jewish Research*, 18 (1949), 179–211; reprinted in Friedman, *Roads to Extinction: Essays on the Holocaust* (New York/Philadelphia: Jewish Publication Society of America, 1980), pp. 500–524.

5. See L. S. Dawidowicz, "Khronikes fun khurbn: Di tsentrale historishe komisye in minkhn," *Di tsukunft*, 55 (1950), 156–159.

6. For an English translation of the law see *State of Israel Government Yearbook* (Jerusalem: Government Printing Press, 1954), pp. 250–251. For an elaboration of Yad Vashem's objectives in the light of its mandate see Benzion Dinur, "Problems Confronting 'Yad Washem' in Its Work of Research," *Yad Vashem Studies*, 1 (1957), 7–30. For a survey of Yad Vashem's activities see Efraim Zuroff, "Yad Vashem: More Than a Memorial, More Than a Name," *Shoa: A Review of Holocaust Studies and Commemorations*, 1 (Winter 1979), 4–9.

7. The following section is based on an earlier essay of mine, "Toward a History of the Holocaust," *Commentary*, 47 (April 1969), 51–56.

8. For more on Polish Jewish historians see Philip Friedman, "Polish Jewish Historiography Between the Two Wars (1918–1939)," *Jewish Social Studies*, 11 (1949), 373–408; reprinted in his *Roads to Extinction*, pp. 467–499.

9. Lord Acton, *Essays on Freedom and Power*, ed. Gertrude Himmelfarb (New York: Meridian, 1955), p. 39.

10. Many thousands of oral histories by survivors recounting their experiences exist in libraries and archives around the world. Their quality and usefulness vary significantly according to the informant's memory, grasp of events, insights, and of course accuracy. Also important in determining the quality of the account is the interviewer's ability to pursue lines of inquiry that elicit information that has been subconsciously or deliberately suppressed or that supplements an already accumulated body of information on

a given subject or place. The longer the time elapsed, the less likely that the informant has retained freshness of recollection or can offer new information. The transcribed testimonies I have examined have been full of errors in dates, names of participants, and places, and there are evident misunderstandings of the events themselves. To the unwary researcher, some of the accounts can be more hazard than help.

For the usefulness of such accounts as basic historical sources see Isaiah Trunk, *Jewish Responses to Nazi Persecution: Collective and Individual Behavior in Extremis* (New York: Stein and Day, 1979), a collection of eyewitness testimonies selected out of a large mass, excerpted, corrected, and, finally, put into a systematic historical framework.

11. Foreword to Jacob Robinson and Philip Friedman, *Guide to Jewish History under Nazi Impact*, Bibliographical Series, no. 1 (New York: Yad Vashem/YIVO Institute for Jewish Research, 1960), xix–xx.

12. See Lucy S. Dawidowicz, *The War Against the Jews, 1933–1945* (New York: Holt, Rinehart & Winston, 1975), pp. 311–313.

13. See Haim Ormian, "The Attitude of Israeli High School Students toward Mendele Moykher Sforim," *YIVO Annual of Jewish Social Science*, 5 (1950), 292–312; Gideon Hausner, *Justice in Jerusalem* (New York: Harper & Row, 1966), pp. 186, 333, 451–452, 453; Edward Alexander, *The Resonance of Dust: Essays on Holocaust Literature and Jewish Fate* (Columbus, Ohio: Ohio State University Press, 1979), pp. 84–89.

14. The flow of memoirs in a variety of languages, especially Yiddish and Hebrew, has been abundant. The first three volumes of the Yad Vashem/YIVO Bibliographical Series attest to the quantity of published materials. Only a very few are here listed as illustrative of this genre: Tuviah Bozikowski, *Tsvishn falndike vent* (Warsaw: Merkaz Hehalutz, 1949); Bernard Goldstein, *Finf yor in varshever geto* (New York: Undzer Tsayt, 1947); A. Sutzkewer, *Vilner geto, 1941–1944* (Paris: Association of Vilner in France, 1946); Melekh Neustadt, *Khurbn un oyfshtand fun di yidn in varshever geto: eydes-bleter un azkores*, 2 vols. (Tel-Aviv: Executive Committee of the General Federation of Jewish Labour in Palestine and the Jewish National Workers' Alliance in U.S.A., 1948); Rachel Auerbach, *Oyf di felder fun treblinke* (Warsaw-Lodz: Central Jewish Historical Commission, 1947). See also Leo W. Schwarz, ed., *The Root and the Bough: The Epic of an Enduring People* (New York: Rinehart & Co., 1949).

15. Philip Friedman, "Der yidisher vidershtand kegn der natsi hershaft," *Yidisher kemfer*, 34 (April 3, 1953), 88–94; "Der shetekh fun der yidisher vidershtand bavegung," 34 (May 8, 1953), 9–11; "In vald un feld," 34 (May 15, 1953), 12–13; "Oyfshtandn in lagern un getos," 34 (May 22, 1953), 10–11, 14; "Jewish Resistance to Nazism," originally read at a conference in 1958 and later published in *European Resistance Movements, 1939–1945*, vol. 1 (Oxford/London: Pergamon Press, 1960); a revised and expanded version was published for the first time in Friedman, *Roads to Extinction*, pp. 387–408.

Isaiah Trunk, "Vegn yidishn vidershtand in varshever geto," *Undzer tsayt* (New York), nos. 186–187 (April–May 1957), 16–18; a revised and expanded version appeared in Trunk, *Shtudyes in yidisher geshikhte in poyln* (Buenos Aires: Yidbukh, 1963), pp. 298–312.

16. One of the two most controversial works was by Bruno Bettelheim, a psychologist and psychoanalyst, the other by Raul Hilberg, a political scientist. Neither was familiar with Jewish history or Jewish traditional life and culture. Neither understood the historian's craft in terms of critical analysis of sources and exploration of complex interacting causal factors. Bettelheim's book, *The Informed Heart: Autonomy in a Mass Age* (Glencoe, Ill.: Free Press, 1960), criticized the behavior of Jews as passive and regressive (pp. 107–175, 177–235, 237–265). Hilberg's book, *The Destruction of the European Jews* (Chicago: Quadrangle, 1961), savagely charged the European Jews with passivity and, in profound ignorance of Jewish history, blamed "Jewish ghetto history," that is, Diaspora history, for that passivity (see esp. pp. 14, 329, 343, 624–625, 662–663, 667, 669). See also H. R. Trevor-Roper's review, "Nazi Bureaucrats and Jewish Leaders," *Commentary*, 33 (April 1962), 354–355

In the controversy that followed the publication of Hannah Arendt's *Eichmann in Jerusalem: A Report on the Banality of Evil*, rev. ed. (New York: Viking, 1965), Arendt was mistakenly accused of holding views similar to Hilberg's on resistance. She did not blame the Jews for lack of resistance, declaring that "no non-Jewish group or people had behaved differently" (pp. 11ff). See also pp. 283–284.

17. E.g., Zvi A. Braun and Dov Levin, *Toledoteha shel mahteret: He-Irgun haloham shel yehudei Kovno bemilhamet ha-olam hashniya* (Jerusalem: Yad Vashem, 1962). See also the series *Yad Vashem Studies* and *Yalkut Moreshet*. In the United States, see Oscar Handlin, "Jewish Resistance to the Nazis," *Commentary*, 34 (November 1962), 398–405.

18. See *Jewish Resistance during the Holocaust: Proceedings of the Conference on Manifestations of Jewish Resistance, Jerusalem, 7–11, 1968* (Jerusalem: Yad Vashem, 1971).

19. Nachman Blumental, "Sources for the Study of Jewish Resistance," ibid., p. 50.

20. E.g., a popular pamphlet by Yehuda Bauer, *They Chose Life: Jewish Resistance in the Holocaust* (New York: The American Jewish Committee, 1973), whose very title is an offense against the murdered Jews in its implication that those who did not engage in armed resistance to the Germans chose death over life. Reuben Ainsztein, *Jewish Resistance in Nazi-Occupied Eastern Europe* (London: Paul Elek, 1974), is a massive work of 969 pages making an excessive case for Jewish muscularity throughout the centuries in order to refute Hilberg's charge of passivity and offering elaborate documentation for Jewish participation in regular and partisan warfare.

21. Stanley M. Elkins, "The Slavery Debate," *Commentary*, 60 (December 1975), 40–54.

22. For an exhaustive treatment of the functions and activities of the Judenräte and the attitudes toward them see Isaiah Trunk, *Judenrat: The Jewish Councils in Eastern Europe under the Nazi Occupation* (New York: Macmillan, 1972). See also Dawidowicz, *The War Against the Jews*, pp.

223–241, for an analysis of the evolution of the Judenrat under the duress of Nazi terror.

23. See a review of the case in Dawidowicz, *The Jewish Presence* (New York: Holt, Rinehart & Winston, 1977), pp. 269–279.

24. Solomon F. Bloom, "Dictator of the Lodz Ghetto," *Commentary*, 7 (February 1949), 111–122; Philip Friedman, "Goaley-sheker be-getaot polin," *Metsuda* (London), 7 (1954), 602–618; Friedman, "Two 'Saviors' Who Failed," *Commentary*, 26 (1958), 479–491; Friedman's "Preliminary and Methodological Aspects of Research on the Judenrat," originally a lecture delivered before the Yad Vashem in 1957, was first published in *Yad Vashem Studies*, 2 (1958), 95–113. All Friedman's essays are now reprinted in his *Roads to Extinction*.

25. Arendt, *Eichmann in Jerusalem*, p. 125.

26. "Eichmann in Jerusalem: An Exchange of Letters between Gershom Scholem and Hannah Arendt," *Encounter*, 22 (January 1964), 51–56.

27. Norman Podhoretz, "Hannah Arendt on Eichmann: A Study in the Perversity of Brilliance," *Commentary*, 36 (September 1963), 201–208.

28. Nachman Blumental, ed., *Darko shel yudenrat: teudot migeto bialystok* (Jerusalem: Yad Vashem, 1962), contains the original Yiddish text and Hebrew translation, with notes and introduction; Blumental, ed., *Teudot migeto lublin* (Jerusalem: Yad Vashem, 1967), contains a Hebrew translation of the Polish text and facsimile of the original typescript, with an apparatus; Adam Czerniaków, *Yoman geto varsha*, ed. Nachman Blumental et al. (Jerusalem: Yad Vashem, 1968), a Hebrew version with a poor facsimile of the original Polish holograph, with an apparatus.

29. Excerpts in an English translation from all three documents are in Dawidowicz, ed., *A Holocaust Reader*, pp. 240–287. An English version of Czerniaków's diary was published in New York in 1979.

30. Isaiah Trunk, *Lodzher geto: a historishe un sotsyologishe shtudye* (New York: Yad Vashem/YIVO, 1962). The *Encyclopedia Judaica*, the *Entsiklopedia shel galuyot*, and the series *Pinkas hakehillot* published by Yad Vashem provide encyclopedic articles of the destroyed European Jewish communities, but no study comparable to Trunk's Lodz exists. A handful of Hebrew and Yiddish books on individual ghettos (Vilna, Kovno, Bialystok, Warsaw) concentrate primarily on the murder of the Jews in those communities and on Jewish resistance.

31. Jacob Robinson, *And the Crooked Shall Be Made Straight: The Eichmann Trial, the Jewish Catastrophe, and Hannah Arendt's Narrative* (New York: Macmillan, 1965).

32. Trunk, *Judenrat*, p. xvii.

33. The same year that Trunk's *Judenrat* appeared, the YIVO published the proceedings of a colloquium held five years earlier: *Imposed Jewish Governing Bodies under Nazi Rule: YIVO Colloquium December 2–5, 1967* (New York: YIVO Institute for Jewish Research, 1972). Some of those papers had meanwhile been published elsewhere.

*Yad Vashem Studies*, 10 (1974), contained three papers on Jewish leadership in the Netherlands, Hungary, and Germany during the war and also a bibliography on the Judenräte. The bibliography listed 214 items, most of them articles or short passages in books. These included survivor accounts, journalistic essays, bibliographies, encyclopedia entries, as well as scholarly papers.

34. A few examples: *Randolph Braham, The Destruction of Hungarian Jewry: A Documentary Account* (New York: World Federation of Hungarian Jews, 1963); Frederick B. Chary, *The Bulgarian Jews and the Final Solution* (Pittsburgh: University of Pittsburgh Press, 1972); Leon Poliakov and Jacques Sabille, *Jews under the Italian Occupation* (Paris: Centre de Documentation Juive Contemporaine, 1955); Jacob Presser, *The Destruction of the Dutch Jews* (New York: E. P. Dutton, 1969); Leni Yahil, *The Rescue of Danish Jewry* (Philadelphia: Jewish Publication Society of America, 1969).

35. See Ismar Schorsch, "German Antisemitism in the Light of Post-War Historiography," *Leo Baeck Institute Year Book XIX* (London: Secker & Warburg, 1974), pp. 257–271.

The following historical works on anti-Semitism were probably produced as a consequence of their authors' preoccupation with the Holocaust. The earliest to appear was Koppel S. Pinson, ed., *Essays on Antisemitism* (New York: Conference on Jewish Relations, 1942); a revised enlarged edition was published in 1946. Joshua Trachtenberg, *The Devil and the Jews: The Medieval Conception of the Jew and Its Relation to Modern Antisemitism* (Cleveland/New York: Meridian Books, 1961), was undertaken in the late 1930s and first published by Yale University Press in 1943. Leon Poliakov, who wrote one of the earliest histories of the Holocaust, *Bréviaire de la haine* (Paris: Calmann-Lévy, 1951), trans. *Harvest of Hate: The Nazi Program for the Destruction of the Jews of Europe* (Syracuse, N.Y.: Syracuse University Press, 1954), has been working on a multivolume work, *The History of Anti-Semitism*, of which three volumes have been published (New York: Vanguard, 1965, 1973, 1977). In addition, he wrote *The Aryan Myth: A History of Racist and Nationalist Ideas in Europe* (New York: Basic Books, 1974). Norman Cohn, *Warrant for Genocide: The Myth of the Jewish World-Conspiracy and the Protocols of the Elders of Zion* (New York: Harper & Row, 1966), and his *Pursuit of the Millennium: Revolutionary Messianism in Medieval and Reformation Europe and Its Bearing on Modern Totalitarian Movements*, rev. ed. (New York: Harper, 1961), were both produced under the impact of the Holocaust. Saul Friedländer's *L'Antisemitisme Nazi: Histoire d'une psychose collective* (Paris: Editions du Seuil, 1971), is one of several books he has written on subjects bearing on the Holocaust. See also his paper, "Some Aspects of the Historical Significance of the Holocaust," *The Jerusalem Quarterly*, 1 (Fall 1976), 36–57. Three works by Jewish historians dealing with German anti-Semitism before the rise of Hitler are: Paul W. Massing, *Rehearsal for Destruction: A Study of Political Anti-Semitism in Imperial Germany* (New York: Harper, 1949); Ismar Schorsch, *Jewish Reactions to German Anti-Semitism, 1870–1914* (New York: Columbia University Press, 1972); Uriel Tal,

*Christians and Jews in Germany: Religion, Politics and Ideology in the Second Reich* (Ithaca, N.Y.: Cornell University Press, 1975).

36. I was led to these passages in Tr. Sabbath 13b by the citations in Elias Tcherikower, "Jewish Martyrology and Jewish Historiography," *YIVO Annual of Jewish Social Science*, 1 (1946), 11.

## Afterword

1. Polybius, *The Histories of Polybius* (London/New York: Macmillan, 1889), 2:182.

2. Hans Kohn, *The Idea of Nationalism: A Study in Its Origins and Background* (New York: Macmillan, 1961), pp. 569–572 et passim. See also Walter Laqueur and George L. Mosse, eds., *Historians in Politics* (London/Beverly Hills, Cal.: Sage Publications, 1974).

3. Quoted in Frederick J. Teggart, *Theory and Processes of History* (Berkeley/Los Angeles, Cal.: University of California Press, 1960), p. 29.

4. Herbert Butterfield, *The Whig Interpretation of History* (New York: Norton, 1965), pp. 3–4.

5. Edward Hallett Carr, *What Is History? The George Macaulay Trevelyan Lectures Delivered in the University of Cambridge January–March 1961* (New York: Knopf, 1964), p. 26.

6. Quoted in Herbert Butterfield, *Man on His Past: The Study of the History of Historical Scholarship* (Boston: Beacon Press, 1960), p. 73n.

7. Isaiah Berlin, *Four Essays on Liberty* (London/New York: Oxford University Press, 1969), pp. 41–117.

So many nineteenth-century English historians became addicted to the term "circumstances" to explain the course of history that it became the subject of parody in Gilbert and Sullivan's *Ruddigore:*

> But be so kind to bear in mind,
> We are the victims of circumstances.

8. G. J. Renier, *History: Its Purpose and Method* (Boston: Beacon Press, 1950), p. 255.

# INDEX